IN ASSOCIATION WITH

Hodder Gibson Model Practice Papers
WITH ANSWERS

PLUS: Official SQA Specimen Paper With Answers

Higher for CfE
# English

2014 Specimen Question Paper & Model Papers

D0259500

HODDER GIBSON
AN HACHETTE UK COMPANY

This book contains the official 2014 SQA Specimen Question Paper for the new CfE Higher English, with associated SQA approved answers modified from the official marking instructions that accompany the paper.

In addition the book contains model practice papers, together with answers, plus study skills advice. These papers, some of which may include a limited number of previously published SQA questions, have been specially commissioned by Hodder Gibson, and have been written by experienced senior teachers and examiners in line with the new CfE Higher syllabus and assessment outlines, Spring 2014. This is not SQA material but has been devised to provide further practice for Higher examinations in 2015 and beyond.

Hodder Gibson is grateful to the copyright holders, as credited on the final page of the Answer Section, for permission to use their material. Every effort has been made to trace the copyright holders and to obtain their permission for the use of copyright material. Hodder Gibson will be happy to receive information allowing us to rectify any error or omission in future editions.

Hachette UK's policy is to use papers that are natural, renewable and recyclable products and made from wood grown in sustainable forests. The logging and manufacturing processes are expected to conform to the environmental regulations of the country of origin.

Orders: please contact Bookpoint Ltd, 130 Park Drive, Abingdon, Oxon OX14 4SE. Telephone: (44) 01235 827720. Fax: (44) 01235 400454. Lines are open 9.00–5.00, Monday to Saturday, with a 24-hour message answering service. Visit our website at www.hoddereducation.co.uk. Hodder Gibson can be contacted direct on: Tel: 0141 848 1609; Fax: 0141 889 6315; email: hoddergibson@hodder.co.uk

This collection first published in 2014 by
Hodder Gibson, an imprint of Hodder Education,
An Hachette UK Company
2a Christie Street
Paisley PA1 1NB

ïBrightRED Hodder Gibson is grateful to Bright Red Publishing Ltd for collaborative work in preparation of this book and all SQA Past Paper, National 5 and Higher for CfE Model Paper titles 2014.

Typeset by PDQ Digital Media Solutions Ltd, Bungay, Suffolk NR35 1BY

Printed in the UK

A catalogue record for this title is available from the British Library

ISBN: 978-1-4718-3718-0

3 2

2015

# Introduction

## Study Skills – what you need to know to pass exams!

### Pause for thought

Many students might skip quickly through a page like this. After all, we all know how to revise. Do you really though?

### Think about this:

"IF YOU ALWAYS DO WHAT YOU ALWAYS DO, YOU WILL ALWAYS GET WHAT YOU HAVE ALWAYS GOT."

Do you like the grades you get? Do you want to do better? If you get full marks in your assessment, then that's great! Change nothing! This section is just to help you get that little bit better than you already are.

There are two main parts to the advice on offer here. The first part highlights fairly obvious things but which are also very important. The second part makes suggestions about revision that you might not have thought about but which WILL help you.

### Part 1

DOH! It's so obvious but …

### Start revising in good time

Don't leave it until the last minute – this will make you panic.

Make a revision timetable that sets out work time AND play time.

### Sleep and eat!

Obvious really, and very helpful. Avoid arguments or stressful things too – even games that wind you up. You need to be fit, awake and focused!

### Know your place!

Make sure you know exactly **WHEN and WHERE** your exams are.

### Know your enemy!

**Make sure you know what to expect in the exam.**

How is the paper structured?

How much time is there for each question?

What types of question are involved?

Which topics seem to come up time and time again?

Which topics are your strongest and which are your weakest?

Are all topics compulsory or are there choices?

### Learn by DOING!

There is no substitute for past papers and practice papers – they are simply essential! Tackling this collection of papers and answers is exactly the right thing to be doing as your exams approach.

### Part 2

People learn in different ways. Some like low light, some bright. Some like early morning, some like evening / night. Some prefer warm, some prefer cold. But everyone uses their BRAIN and the brain works when it is active. Passive learning – sitting gazing at notes – is the most INEFFICIENT way to learn anything. Below you will find tips and ideas for making your revision more effective and maybe even more enjoyable. What follows gets your brain active, and active learning works!

### Activity 1 – Stop and review

#### Step 1

When you have done no more than 5 minutes of revision reading STOP!

#### Step 2

Write a heading in your own words which sums up the topic you have been revising.

#### Step 3

Write a summary of what you have revised in no more than two sentences. Don't fool yourself by saying, "I know it, but I cannot put it into words". That just means you don't know it well enough. If you cannot write your summary, revise that section again, knowing that you must write a summary at the end of it. Many of you will have notebooks full of blue/black ink writing. Many of the pages will not be especially attractive or memorable so try to liven them up a bit with colour as you are reviewing and rewriting. **This is a great memory aid, and memory is the most important thing.**

## Activity 2 — Use technology!

Why should everything be written down? Have you thought about "mental" maps, diagrams, cartoons and colour to help you learn? And rather than write down notes, why not record your revision material?

What about having a text message revision session with friends? Keep in touch with them to find out how and what they are revising and share ideas and questions.

Why not make a video diary where you tell the camera what you are doing, what you think you have learned and what you still have to do? No one has to see or hear it, but the process of having to organise your thoughts in a formal way to explain something is a very important learning practice.

Be sure to make use of electronic files. You could begin to summarise your class notes. Your typing might be slow, but it will get faster and the typed notes will be easier to read than the scribbles in your class notes. Try to add different fonts and colours to make your work stand out. You can easily Google relevant pictures, cartoons and diagrams which you can copy and paste to make your work more attractive and **MEMORABLE**.

## Activity 3 – This is it. Do this and you will know lots!

### Step 1

In this task you must be very honest with yourself! Find the SQA syllabus for your subject (www.sqa.org.uk). Look at how it is broken down into main topics called MANDATORY knowledge. That means stuff you MUST know.

### Step 2

BEFORE you do ANY revision on this topic, write a list of everything that you already know about the subject. It might be quite a long list but you only need to write it once. It shows you all the information that is already in your long-term memory so you know what parts you do not need to revise!

### Step 3

Pick a chapter or section from your book or revision notes. Choose a fairly large section or a whole chapter to get the most out of this activity.

With a buddy, use Skype, Facetime, Twitter or any other communication you have, to play the game "If this is the answer, what is the question?". For example, if you are revising Geography and the answer you provide is "meander", your buddy would have to make up a question like "What is the word that describes a feature of a river where it flows slowly and bends often from side to side?".

Make up 10 "answers" based on the content of the chapter or section you are using. Give this to your buddy to solve while you solve theirs.

### Step 4

Construct a wordsearch of at least 10 X 10 squares. You can make it as big as you like but keep it realistic. Work together with a group of friends. Many apps allow you to make wordsearch puzzles online. The words and phrases can go in any direction and phrases can be split. Your puzzle must only contain facts linked to the topic you are revising. Your task is to find 10 bits of information to hide in your puzzle, but you must not repeat information that you used in Step 3. DO NOT show where the words are. Fill up empty squares with random letters. Remember to keep a note of where your answers are hidden but do not show your friends. When you have a complete puzzle, exchange it with a friend to solve each other's puzzle.

### Step 5

Now make up 10 questions (not "answers" this time) based on the same chapter used in the previous two tasks. Again, you must find NEW information that you have not yet used. Now it's getting hard to find that new information! Again, give your questions to a friend to answer.

### Step 6

As you have been doing the puzzles, your brain has been actively searching for new information. Now write a NEW LIST that contains only the new information you have discovered when doing the puzzles. Your new list is the one to look at repeatedly for short bursts over the next few days. Try to remember more and more of it without looking at it. After a few days, you should be able to add words from your second list to your first list as you increase the information in your long-term memory.

## FINALLY! Be inspired...

Make a list of different revision ideas and beside each one write **THINGS I HAVE** tried, **THINGS I WILL** try and **THINGS I MIGHT** try. Don't be scared of trying something new.

And remember – "FAIL TO PREPARE AND PREPARE TO FAIL!"

# Higher English

## The course

The Higher English course aims to enable you to develop the ability to:

- listen, talk, read and write, as appropriate to purpose, audience and context
- understand, analyse and evaluate texts, including Scottish texts, as appropriate to purpose and audience in the contexts of literature, language and media
- create and produce texts, as appropriate to purpose, audience and context
- apply knowledge and understanding of language.

## The basics

The grade you finally get for Higher English depends on three things:

- The two internal Unit Assessments you do in school or college: "Analysis and Evaluation" and "Creation and Production"; these don't count towards the final grade, but you must have passed them before you can get a final grade.
- Your Portfolio of Writing – this is submitted in April for marking by SQA and counts for 30% of your final grade.
- The two exams you sit in May – that's what this book is all about.

## The exams

### Reading for Understanding, Analysis and Evaluation

- exam time: 1 hour 30 minutes
- total marks: 30
- weighting in final grade: 30%
- what you have to do: read two passages and answer questions about the ideas and use of language in one of them (25 marks), and then compare the ideas in both passages (5 marks)

### Critical Reading

- exam time: 1 hour 30 minutes
- total marks: 40 (20 marks for each Section)
- weighting in final grade: 40%
- what you have to do: Section 1: read an extract from one of the Scottish Texts which are set for Higher and answer questions about it; Section 2: write an essay about a work of literature you have studied during your course.

## 1 Reading for Understanding, Analysis and Evaluation

*Questions which ask for understanding (e.g. questions which say "Identify ... " or "Explain what ... " etc.)*

- Keep your answers fairly short and pay attention to the number of marks available.
- Use your own words as far as possible. This means you mustn't just copy chunks from the passage – you have to show that you understand what it means by rephrasing it in your own words.

*Questions about language features (e.g. questions which say "Analyse how ... ")*

- This type of question will ask you to comment on features such as Word Choice, Imagery, Sentence Structure and Tone.
- You should pick out a relevant language feature and make a valid comment about its impact. Try to make your comments as specific as possible and avoid vague comments (such as "It is a good word to use because it gives me a clear picture of what the writer is saying"). Remember that you will get no marks just for picking out a word, image or feature of a sentence structure – it's the comment that counts.
- Some hints:
  - **Word choice:** Always try to pick a single word and then give its connotations, i.e. what it suggests.
  - **Sentence structure:** Don't just name the feature – try to explain what effect it achieves in that particular sentence.
  - **Imagery:** Try to explain what the image means literally and then go on to explain what the writer is trying to say by using that image.
  - **Tone** This is always difficult – a good tip is to imagine the sentence or paragraph being read out loud and try to spot how the words or the structure give it a particular tone.

## The last question

- Make sure you follow the instruction about whether you're looking for agreement or disagreement (or possibly both).
- When you start on Passage 2, you will have already answered several questions on Passage 1, so you should know its key ideas quite well; as you read Passage 2, try to spot important ideas in it which are similar or different (depending on the question).
- Stick to **key ideas** and don't include trivial ones; **three** relevant key ideas will usually be enough – your task is to decide what the most significant ones are.

# 2 Critical Reading

## Section 1 – Scottish Text

The most important thing to remember here is that there are two very different types of question to be answered:

- Three or four questions (for a total of 10 marks) which focus entirely on the extract.
- One question (for 10 marks) which requires knowledge of the whole text (or of another poem or short story by the same writer).

The first type of question will often ask you to use the same type of close textual analysis skills you used in the Reading part of your Analysis and Evaluation Unit. The golden rules are to read each question very carefully and do exactly as instructed, and to remember that (just like the "Anlaysis" questions in the Reading for Understanding, Analysis and Evaluation paper) there are no marks just for picking out a word or a feature – it's the comment that matters.

The second type of question requires you to discuss common features (of theme and/or technique) in the extract and elsewhere in the writer's work. You can answer this question with a series of bullet points or by writing a mini-essay, so choose the approach you feel most comfortable with.

Finally, a bit of advice for the Scottish Text question: when you see the extract in the exam paper, don't get too confident just because you recognise it (you certainly should recognise it if you've studied properly!). And even if you've answered questions on it before, remember that the questions in the exam are likely to be different, so stay alert.

## Section 2 – Critical Essay

A common mistake is to rely too heavily on ideas and whole paragraphs you have used in practice essays and try to use them for the question you have chosen in the exam. The trick is to come to the exam with lots of ideas and thoughts about at least one of the texts you have studied and use these to tackle the question you choose from the exam paper. You mustn't use the exam question as an excuse to trot out an answer you've prepared in advance.

### Structure

Every good essay has a structure, but there is no "correct" structure, no magic formula that the examiners are looking for. It's **your** essay, so structure it the way **you** want. As long as you're answering the question all the way through, then you'll be fine.

### Relevance

Be relevant to the question **all of the time** – not just in the first and last paragraphs.

### Central Concerns

Try to make sure your essay shows that you have thought about and understood the central concerns of the text, i.e. what it's "about" – the ideas and themes the writer is exploring in the text.

### Quotation

In poetry and drama essays, you're expected to quote from the text, but never fall into the trap of learning a handful of quotations and forcing them all into the essay regardless of the question you're answering. In prose essays, quotation is much less important, and you can show your knowledge more effectively by referring in detail to what happens in key sections of the novel or the short story.

### Techniques

You are expected to show understanding of how various literary techniques work within a text, but simply naming them will not get you marks, and structuring your essay around techniques rather than around relevant ideas in the text is not a good idea.

## Good luck!

Remember that the rewards for passing Higher English are well worth it! Your pass will help you get the future you want for yourself. In the exam, be confident in your own ability. If you're not sure how to answer a question, trust your instincts and just give it a go anyway – keep calm and don't panic! GOOD LUCK!

## HIGHER FOR CfE

# 2014 Specimen
# Question Paper

National
Qualifications
SPECIMEN ONLY

SQ14/H/01

English
Reading for Understanding,
Analysis and Evaluation

Date — Not applicable

Duration — 1 hour 30 minutes

**Total marks — 30**

Attempt ALL questions.

Write your answers clearly in the answer booklet provided. In the answer booklet you must clearly identify the question number you are attempting.

Use **blue** or **black** ink.

Before leaving the examination room you must give your answer booklet to the Invigilator; if you do not, you may lose all the marks for this paper.

The following two passages focus on the importance of trees.

**Passage 1**

*In the first passage Janice Turner, writing in The Times newspaper, considers the value of trees.*

Read the passage below and attempt the questions which follow.

Watching the tree surgeon from the window, I felt I was witnessing a crime. One I'd authorised, like a Mafia hit. The holm oak — a dense, virulent, evergreen ball — loomed over the garden like a storm cloud. It had to be cut back. But as the chainsaw whined and branches tumbled, I wondered if I really had the right.

5   I'm a resolute city-dweller, but trees seem ever more precious these days, a rebuke to built-in obsolescence, a steady point in a churning world. My pear and apple trees are remnants from when South London orchards ran all the way down to meet the sea. The walnut reaches out a mammoth limb from my neighbour's garden to mine like God's arm on the ceiling of the Sistine Chapel in Rome.

10  They are our living past, clocking up the years, ring by ring. Trees are calming like cathedrals, reassuring us that they will endure even though we will not. No wonder the ancients believed they were gods; there are worse things to worship than a tree.

And this week, reading how some protesters had been arrested trying to prevent ancient woodland being destroyed to make way for a three-mile link road to Hastings, I thought: yes, I'd
15  go to prison for a tree. Indeed, the protesters who are digging tunnels in the mud and standing before the diggers are not "eco-warriors" or "hippies". Among them are young families, retired folk and ordinary dog-walkers. "Local grandmothers", it was reported, came to swing in giant hammocks strung between the 400-year-old oaks.

But this is their last stand. They can only slow the developers. By March the trees will be
20  felled. Local people have fought for 20 years to save them, but they are on the wrong side of what the government is determined to market as progress, however short-term and dubious the economic benefits. The Chancellor of the Exchequer gave £56.8 million of government money for this very road, which will fill up with extra traffic, as new roads do, and lead in time to a spanking new industrial estate, although Hastings town already has plenty of boarded-up
25  premises from which to trade.

Development versus the trees. The government tells us that those who want to protect open countryside and woodland from being turned into endless Lego-brick estates are not conservationists, they are selfish, privileged people who, sitting comfortably in their own cheaply bought piles, have no care for struggling young couples who can't afford a family home.
30  Anyway, what's a bunch of trees?

But people with no respect for trees show a special kind of arrogance: they think they're bigger than history. I'd argue that cutting down an ancient oak is worse than killing most types of animal. Certainly the more numerous species such as dogs, cows, monkeys or cats. A chainsaw slicing into a 300-year-old trunk is more brutal and grotesque than hunting 100 foxes. Chopping
35  down a fine old tree is more like shooting an elephant or harpooning a whale: the aching poignancy of an enormous creature whose size and strength nonetheless cannot save it. Except even the mightiest mammal can be bred to maturity in a few years. Not so a tree.

Yet it is astonishing, given how much people love them — planting them to mark special moments or honour dead loved ones, measuring their lives by their seasonal changes — that
40  officialdom loathes trees. Insurance companies fretting about subsidence would rather you took them all down just in case. Councils detest them, employing municipal butchers to hack away at whole groves. Embarrassed stumps with a couple of twigs are all that remain.

It's a wonder any tree survives a health and safety audit.  One City Council tried to remove a whole row of horsechestnuts because conkers fell on cars and children might slip on leaves.  Our
45 local primary school cut down a fine tree beneath which generations of children had played, because the new head deemed its twigs and leaves too messy.  A posh gardener once suggested we cut down most of our trees and start again with fresh, more groovy varieties. This misunderstood the very point:  trees are the antithesis of fickle fashion. But some crass homeowners can't bear the fluff-balls from plane trees messing up their hall carpet or the lime
50 sap puking down on their shiny car bonnets.  Neater to reach for the axe.  Maybe garden centres should start selling plastic ones:  say goodbye to autumnal hell.

Visiting Burma, I learnt that its teak forests were flogged off to China by the generals, who were desperate for quick cash, like a beautiful girl being forced to sell her hair. Iceland is barren because Vikings cut them all down in a year and Peru is logging away its resources.

55 Our country's trees will tumble to make way for the machines of progress.  But for how much economic growth is it worth mowing down a wood?  Trees are beyond priceless:  they are our history inscribed in the natural world. Which rich men, planting beautiful orchards to their own glorious memory, have always known.

*Adapted from an article in The Times newspaper, January 2013.*

MARKS

**Questions**

1. Re-read lines 1–12

   (a) From the first paragraph, identify two feelings the writer had as she watched the tree in her garden being cut back.

   2

   (b) Analyse how the writer's use of language in lines 5–12 emphasises the importance of trees. You should refer in your answer to such features as sentence structure, word choice, imagery, contrast, tone . . .

   4

2. Re-read Lines 13–25

   According to the writer in lines 13–18, in what ways are the protestors different from how we might expect them to be?

   2

3. **By referring to at least two features of language in lines 19–25** analyse how the writer conveys her feelings of unhappiness about the Hastings development. You should refer in your answer to such features as sentence structure, word choice, contrast, tone . . .

   3

4. Re-read lines 26–37

   (a) From lines 26–30 identify two claims the government makes about the protestors.

   2

   (b) **By referring to at least two features of language in lines 31–37**, analyse how the writer conveys the strength of her belief in tree conservation.

   4

5. Re-read lines 38–54

   (a) Identify any **four** reasons given in these lines for cutting down trees. You should use your own words as far as possible.

   4

   (b) By referring to at least one example, analyse how the writer's use of imagery emphasises her opposition to cutting down trees.

   2

6. Evaluate the final paragraph's effectiveness as a conclusion to the passage as a whole.

   2

**Passage 2**

*In the second passage below, the science writer Colin Tudge gives his own views on trees.*

Read the passage and attempt the question which follows.  While reading, you may wish to make notes on the main ideas and/or highlight key points in the passage.

In New Zealand a few years ago I experienced more powerfully than ever the sheer gravitas of trees:  in the presence of the world's largest kauri.  Kauris are conifers, the biggest of their family.  The great trunk of the kauri rises like a lighthouse out of the gloom:  fifteen metres in circumference — it would touch all four walls in an average living room — and straight up,
5  leafless, for twenty metres or so.  And then on its great horizontal boughs rests a virtual park, a floating island with an entire ecosystem of ferns and flowers.  Kauris are about 2000 years old.  For the first 1400 years of the kauri's life, moas strutted their stuff around its base.  Moas included the world's tallest-ever birds, like giant emus, which were preyed upon by commensurately huge but short-winged eagles.  The moas and their attendant eagles are now
10  long gone.  The kauri lives on.

The remaining kauri forest has been horribly reduced these past two hundred years, but the way modern New Zealanders look after the trees that are left to them is a model for all the world.  Rare trees are no longer felled but existing planks are prized and meticulously re-cycled.  Meanwhile, you can follow slatted wooden paths among the vast conifers.  That's conservation;
15  that's intelligent ecotourism.

Similarly, if new farming economies are to come about, then trees must be at the centre of them. Yet, tree-based farming systems have to fight for survival against the massed ranks of the powers-that-be. How ludicrous.  The world's most powerful governments have made themselves answerable to the big companies — and they take pride in this.  They call it "realism".

20  So although the things that need doing seem obvious, governments — and the big corporations whose interests they serve — have a quite different agenda. If we want life to be agreeable or indeed to continue at all we just have to ignore the pressures from our ostensible leaders, and do things the way they should be done:  building new ways of life, whatever the pressures from on high.  Again, trees show the way.

25  Outstanding among the world's many popular initiatives is the Greenbelt Movement, a campaign among Kenyan women to re-plant trees in places they used to grow.  Now they have planted 30 million.  They have transformed landscapes and changed entire economies and the whole tenor of life.  This kind of thing, very simple, and achieved in the teeth of the modern economy (for who makes money out of it?), contributes far more to human wellbeing than, say, cheap white
30  goods from China, on which the economy of the modern world, egged on by our world leaders, is being built.

The broadest issue of all is the western conceit that we can "conquer" nature, or indeed control it.  This idea truly took off in the 19th century, and yet is taken still as a mark of modernity.  In 1879 the poet Gerard Manley Hopkins lamented the felling of poplars:  "O if we but knew what
35  we do/When we delve or hew — Hack and rack the growing green!"  We still don't know what we are doing but the hacking and racking continue more vigorously than ever.  The only halfway sane approach if we want this world to remain habitable, is to approach it humbly.  Trees teach humility.  We need to take the world far more seriously.  It would be a good idea to begin with trees.

*Adapted from an article published on Colin Tudge's website in 2005.*

**Question**                                              **MARKS**

7. Both writers express their views about the importance of trees. Identify key areas on which they agree. In your answer, you should refer in detail to both passages.   **5**

You may answer this question in continuous prose or in a series of developed bullet points.

### [END OF SPECIMEN QUESTION PAPER]

National
Qualifcations
SPECIMEN ONLY

**SQ14/H/02**

**English**
**Critical Reading**

Date — Not applicable

Duration — 1 hour 30 minutes

**Total marks — 40**

**SECTION 1 — Scottish Text — 20 marks**

Read an extract from a Scottish text you have previously studied and attempt the questions.

Choose ONE text from either

Part A — Drama        Pages 2—9
or
Part B — Prose        Pages 10—19
or
Part C — Poetry       Pages 20—31

Attempt ALL the questions for your chosen text.

**SECTION 2 — Critical Essay — 20 marks**

Attempt ONE question from the following genres — Drama, Prose, Poetry, Film and Television Drama, or Language.

Your answer must be on a different genre from that chosen in Section 1.

You should spend approximately 45 minutes on each Section.

Write your answers clearly in the answer booklet provided. In the answer booklet you must clearly identify the question number you are attempting.

Use **blue** or **black** ink.

Before leaving the examination room you must give your answer booklet to the Invigilator; if you do not, you may lose all the marks for this paper.

## SECTION 1 — SCOTTISH TEXT — 20 marks

Choose ONE text from Drama, Prose or Poetry.

Read the text extract carefully and then attempt ALL the questions for your chosen text.

You should spend about 45 minutes on this Section.

## PART A — SCOTTISH TEXT — DRAMA

### Text 1 — Drama

If you choose this text you may not attempt a question on Drama in Section 2.

Read the extract below and then attempt the following questions.

### *The Slab Boys* by John Byrne

*In this extract, which is taken from Act 1 of the play, the discovery of Phil's folio causes conflict in the Slab Room.*

(*Alan turns over the folio . . . idly looks inside.*)

| | | |
|---|---|---|
| Alan: | (*Taking out drawings*) Hey, these aren't yours, are they? | |
| Spanky: | No, they must be Phil's . . . ho, put them back. If he catches you going through his stuff he'll break your jaw. | |
| 5　Alan: | I'm not touching them. Hey some of these are not bad . . . look at this one . . . | |
| Spanky: | I'm telling you Alec . . . (*Crosses to have a look.*) God they are good, aren't they? There's one of Elvis...'s dead like him, isn't it? Right . . . shut the folder or I'll get the blame. I get the blame for everything around here . . . | |
| Alan: | Hey . . . how about that red chalk drawing? | |
| 10　Spanky: | That's his old man . . .I recognise his ears . . . like Dumbo. And there's one of his maw. Christ, you can tell, can't you? | |
| Alan: | Tell what? | |
| Spanky: | Nothing . . . tell it's his mother. Shut that folder, I said. | |
| Alan: | Look at the way he's done those hands. Whenever I have a bash at hands they turn out looking like fankled pipecleaners . . . | |
| 15 | | |
| Spanky: | Which is exactly how your features are going to look if Phil comes back. Get that shut . . . I'm not telling you again. | |
| Alan: | I wonder how he got that effect? | |
| Spanky: | What effect? | |
| 20　Alan: | There . . . The way he's got the nose coming forward from the head . . . | |
| Spanky: | Mines comes forward . . . | |
| Alan: | Some of these are quite accomplished . . . | |
| Spanky: | Aw . . . 'quite accomplished', are they? And what d'you know about it? | |
| Alan: | Not a great deal but anyone can see they're rather good. He's wasting his time in here . . . | |
| 25 | | |

*Page two*

Spanky:    Yeh, you have a word with him kiddo . . . I'm sure he'll appreciate it.  Now for the last time, are you going to shut that folder or . . .

(*Enter Curry*)

Curry:    I've just been having a natter with your dad, Alan . . .

30    Alan:    Oh . . .? (*Tries to gather up drawings*)

Curry:    On the phone.  You never let on Bob Downie was your father . . . eh?

Godstruth, see you young fellows . . . Chief Designer at Templars . . .?  I'd have been as proud as punch . . . Hullo, what's this?  Some of your artwork?  Let's have a butcher's . . .

35    Alan:    No, these aren't . . .

Curry:    Tch, tch, tch, tch . . . a chip off the old block, eh?

Alan:    I'm afraid they aren't . . .

Curry:    A right talented pair of buggers . . . I remember when Bob Downie used to work here he was always . . .

40    Alan:    These aren't mine, Mr Curry.

Curry:    What?

Spanky:    Yeh, they're not his.

Alan:    I was just . . .

Curry:    Who belongs to them then?  They aren't yours, Farrell, that's for sure.  You've
45    got trouble trying to draw water from that tap over there . . .

Alan:    They were just lying around . . .

Curry:    And they can't be Hector's.  Too bold for him . . .

Alan:    I think they must be . . .

Curry:    (*Interrupting him*) You're not going to tell me they're McCann's.  What's this . . .
50    (*Turns drawing over*)  That's the Art School stamp isn't it?  Jimmy Robertson and I used to go up to Saturday morning classes together . . . [*Reads*] 'Glasgow School of Art . . . First Year Entrance Exam . . . Nineteen Fifty Sev . . .' What??

Spanky    Eh?

55    Curry:    Whose are these??  Come on . . .

Spanky:    How should I know?

Curry:    (*Finding label on front of folder*) "P. J. McCann, 19 Darkwood Crescent, Ferguslie Park . . ." So that's what the loafer's been up to.  A flyman, eh?

Well we'll soon see about this . . . Farrell!

60    Spanky:    What?

Curry:    Away down to the ablutions and fetch that crony of yours up here.

Spanky:    I'll need to wash my hands first.

Curry:    Get a move on! Tell him to drag that miserable carcase of his up those flaming stairs.  You and McKenzie can take an arm and a leg each if he can't manage.

65    Spanky:    And just leave the rest of his body down there?

MARKS

Curry:    Get those mitts washed! Bloody corner boy. Now, Alan, where were we? Ah, yes . . . now, I'm going to rough in a few roses here. I dare say your dad's covered some of this ground with you . . . still, no harm in seeing it again, eh? I showed Bob Downie a few tricks while he was with us. Expect he told you, eh? Now, what's the first . . . Farrell, will you gee yourself up a bit! You'd think it was a damned bath you were having! Right Alan . . . what's the first thing we do when we're starting a charcoal sketch.

70

**Questions**

1.  By referring closely to two examples of dialogue from lines 3–17, explain what Spanky's comments suggest about Phil.

    2

2.  Throughout the play, Curry often reminisces about various incidents in his life. By referring to two examples of dialogue in this extract, explain what these memories suggest about him.

    2

3.  Describe the contrasting attitudes shown by Curry to the Slab Boys and to Alan. Explain how this is shown by referring closely to the extract.

    4

4.  Choose any example of humour in this extract and explain how it is used to engage the audience's sympathy for Spanky.

    2

5.  By referring to this extract and elsewhere in the play, discuss how the theme of frustrated ambition is developed in the text.

    10

**OR**

**Text 2 — Drama**

If you choose this text you may not attempt a question on Drama in Section 2.

Read the extract below and then attempt the following questions.

**The Cheviot, the Stag and the Black, Black Oil by John McGrath**

|  |  |  |
|---|---|---|
| *Fiddle plays:* | | "The Lord is my Shepherd". *The Company hum quietly as one of the actors is dressed as* The MINISTER *and the* OLD MAN *places his pulpit in position.* |

5

10

15

20

MINISTER:    Dearly beloved Brethren, we are gathered here today in the sight of the Lord and in the house of the Lord, to worship the Lord and sing His praises, for He is indeed, the Lord and Shepherd of our souls. Oh you are sheep, sheep who have gone astray, who have wandered from the paths of righteousness and into the tents of iniquity. Oh guilty sinners, turn from your evil ways. How many times and on how many Sabbaths have I warned you from this very pulpit of your wickedness and of the wrath of the Almighty. For I will repay, saith the Lord. The troubles that are visiting you are a judgement from God, and a warning of the final judgement that is to come. Some of you here today are so far from the fold, have so far neglected the dignity of your womanhood, that you have risen up to curse your masters, and violate the laws of the land. I refer of course to the burning of the writs. And everybody here gathered knows to which persons I am referring. There will be no more of this foolishness. Be warned. Unless you repent, you are in great danger of the fire, where there will be much wailing and gnashing of teeth. On that fearful day when God divides the sheep from the goats, every one of us, and particularly those whom I have spoken of today, will have to answer for their flagrant transgression of authority.

*He goes off.*

OLD MAN:    And it worked . . .

25  SECOND GIRL:    Everywhere, except in Knockan, Elphin and Coigeach.

FIRST GIRL *comes on stage and says, to mounting cheers from the others.*

30

FIRST GIRL:    Here the people made a stout resistance, the women disarming about twenty policemen and sheriff-officers, burning the summonses in a heap, and ducking the representatives of the law in a neighbouring pool. (*Big cheer.*) The men formed a second line of defence — (*Groan*) — in case the women should receive any ill-treatment. (*More groans.*) They, however, never put a finger on the officers of the law — all of whom returned home without serving a single summons or evicting a single crofter!

35  *A big hooch from the Company, the fiddle strikes up and they leap onto the stage to dance to celebrate this victory, the women leading off.*

*At the end, all go off except the actor playing the* OLD MAN, *who comes to the mike and talks to the audience as himself.*

MARKS

OLD MAN.  What was really going on?  There is no doubt that a change had to come
40 to the Highlands:  the population was growing too fast for the old,
inefficient methods of agriculture to keep everyone fed.  Even before
the Clearances, emigration had been the only way out for some. But this
coincided with something else: English — and Scottish — capital was
growing powerful and needed to expand.  Huge profits were being made
45 already as a result of the Industrial Revolution, and improved methods of
agriculture.  This accumulated wealth had to be used, to make more
profit — because this is the law of capitalism.  It expanded all over the
globe.  And just as it saw in Africa, the West Indies, Canada, the Middle
East and China, ways of increasing itself, so in the Highlands of Scotland
50 it saw the same opportunity.  The technological innovation was there:
the Cheviot, a breed of sheep that would survive the Highland winter
and produce fine wool.  The money was there.  Unfortunately, the
people were there too.  But the law of capitalism had to be obeyed.

## Questions

6. Explain how the minister's speech reveals that he regards himself as a force of
authority and control.                                                                                            3

7. By referring closely to an example of stage directions or dialogue, analyse how
humour is used in lines 26—34.                                                                          2

8. Music is evident on two occasions in this short extract.  In each case, explain what
the music contributes to the scene.                                                                    2

9. In lines 39—54, the Old Man presents a series of financial details.  By referring to at
least two examples, explain how these details are relevant to the themes of the
play.                                                                                                                      3

10. The role of women is a significant issue in this play.  By referring to this extract and
elsewhere in the play, discuss how this theme is developed.                              10

OR

Text 3 — Drama

If you choose this text you may not attempt a question on Drama in Section 2.

Read the extract below and then attempt the following questions.

*Men Should Weep* by Ena Lamont Stewart

Isa comes out of the bedroom.  She has a tawdry lacy, low-cut slip on, and over it a dirty film starish négligée

|       |         |                                                                                                  |
|-------|---------|--------------------------------------------------------------------------------------------------|
|       | ISA:    | Whit's a the row?                                                                                |
|       | MAGGIE: | (*emptying the contents of her purse on the table*) Alec's shiverin; he can                      |
| 5     |         | hardly staun on his feet.  Rin doon quick and get's a gill o whisky.                             |
|       | ISA:    | A *gill*?  There's no much in a gill.                                                             |
|       | MAGGIE: | An get a packet o Woodbine tae.  An here!  You've tae leave aff tormentin him!                    |
|       | ISA:    | Me?  Tormentin him?  I'm no tormentin him!                                                        |
| 10    | MAGGIE: | Aye are ye!  Threatenin tae leave him when ye ken he's that daft aboot ye.  Goad kens why, for ye're a worthless slut if ever there wis yin. |
|       | ISA:    | You keep yer insultin names tae yersel, ye dirty aul bitch!                                       |
|       | MAGGIE: | I'll learn ye tae ca me a bitch!  (*She slaps Isa's face.*)                                       |

At this moment John comes in

|       |         |                                                                                                  |
|-------|---------|--------------------------------------------------------------------------------------------------|
| 15    | JOHN:   | Here!  Whit's a this?                                                                             |
|       | ISA:    | She hit me!  She's that rotten tae me!                                                            |
|       | JOHN:   | Maggie!  Whit dae ye think ye're daein?                                                           |
|       | MAGGIE: | Naethin she didnae deserve.  She ca'd me a bitch.                                                 |
|       | JOHN:   | Well, ye're certainly actin like yin.                                                             |
| 20    | MAGGIE: | John!                                                                                             |
|       | JOHN:   | Ma Goad!  Whit a hell o a hoose tae come hame tae!                                                |
|       | MAGGIE: | It's no ma fault!  I've din a hale copper-fu o washin an scrubbed three floors an the hale lot o yous had naethin tae dae but lie in yer beds!  Ye couldna even wash up a dish for me.  It's me that aye has tae dae twa jobs when you |
| 25    |         | get the sack.                                                                                     |
|       | JOHN:   | Aw, shut up harpin on that string.  It's no ma fault.  I've been oot lookin for work.            |
|       | MAGGIE: | Aye, I've seen yous men lookin for work.  Haudin up the street corners, ca'in doon the Government . . . tellin the world whit you'd dae if you wis rinnin the |
| 30    |         | country . . .                                                                                     |
|       | JOHN:   | Shut yer mouth or I'll shut it for ye!                                                            |
|       | MAGGIE: | (*shocked*) John!  (*Pause*)  Whit I meant wis . . . ye could have tidied the place up afore ye went oot. |
|       | JOHN:   | Tae Hell wi this Jessie business every time I'm oot o a job!  I'm no turnin                       |
| 35    |         | masel intae a bloomin skivvy!  I'm a man!                                                         |

| ISA: | (*softly*) Quite right.  A woman disnae respect a man that's nae a man.  (*To Maggie*) Well, whit aboot this whisky? |
| JOHN: | Whit's this?  Whisky?  There's nae drink comin intae this hoose! |
| ISA: | It's for Alec.  He's nae weel, she says. |
| 40 MAGGIE: | He's lyin doon. |
| JOHN: | If he's nae weel it's mair likely because his system's poisoned wi the stuff a'ready.  Alec!  Get oot o that bed an show yer face! |
| MAGGIE: | I tell't ye he's nae weel, John. |

*John goes across to the bed and drags Alec out.*

| 45 JOHN: | Get outside and breathe some fresh air, at least whit passes for fresh air roon here.  Ye're getting nae whisky.  D'ye understan? |
| MAGGIE: | (*turning on him fiercely*) Who earned that money?  You or me? |

*John, as if he had been shot, drops Alec and turns away, slumps down in a chair and puts his head in his hands.*

50 *Alec craftily sneaks some of Maggie's cash and slinks out.*

*Maggie, resentful, eyes first Isa and then the demoralised John.*

| ISA: | That's the stuff!  He's needin somebody tae tak him in haun.  He's beyond me. (*She cries, not very convincingly*).  I canne dae naethin wi him. |
| MAGGIE: | Oh, wull ye listen tae her!  See they crocodile tears?  It's a wunner ye can 55 squeeze oot a drap frae they wee marble eyes! |
| JOHN: | Don't cry, Isa; he's nae worth it. |
| MAGGIE: | It's her that's the worthless yin!  If she'd leave him alane … … |
| JOHN: | Maggie!  That's no fair!  She's upset. |
| MAGGIE: | (*bitterly hurt at John's perfidy*) Oh, yous men!  Big saft idiots the lot o ye. |
| 60 JOHN: | It's your fault.  You spoiled him frae the day he wis born.  He's still your wee pet lamb no matter whit he gets up tae. |
| ISA: | Aye, he's jist a great big baby.  If he disnae get whit he wants, he greets; tears rinnin doon his cheeks.  It fair scunners me.  I like a man tae be a man.  Staun up for hissel. |
| 65 MAGGIE: | (*to John*) And I like a man . . . (*Her voice breaking*) . . . tae stand up for his wife. |

*She seizes her coat and hauls it on, jams on her terrible old hat (this should be black or dark brown) and goes to the table to pick up her money:  when she sees how little Alec has left her, she can't help making a small sound.*

MARKS

**Questions**

11. By referring closely to the dialogue between Maggie and Isa in lines 3—13, explain what is revealed about the difference between Maggie's attitudes to Isa and to Alec.    **2**

12. Much of the dialogue in lines 20—66 is about how a man is expected to behave. With close reference to the text, discuss Maggie, Isa and John's differing attitudes to this issue.    **3**

13. Analyse how the stage directions in lines 48—49 add to our understanding of John's character.    **3**

14. Maggie is disappointed by John's behaviour in this scene.  By referring closely to this scene, explain two examples of his behaviour which she finds disappointing.    **2**

15. Discuss this scene's importance to the development of Maggie's character.  You should refer to this extract and in more detail to the play as a whole.    **10**

## SECTION 1 — SCOTTISH TEXT — 20 marks

Choose ONE text from Drama, Prose or Poetry.

Read the text extract carefully and then attempt ALL the questions for your chosen text.

You should spend about 45 minutes on this Section.

## PART B — SCOTTISH TEXT — PROSE

Text 1 — Prose

If you choose this text you may not attempt a question on Prose in Section 2.

Read the extract below and then attempt the following questions.

*In Church* by Iain Crichton Smith

He was grateful now for the silence and for the wood which had a certain semblance of order after the scarred ground worked over and over, continuously revised by shells, so that it looked like carbon paper scribbled over endlessly by a typewriter that never stopped.

5   He looked up again and as he did so he saw two birds attacking another one.  They seemed to synchronise their movements and they were low enough for him to see their beaks quite clearly.  The third tried to fly above them but they attacked, probing upwards from below.  He could no longer see the plane, just the birds.  The third bird was weakening.  He couldn't make out whether it was a buzzard or a crow.  The other two
10  birds were zeroing in at it all the time, pecking and jabbing, going for the head.

He couldn't stand watching the fight any more and turned away into the wood, and it was then that he saw it — the church. It was completely intact though quite small and with gravestones beside it. It was strange to see it, like a mirage surrounded by trees whose brown leaves stirred faintly in the slight breeze.  From the sky above, the birds had
15  departed:  perhaps the two had killed the third one or perhaps it had escaped.  It reminded him of a dogfight he had seen between a German triplane and a British Sopwith Camel.  After a long duel, the German triplane had destroyed the British plane but was in turn shot down by another British fighter.  The triplane made a perfect landing.  The British troops rushed up to find the pilot seated at the controls, upright, disciplined,
20  aristocratic, eyes staring straight ahead, and perfectly dead.  Later they found the bullet which had penetrated his back and come out at the chest.

He pushed open the door of the church and stood staring around him. He had never been in a church like this before with the large effigy of the Virgin Mary all in gold looking down at him, hands crossed.  The stained glass windows had pictures of Christ in green
25  carrying a staff and driving rather shapeless yellow sheep in front of him. In one of the panes there was another picture of him holding out his hands in either a helpless or a welcoming gesture.  There were no Bibles or hymn books on the seats as if no one had been there for some time.  At the side there was a curtained alcove which he thought might be a confessional.  He pulled the curtains aside but there was no one there.

30  He sat down and gazed for a long time at the huge golden cross which dominated the front of the church.  The silence was oppressive.  It was not at all like the churches at home.  There was more ornament, it was less bare, more decorated.  The churches at home had little colour and less atmosphere than this.  He could feel in his bones the presence of past generations of worshippers, and then he heard the footsteps.

MARKS

35  He turned round to see a man in a black gown walking towards him.  There was a belt of rope round his gown and his hands could not be seen as they seemed to be folded inside his gown.  The face was pale and ill looking.

"What do you want, my son?" said the voice in English.

**Questions**

16.  Analyse how Iain Crichton Smith uses both word choice and sentence structure in the first two paragraphs (lines 1—10) to emphasise:

(i)  war's futility

(ii)  cruelty                                                                                      4

You should comment on both word choice and sentence structure in each part of your answer.

17.  Explain how the anecdote about the dogfight in paragraph 3 develops the theme of the futility of war.                                                                      2

18.  Analyse how Iain Crichton Smith conveys the narrator's unfamiliarity with his surroundings. (lines 22—38)                                                             4

19.  In his stories set in wartime, Iain Crichton Smith develops the theme of the destructive nature of war.  By referring to this and at least one other story by Crichton Smith, discuss how he develops this theme.                                 10

**OR**

**Text 2 — Prose**

If you choose this text you may not attempt a question on Prose in Section 2.

Read the extract below and then attempt the following questions.

*A Time to Keep* **by George Mackay Brown**

I dug out a new field at the side of the house — because no-one on God's earth could plough such a wilderness — and all the while I was tearing up stones and clumps of heather I thought to myself, "What a fool! Sure as hell the laird will raise your rent for this day's work." And my spade rang against stones or sank with a squelch into a sudden
5    bit of bog.

I looked up once and saw a dozen women trooping across the fields to the school.

It was Good Friday.

I looked up another time and saw a horseman riding between the hills. It was the laird. He turned his horse towards the school also. The Easter service was being held
10    there.

Two of my lambs had been born dead that morning. They lay, red bits of rag, under the wall. I would bury them afterwards.

There was one stone in the new field that just showed a gray curve through the heather. I took the biggest hammer in the barn and was an hour breaking it up and
15    tearing the sharp bits out of the ground.

That was enough labour for one day. The sun was going down. I turned for home.

Ingi was not in. The house was dead. The pot sat black upon a black fire. My shoulders ached with the misery and foolishness of increasing my own rent. I was very hungry too.

20    Ingi was at the service with the laird and the other women, listening to the story of the lash and the whins and the nails and the last words. All the women were there sitting before the missionary with open mouths, listening to that fairy tale. I and a few others in the island knew better. Mr Simpson, B.Sc., from Glasgow had not been our schoolmaster four winters for nothing.

25    I spent the rest of that day in the ale-house with half a dozen other ploughmen.

And how I got home to the croft again I do not know. I woke up in the morning on the rack of my own bed, with all my clothes on.

There was a jam jar with new daffodils in it in the window.

Ingi heard my awakening, a groan and a creak.

30    She rose up quickly from the chair where she was peeling potatoes and put her cold hand on my forehead. "You'll be fine now," she said. "Bella had two lambs in the night, such bonny peedie things! Your throat must be dry. I'll get you some water."

Bella was the old ewe. None of her lambs, so I had been told when I bought her, ever died.

35    "You listen to me," I said to Ingi. "You spend too much money every Wednesday at that grocery van. Don't you buy any more jars of jam, and sponge-cakes from the bake-house in Hamnavoe. We're poor people. Remember that."

The daffodils in the window were like a dozen old women shawled in brightness.

The fire burned high in the hearth and the kettle sang.

40    I closed my eyes.

MARKS

## Questions

20. By referring closely to lines 1—15 analyse how George Mackay Brown conveys:

    (i) the poverty of the land

    (ii) the narrator's inadequacy as a farmer.                                    4

21. By referring to at least two examples, analyse how George Mackay Brown uses sentence structure to develop the narrator's worsening mood in the extract.                                    4

22. By referring closely to one example of Ingi's actions or speech, explain how she influences or tries to influence his mood.                                    2

23. In his short stories, George Mackay Brown creates characters who are flawed but nonetheless engage the reader's sympathy. By referring to this story and at least one other by George Mackay Brown, discuss how he achieves this.                                    10

OR

### Text 3 — Prose

If you choose this text you may not attempt a question on Prose in Section 2.

Read the extract below and then attempt the following questions.

### *The Trick is to Keep Breathing* by Janice Galloway

*In this extract, Joy attends her first appointment with a psychiatrist, having been referred by her GP, Dr Stead.*

I knew right away this was going to be a disappointment.

Lesson 1:  Psychiatrists aren't as smart as you'd think.

I knew three things right away:

1.    I hate facile questions (So-why-do-you-think-you're-here is so easy to subvert);

5   2.    You have to try: it's the whole purpose of being here; and

3.    You have to be on your guard.  There is no defence against the arbitrariness of things.  You have to be suspicious of everything.

All three things whispered in my ears like Angels and Devils in a TV cartoon which made it very difficult to think straight.  Dr One didn't know that.  All he knew was I wasn't
10  answering.

So, he said.  Why do you think you've been sent to us?

He thought I wasn't trying.

Lesson 2:  Psychiatrists are not mind-readers.  They just try to look as though they are.

He tried another tack.

15      Tell me from the beginning what you think is making you feel bad, he said. Take your time and tell it in your own words.

For some reason, I hadn't expected this.  I'd done that story so many times I knew it like a nursery rhyme but now my throat was contracting.  I couldn't think about even the first line without feeling I was about to short-circuit.  On top of everything else I was ashamed
20  of how stupid I'd been.  I hadn't thought it through.  It was perfectly logical he should start like this yet I hadn't seen it coming.  The devils whispered What did you expect? A course of shock therapy the minute you walked in the door?   The angels whispered Try. Dr Stead went to a lot of trouble to get you this appointment.  You have to try.  There was only one way out of this.  My mouth knew more than the rest of me put together.  I had to
25  trust my mouth.  I closed my eyes and the mouth said

My mother walked into the sea.

I remember the voice:  chiselled as crystal.  Cold as a razor.  I hadn't known it would start like this but then I was redundant.  The voice didn't need me.  It didn't even like me.  I let the story come out in this disembodied glass voice and listened, out of harm's way in
30  the corner of the room.

She didn't die right away.  At the funeral, the man I lived with shook my hand.  I left him.  I had an affair with a married man.  He left his wife to come and stay with me. Things were difficult.  My house started caving in and we had to move somewhere else.  Then we went away and he drowned

MARKS

35 The end of the story seemed to come up too soon.  I heard the last bit twisting out of kilter then stopping without warning.  The room felt suddenly eerie:  like the Bates Motel in Psycho.  If you listened hard you could probably hear the liver-coloured furniture breathing, little creaks and rustles where people had been before.  I had to think hard to remember where I was.

40                     He drowned.

Something was happening to my stomach.  As though I'd stamped my foot down hard at the end of a staircase and the floor wasn't where I thought it was.  The side of the pool, the circle of men, blue eyes and the sky.  I suddenly remembered what I was saying wasn't a story.  It wasn't the furniture breathing, it was me.  What I was saying was true.

45                     Lesson 3:  Psychiatrists give you a lot of rope knowingly.


**Questions**


24.  By referring closely to lines 1—13, explain how Galloway makes the reader aware of Joy's attitude towards the psychiatrist.                                                                2


25.  "Tell me from the beginning . . . in your own words." (lines 15—16)

     Referring closely to at least two examples in lines 15—30, analyse how the writer conveys Joy's state of mind at this point.                                                           4


26.  Referring closely to at least two examples from lines 31—45, analyse how the writer highlights the significance of Michael's death.                                                  4


27.  By referring to this extract and elsewhere in the novel, discuss how Galloway develops the theme of loss.                                                                        10

OR

Text 4 — Prose

If you choose this text you may not attempt a question on Prose in Section 2.

Read the extract below and then attempt the following questions.

**Sunset Song** by Lewis Grassic Gibbon

*In this extract, which is from Part I I (Drilling), Peesie's Knapp is on fire.*

And faith, quick though they were, it was father that saved Chae Strachan's folk.  He was first down at the blazing Knapp, John Guthrie; and he ran round the biggings and saw the flames lapping and lowing at the kitchen end of the house, not a soul about or trying to stop them though the noise was fair awful, the crackling and burning, and the winter air
5   bright with flying sticks and straw.  He banged at the door and cried *Damn't to hell do you want to be roasted*?  and when he got no answer he smashed in the window, they heard him then and the bairns scraiched, there was never such a lot for sleep, folk said, Chae'd have slept himself out of this world and into hell in his own firewood if John Guthrie hadn't roused him then.  But out he came stumbling at last, he'd only his breeks
10  on; and he took a keek at John Guthrie and another at the fire and cried out *Kirsty, we're all to hell*!  and off he tore to the byre.

But half-way across the close as he ran the barn swithered and roared and fell, right in front of him, and he'd to run back, there was no way then of getting at the byre.  By then Long Rob of the Mill came in about, he'd run over the fields, louping dykes like a hare,
15  and his lungs were panting like bellows, he was clean winded.  He it was that helped Mrs Strachan with the bairns and such clothes as they could drag out to the road while Chae and John Guthrie tried to get at the byre from another angle:  but that was no good, the place was already roaring alight.  For a while there was only the snarling of the fire eating in to the wooden couplings, the rattle of falling slates through the old charred
20  beams, and then, the first sound that Will and Chris heard as they came panting down the road, a scream that was awful, a scream that made them think one of the Strachans was trapped down there.  And at that sound Chae covered his ears and cried *Oh God, that's old Clytie*, Clytie was his little horse, his sholtie, and she screamed and screamed, terrible and terrible, Chris ran back to the house trying not to hear and to help poor
25  Kirsty Strachan, snivelling and weeping, and the bairns laughing and dancing about as though they were at a picnic, and Long Rob of the Mill smoking his pipe as cool as you please, there was surely enough smell and smoke without that?  But pipe and all he dived in and out of the house and saved chairs and dishes and baskets of eggs; and Mistress Strachan cried *Oh, my sampler*!  and in Rob tore and rived that off a blazing wall, a
30  meikle worsted thing in a cracked glass case that Mistress Strachan had made as a bairn at school.

MARKS

**Questions**

28.  By close reference to the text, explain how two aspects of John Guthrie's and Long Rob's character are revealed in this extract.

4

29.  By referring to at least two examples from **paragraph one** analyse how the writer conveys a sense of urgency.

2

30.  By referring to at least two examples from **paragraph two** analyse how the writer conveys the ferocity of the fire.

4

31.  The community is presented positively in this extract.  By referring to this extract, and elsewhere in the novel, discuss how Grassic Gibbon conveys positive aspects of the community.

10

**OR**

**Text 5 — Prose**

If you choose this text you may not attempt a question on Prose in Section 2.

Read the extract below and then attempt the following questions.

### *The Cone Gatherers* by Robin Jenkins

*In this extract, Mr Tulloch arrives to speak with the brothers after their expulsion from the beach hut by Lady Runcie Campbell.*

When he caught sight of Neil ahead of him, he halted and watched from behind a slender spruce long ago wind-blown, with its roots in the air.  From that distance, judged only by his gait, Neil appeared like an old man.  He was gathering beech seed, which he had been instructed to do whenever bad weather kept him from climbing.  He would cautiously go
5   down on his haunches, wait, apparently to gather strength and endurance against the pain of that posture, and then would begin to pick up the seed-cases or mast, squeeze each one with his fingers to find if it were fertile, and drop it if it were not.  The watching forester knew most of them would not be, unless this luckily was the tree's year of fertility: otherwise as many as ninety out of a hundred would be barren.  To fingers
10   crippled with rheumatism it would not be easy to examine them with the necessary patience.  When that area had been searched, Neil hobbled on his haunches to another. Thus he would go on until break-time.  Such fidelity to so simple but indispensable a task was to the forester as noble and beautiful a sight as was to be seen in that wood so rich in magnificent trees.  To praise it would be to belittle it, so inadequate were words; but to
15   fail to appreciate it or to refuse to defend it, would be to admit the inadequacy of life itself.

He stepped out from behind the hanging roots, and without hurry approached the intent seed-gatherer.

Neil looked up, saw him, stared a moment, and then went on with his inspection of the
20   beech nut.  That one was fertile.  He held it out to his employer.

"That's the first good one in the last half hour, Mr Tulloch," he said.

"Well, it's a slow business, Neil," replied the forester, smiling, "but look at the result." Walking forward he touched the huge grey trunk.

Behind him Neil began to sob.  He did not turn to look, but kept stroking the tree.

25   "Don't fret over it, Neil," he said.

"It's not for me," sobbed Neil.  "It's for Calum."  And he began to pour out an account of the expulsion from the beach hut, all mixed up with the story of the insult in the hotel bar.  The forester had heard about that episode from one of his workers, but he had been given to believe that the soldier had apologised, and that afterwards the sympathy of
30   nearly everybody in the pub had been with the brothers.

"I'm responsible for him, Mr Tulloch," said Neil.  "If you were to ask me to whom I'm to give account for the way I've looked after him, I couldn't tell you; but I'm responsible just the same."

"No man on earth has ever looked after his brother so well," replied Tulloch.  "We all
35   know that.  You can give a good account, no matter to whom."

He turned round and saw, with a shock he did not show, how stooped and contorted Neil was then, by rheumatism and despair: it was as if, in some terrible penance, he was striving to become in shape like his brother.

*Page eighteen*

MARKS

"Why is it, Mr Tulloch," he asked, "that the innocent have always to be sacrificed?"

40    "Is that really true, Neil?"

"Aye, it's true.   In this war, they tell me, babies are being burnt to death in their cradles."

The forester was silent; his own brother had been killed at the time of Dunkirk.

"I suppose it's so that other babies will be able to grow up and live like free men," he
45    said.   "But I see what you mean; in a way, aye, the innocent have to be sacrificed."

"We were driven out like slaves, Mr Tulloch.   Her dog was to be saved from the storm, but not my brother."

"I think maybe she was taken by surprise, Neil.   She didn't expect to find you there. After all, you did get in by the window.   Maybe she got a bit of a shock."

50    "Did she think we were monkeys that would bite her?"

"I think she was in the wrong, Neil, but I would like to be fair to her.   She's a good woman really; but she's got a code to live by."

Neil shook his head dourly.

"My brother's the shape God made him,' he said.   'What right has she, great lady though
55    she is, to despise him?"

"No right at all, Neil.   But don't think about it anymore.   I'm seeing her this afternoon, and I'm going to tell her I'm taking you back to Ardmore."


## Questions

32.    By referring closely to lines 1—38, analyse how Jenkins evokes both sympathy and admiration for Neil.    4

33.    By referring closely to lines 39—55, explain the reasons for Neil's attitude to Lady Runcie Campbell.    4

34.    Explain the reasons for Mr. Tulloch's attitude to Lady Runcie Campbell and the 'code' by which she makes decisions, referring to lines 39—57 in your answer.    2

35.    Neil's words "Why is it...that the innocent have always to be sacrificed?" clarify one of the central concerns of the text.

With reference to such features as setting, characterisation and narrative in this extract and elsewhere in the novel, discuss how Jenkins develops our understanding of this central concern.    10

**SECTION 1 — SCOTTISH TEXT — 20 marks**                                    MARKS

**Choose ONE text from Drama, Prose or Poetry.**

**Read the text extract carefully and then attempt ALL the questions for your chosen text.**

**You should spend about 45 minutes on this Section**

### PART C — SCOTTISH TEXT — POETRY

Text 1 — Poetry

If you choose this text you may not attempt a question on Poetry in Section 2.

Read the extract below and then attempt the following questions.

**Holy Willie's Prayer by Robert Burns**

*This extract begins at stanza five of the poem.*

Yet I am here a chosen sample,
To show thy grace is great and ample;
I'm here, a pillar o' Thy temple,
    Strong as a rock,
5  A guide, a buckler, and example,
      To a' Thy flock.

O Lord, Thou kens what zeal I bear,
When drinkers drink, an swearers swear,
An' singin' there, an' dancin' here,
10     Wi' great an' sma';
For I am keepet by Thy fear,
    Free frae them a'.

But yet, O Lord! confess I must ___
At times I'm fash'd wi' fleshly lust:
15  And sometimes too, in wardly trust,
    Vile self gets in:
But Thou remembers we are dust,
    Defil'd wi' sin.

O Lord!  yestreen, Thou kens, wi' Meg —
20 Thy pardon I sincerely beg !
O! may't ne'er be a livin' plague
    To my dishonour !
An' I'll ne'er lift a lawless leg
    Again upon her.

MARKS

25　Besides, I farther maun allow,

　　　Wi' Leezie's lass, three times I trow;

　　　But Lord, that Friday I was fou,

　　　　　　　When I came near her;

　　　Or else, Thou kens, Thy servant true

30　　　　　Wad never steer her.

　　　Maybe Thou lets this fleshly thorn

　　　Buffet Thy servant e'en and morn,

　　　Lest he o'er proud and high should turn,

　　　　　　　That he's sae gifted;

35　If sae, Thy han' maun e'en be borne,

　　　　　　　Until Thou lift it.

　　　Lord, bless Thy chosen in this place,

　　　For here Thou hast a chosen race:

　　　But God confound their stubborn face,

40　　　　　And blast their name,

　　　Wha bring Thy elders to disgrace

　　　　　　　An' open shame.


## Questions

**36.**　Explain what Holy Willie means when he calls himself "a chosen sample".　　　　　2

**37.**　Holy Willie's words and feelings/actions contradict one another.

　　　With reference to two examples from lines 1—30 from this extract, analyse how Burns conveys this contradiction.　　　4

**38.**　The tone changes in lines 31—42.　With reference to two examples from lines 31—42, identify the change of tone used by Holy Willie.　　　4

**39.**　Burns creates a variety of characters in his poetry.　From your reading of this poem and at least one other by Burns, discuss the contrast between Holy Willie and at least one other character.　　　10

**OR**

**Text 2 — Poetry**

If you choose this text you may not attempt a question on Poetry in Section 2.

Read the poem below and then attempt the following questions.

**Originally by Carol Ann Duffy**

We came from our own country in a red room
which fell through the fields, our mother singing
our father's name to the turn of the wheels.
My brothers cried, one of them bawling, *Home,*
5   Home, as the miles rushed back to the city,
the street, the house, the vacant rooms
where we didn't live any more.  I stared
at the eyes of a blind toy, holding its paw.

All childhood is an emigration.  Some are slow,
10  leaving you standing, resigned, up an avenue
where no one you know stays.  Others are sudden.
Your accent wrong.  Corners, which seem familiar,
leading to unimagined pebble-dashed estates, big boys
eating worms and shouting words you don't understand.
15  My parents' anxieties stirred like a loose tooth
in my head.  *I want our own country*, I said.

But then you forget, or don't recall, or change,
and, seeing your brother swallow a slug, feel only
a skelf of shame.  I remember my tongue
20  shedding its skin like a snake, my voice
in the classroom sounding just like the rest.  Do I only think
I lost a river, culture, speech, sense of first space
and the right place? Now, *Where do you come from?*
strangers ask.  *Originally?*  And I hesitate.

MARKS

**Questions**

40. By referring closely to **stanza 1** analyse the use of poetic technique to emphasise the dramatic impact moving to another country had on the family.    2

41. Look at **stanza 2**.

    "All childhood is an emigration"

    Explain fully what the poet means by this.    2

42. In lines 12—16 analyse the use of poetic technique to convey the distress of the family members caused by their "sudden" emigration to a new environment.    3

43. Evaluate the effectiveness of **stanza 3** as a conclusion to the poem.  Your answer should deal with ideas and/or language.    3

44. Discuss how Carol Ann Duffy uses contrast in this poem and at least one other to highlight the poems' main concerns.    10

**OR**

**Text 3 — Poetry**

If you choose this text you may not attempt a question on Poetry in Section 2.

Read the poem below and then attempt the following questions.

*For My Grandmother Knitting* **by Liz Lochhead**

There is no need they say
but the needles still move
their rhythms in the working of your hands
as easily
5   as if your hands
were once again those sure and skilful hands
of the fisher-girl.

You are old now
and your grasp of things is not so good
10   but master of your movements then
deft and swift
you slit the still-tickling quick silver fish.
Hard work it was too
of necessity.

15   But now they say there is no need
as the needles move
in the working of your hands
once the hands of the bride
with the hand-span waist
20   once the hands of the miner's wife
who scrubbed his back
in a tin bath by the coal fire
once the hands of the mother
of six who made do and mended
25   scraped and slaved slapped sometimes
when necessary.

But now they say there is no need
the kids they say grandma
have too much already
30   more than they can wear
too many scarves and cardigans —

MARKS

gran you do too much

there's no necessity...

At your window you wave

35 them goodbye Sunday.

With your painful hands

big on shrunken wrists.

Swollen-jointed. Red. Arthritic. Old.

But the needles still move

40 their rhythms in the working of your hands

easily

as if your hands remembered

of their own accord the pattern

as if your hands had forgotten

45 how to stop.


## Questions

45. By referring to **two** examples from lines 1—14, analyse the use of poetic technique in clarifying the main ideas of the poem.

2

46. In lines 15—26 the poet expands upon the life of the grandmother when she was younger.

Choose two poetic techniques and analyse how they help convey the grandmother's life as a younger woman.

3

47. By referring closely to lines 27—33 identify the attitude of the grandchildren to their grandmother and explain how this is conveyed.

2

48. Evaluate how effective you find lines 34—45 as a conclusion to the poem.

Your answer should deal with ideas and/or language.

3

49. By referring to this poem and at least one other by Lochhead, discuss the importance of the theme of memory in her work.

10

OR

**Text 4 — Poetry**

If you choose this text you may not attempt a question on Poetry in Section 2.

Read the poem below and then attempt the following questions.

***Sounds of the Day* by Norman MacCaig**

When a clatter came,
  it was horses crossing the ford.
When the air creaked, it was
  a lapwing seeing us off the premises
5  of its private marsh.  A snuffling puff
Ten yards from the boat was the tide blocking and
  unblocking a hole in a rock.
When the black drums rolled, it was water
  falling sixty feet into itself.

10  When the door
  scraped shut, it was the end
  of all the sounds there are.

  You left me
  beside the quietest fire in the world.

15  I thought I was hurt in my pride only,
  forgetting that,
  when you plunge your hand in freezing water,
  you feel
  a bangle of ice around your wrist
20  before the whole hand goes numb.

MARKS

Questions

50. By referring closely to lines 1–9, analyse MacCaig's use of poetic technique to create a vivid sense of place.

4

51. By referring closely to lines 10–12, analyse MacCaig's use of poetic technique to convey the abrupt change in the persona's circumstance.

2

52. By referring closely to the lines 13–20, analyse how MacCaig highlights the impact which the parting has on the persona.

4

53. By referring to this poem and at least one other by Norman MacCaig, discuss his use of contrast to explore theme in his work.

10

**OR**

**Text 5 — Poetry**

If you choose this text you may not attempt a question on Poetry in Section 2.

Read the poem below and then attempt the following questions.

*Heroes* **by Sorley MacLean**

I did not see Lannes at Ratisbon

nor MacLennan at Auldearn

nor Gillies MacBain at Culloden,

but I saw an Englishman in Egypt.

5  A poor little chap with chubby cheeks

and knees grinding each other,

pimply unattractive face —

garment of the bravest spirit.

He was not a hit "in the pub

10  in the time of the fists being closed,"

but a lion against the breast of battle,

in the morose wounding showers.

His hour came with the shells,

with the notched iron splinters,

15  in the smoke and flame,

in the shaking and terror of the battlefield.

Word came to him in the bullet shower

that he should be a hero briskly,

and he was that while he lasted

20  but it wasn't much time he got.

He kept his guns to the tanks,

bucking with tearing crashing screech,

until he himself got, about the stomach,

that biff that put him to the ground,

25  mouth down in sand and gravel,

without a chirp from his ugly high-pitched voice.

No cross or medal was put to his

chest or to his name or to his family;

there were not many of his troop alive,

30 and if there were their word would not be strong.

And at any rate, if a battle post stands,

many are knocked down because of him,

not expecting fame, not wanting a medal

or any froth from the mouth of the field of slaughter.

35 I saw a great warrior of England,

a poor manikin on whom no eye would rest;

no Alasdair of Glen Garry;

and he took a little weeping to my eyes.

## Questions

54. By referring closely to the first stanza, evaluate its effectiveness as an opening to the poem.

2

55. By referring closely to lines 5–11 **and** lines 35–38, discuss the speaker's attitude towards the English soldier.

4

56. By referring to at least **two** examples from lines 12–26, analyse the use of poetic technique to convey the horror of war.

4

57. MacLean often chooses to write about people or places. Referring closely to this poem and to another poem or poems by MacLean, discuss how the poet develops a theme or themes through his observation of people or places.

10

**OR**

**Text 6 — Poetry**

If you choose this text you may not attempt a question on Poetry in Section 2.

Read the poem below and then attempt the following questions.

**The Ferryman's Arms by Don Paterson**

About to sit down with my half-pint of Guinness
I was magnetized by a remote phosphorescence
and drawn, like a moth, to the darkened back room
where a pool-table hummed to itself in the corner.
5  With ten minutes to kill and the whole place deserted
I took myself on for the hell of it.  Slotting
a coin in the tongue, I looked round for a cue —
while I stood with my back turned, the balls were deposited
with an abrupt intestinal rumble; a striplight
10  batted awake in its dusty green cowl.
When I set down the cue-ball inside the parched D
it clacked on the slate; the nap was so threadbare
I could screw back the globe, given somewhere to stand.
As physics itself becomes something negotiable
15  a rash of small miracles covers the shortfall.
I went on to make an immaculate clearance.
A low punch with a wee dab of side, and the black
did the vanishing trick while the white stopped
before gently rolling back as if nothing had happened,
20  shouldering its way through the unpotted colours.

The boat chugged up to the little stone jetty
without breaking the skin of the water, stretching,
as black as my stout, from somewhere unspeakable,
to here, where the foaming lip mussitates endlessly,
25  trying, with a nutter's persistence, to read
and re-read the shoreline.  I got aboard early,
remembering the ferry would leave on the hour
even for only my losing opponent;
but I left him there, stuck in his tent of light, sullenly
30  knocking the balls in, for practice, for next time.

MARKS

Questions

58. The main themes of the poem are introduced in the title and first six lines

    Identify **one** main theme and show how poetic technique is used to introduce this theme.

    3

59. By referring closely to lines 6–20, analyse the use of poetic technique to achieve a change of mood from alienation and uncertainty to one of confidence.

    4

60. Evaluate the effectiveness of the second stanza as a conclusion to the poem.

    3

61. In this poem, Paterson uses an apparently ordinary experience to explore a deeper truth about humanity.

    By referring to this and another poem or poems by Don Paterson you have studied discuss how he uses poetry to explore the deeper truths behind ordinary experience.

    10

[END OF SECTION 1]

## SECTION 2 — CRITICAL ESSAY — 20 marks

Attempt ONE question from the following genres — Drama, Prose, Poetry, Film and Television Drama, or Language.

You may use a Scottish text but <u>NOT</u> the one used in Section 1.

Your answer must be on a different genre from that chosen in Section 1.

You should spend approximately 45 minutes on this Section.

### DRAMA

> Answers to questions on **drama** should refer to the text and to such relevant features as characterisation, key scene(s), structure, climax, theme, plot, conflict, setting . . .

1. Choose a play in which a central character struggles to cope with social convention **or** financial difficulties **or** family duties.

   Briefly explain the reasons for the character's struggle and discuss how the dramatist's presentation of this struggle enhances your understanding of character and/or theme in the play as a whole.

2. Choose a play in which the concluding scene provides effective clarification of the central concerns.

   By referring in detail to the concluding scene, discuss in what ways it is important for your understanding of the play as a whole.

3. Choose a play in which the conflict between two characters is an important feature.

   Briefly explain the nature of this conflict and discuss how the dramatist's presentation of this feature enhances your understanding of the play as a whole.

## PROSE — FICTION

> Answers to questions on **prose fiction** should refer to the text and to such relevant features as characterisation, setting, language, key incident(s), climax, turning point, plot, structure, narrative technique, theme, ideas, description . . .

4.  Choose a novel or short story in which there is a disturbing or violent incident.

    Explain briefly what happens during this incident and discuss to what extent the disturbing or violent nature of the incident is important to your understanding of the text as a whole.

5.  Choose a novel or short story in which a specific location or setting is crucial to the plot.

    Discuss how the writer makes you aware of the setting's importance and how this feature is used to enhance your appreciation of the text as a whole.

6.  Choose a novel or short story in which a central character is presented as a menacing or threatening presence.

    Discuss how the writer's presentation of this character adds to your understanding of the text as a whole.

## PROSE — NON-FICTION

> Answers to questions on **prose non fiction** should refer to the text and to such relevant features as ideas, use of evidence, stance, style, selection of material, narrative voice . . .

7.  Choose a piece of **travel writing** in which the writer's use of language engages your interest in his/her portrayal of a country or culture.

    Discuss how the writer uses language to successfully engage your interest in this portrayal.

8.  Choose a work of **biography** or **autobiography** in which the writer's description of an emotional experience creates a powerful impression.

    Briefly explain the emotional experience and then discuss how the writer's description of this experience creates this powerful impression.

9.  Choose a piece of **journalism** in which the writer persuades his or her reader to a point of view by effective use of language.

    Briefly explain the writer's point of view, and then discuss how the writer's use of language is effective in persuading the reader.

## POETRY

> Answers to questions on **poetry** should refer to the text and to such relevant features as word choice, tone, imagery, structure, content, rhythm, rhyme, theme, sound, ideas . . .

10. Choose a poem in which the poet explores one of the following emotions: grief, happiness, love, alienation.

    Discuss how the poet's exploration of the emotion has deepened your understanding of it.

11. Choose two poems which deal with the same theme.

    Discuss how the theme is explored in each poem and explain which poem you believe offers a more memorable exploration of the theme.

12. Choose a poem which features a relationship.

    Discuss how the poet's presentation of this relationship adds to your understanding of the central concern(s) of the poem.

## FILM AND TELEVISION DRAMA

> Answers to questions on **film and television drama**\* should refer to the text and to such relevant features as use of camera, key sequence, characterisation, mise-en-scène, editing, setting, music/sound, special effects, plot, dialogue, . . .

13. Choose a film or television drama in which a central character is in difficulty.

    Briefly explain what the difficulty is, and then discuss how the film or programme makers' presentation of the character's difficulties enhances your understanding of a central concern of the text.

14. Choose a film or television drama which contains a particularly memorable or thrilling chase sequence.

    Explain how the memorable or thrilling aspect of this chase was achieved by the film or programme makers and then discuss the significance of this sequence in your appreciation of the text as a whole.

15. Choose a film or television drama which presents an epic voyage or a difficult quest.

    Explain how the film or programme makers evoke the epic nature of the voyage or the difficulty of the quest and discuss how this evocation enhances your appreciation of the text as a whole.

\* "television drama" includes a single play, a series or a serial.

## LANGUAGE

Answers to questions on **language** should refer to the text and to such relevant features as register, accent, dialect, slang, jargon, vocabulary, tone, abbreviation . . .

16. Choose a particular area of journalism such as sports reporting, investigative journalism, motoring journalism, science reporting.

    Identify the key features of the language used in this particular journalistic area and discuss that area's contribution to effective reporting.

17. Choose a form or forms of electronic communication such as e-mail, social networking, text messaging, online forums.

    Identify some of the distinctive features of the language used and discuss to what extent these features contribute to effective communication.

18. Choose a political speech which makes use of persuasive language.

    By referring to specific features of language in this speech, discuss to what extent you feel the speech is successful in achieving its purpose of persuasion.

[END OF SECTION 2]

[END OF SPECIMEN QUESTION PAPER]

# Model Paper 1

Whilst this Model Practice Paper has been specially commissioned by Hodder Gibson for use as practice for the Higher (for Curriculum for Excellence) exams, the key reference document remains the SQA Specimen Paper 2014.

Please note that in the Reading for Understanding, Analysis and Evaluation sections, these model papers use passages from previous Official SQA Papers, but with different questions in line with assessment criteria for the new Higher. There are three Model Papers, but for reasons of space, the third Model Paper does not cover the Scottish Text element.

HODDER
GIBSON
LEARN MORE

National
Qualifications
MODEL PAPER 1

# English
# Reading for Understanding,
# Analysis and Evaluation

Date — Not applicable

Duration — 1 hour 30 minutes

**Total marks — 30**

Attempt ALL questions.

Write your answers clearly in the answer booklet provided.  In the answer booklet you must clearly identify the question number you are attempting.

Use **blue** or **black** ink.

Before leaving the examination room you must give your answer booklet to the Invigilator; if you do not, you may lose all the marks for this paper.

**HODDER**
GIBSON
LEARN MORE

The following two passages focus on the First World War.

**Passage 1**

*The first passage is taken from the introduction to Peter Parker's book "The Last Veteran", published in 2009. The book tells the life story of Harry Patch, who fought in the First World War, and eventually became the last surviving soldier to have fought in the trenches. He died in 2009, aged 111.*

Read the passage below and attempt the questions which follow.

At 11 a.m. on Monday, 11th November 1918, after four and a quarter years in which howitzers boomed, shells screamed, machine guns rattled, rifles cracked, and the cries of the wounded and dying echoed across the battlefields of France and Belgium, everything suddenly fell quiet. A thick fog had descended that morning, and in the muffled landscape the stillness seemed
5   almost palpable.

For those left alive at the Front — a desolate landscape in which once bustling towns and villages had been reduced to piles of smoking rubble, and acre upon acre of woodland reduced to splintered and blackened stumps — there was little cause for rejoicing. The longed-for day had finally arrived but most combatants were too enervated to enjoy it. In the great silence,
10   some men were able to remember and reflect on what they had been through. Others simply felt lost. The war had swallowed them up: it occupied their every waking moment, just as it was to haunt their dreams in the future.

There have been other wars since 1918, and in all of them combatants have had to endure privation, discomfort, misery, the loss of comrades and appalling injuries. Even so, the First
15   World War continues to exert a powerful grip upon our collective imagination. In Britain the international catastrophe that was the First World War has been adopted as a peculiarly national trauma.

When remembering the War, the British continue to talk about a lost generation. The statistics are, of course, extraordinary: over thirty per cent of British men who were aged between
20   twenty and twenty-four in 1914 were killed in action or died of wounds; on the first day of the Battle of the Somme alone, 20,000 British soldiers were killed.

There is a sense that we have never quite recovered from this loss. Not only was the flower of British youth cut down in Picardy and Flanders, but an almost prelapsarian state of innocence was destroyed for ever between the years 1914–1918. Cast out of our pre-war Eden, where it
25   was somehow always perfect summer weather, we have ever after tended to look yearningly back rather than expectantly forward.

The War continues to occupy a tremendously large place in our sense of the world and its history. It has become a seemingly endless resource not only for historians, but for novelists, poets, dramatists, filmmakers and composers. The sounds and images of the First World War
30   are engraved on the national consciousness. We recognise them instantly: the foreign place names such as the Somme, Ypres and Passchendaele; the lines of men at the recruiting offices on 4th August 1914; the rows of crosses in war cemeteries; the scarlet poppies blowing in a landscape rendered unrecognisable by shellfire.

Our popular notion of the First World War is that it was indeed uniquely horrible; that it was
35   conducted by an incompetent High Command that repeatedly sacrificed thousands of men in

order to gain a few yards of churned earth; that it was characterised by "mud, blood and futility".  There is, however, another view of the conflict: that not all the generals were callous incompetents, not all ordinary soldiers hapless and unwilling victims.  Nowadays, revisionist historians insist that some of the battles were brilliantly planned and fought. They remind us
40 that we did, after all, win the war.

By giving an overview of campaigns and strategy, military historians can tell us what the war was about; although what really interests us is what the war was *like*.  For that we have always turned to those who were there, notably the poets and memoirists, but latterly to those more ordinary people, the diminishing band of living witnesses.  The gulf between military history
45 and personal experience was exemplified by the man who became Britain's Last Veteran, Harry Patch.

For Harry, the War was not about military intelligence or plan of attack.  He may have forgotten exact dates and places but he knew what a battlefield was *like*.  It was, he said, about wading around in filth with no opportunity to change your lice-ridden clothes for months.  It was
50 about discomfort and exhaustion and fear and having your friends quite literally "blown to pieces".  Revisiting the battlefields he commented, "Millions of men came to fight in this war. I didn't know whether I would last longer than five minutes.  We were the Poor Bloody Infantry — and we were expendable.  What a waste.  What a terrible waste."

*Adapted from the introduction to Peter Parker's book "The Last Veteran", 2009*

**Questions**

1.  Re-read lines 1—12.

    (a) By referring to **at least two features of language** in these lines, analyse how the writer conveys the destructive nature of the First World War.  In your answer you should refer to such features as word choice, sentence structure and sound.  **4**

    (b) According to the writer, what effects did the war have on "those left behind"?  **3**

2.  In lines 13—17, what does the writer suggest is surprising about the way people in Britain view the First World War?  **3**

3.  Re-read lines 18—26.

    In your own words, identify **three** important ways the First World War affected Britain.  **3**

4.  Analyse how the writer's use of language in lines 27—33 conveys how important the First World War has become to us.  **4**

5.  By referring to lines 34—40, explain in your own words the two opposing views of the First World War.  **4**

6.  Read lines 41—53.

    Evaluate the effectiveness of these two paragraphs as a thought-provoking and emotional conclusion to the passage as a whole.  In your answer you should refer to ideas and language.  **4**

**Passage 2**

Publisher's note: Ellipses [...] are used in Passage 2 to indicate where the original article has been edited slightly. This does not affect your reading of the passage or the way the questions should be answered. At the copyright holder's request, Passage 2 differs very slightly from that used in the 2014 Higher English SQA exam, but this does not affect in any way the answering of any of the questions.

*In the second passage below, the Scottish novelist and filmmaker William Boyd, writing in the New York Times newspaper in February 2012, looks at why the First World War continues to be of such interest to us.*

Read the passage and attempt the question which follows. While reading, you may wish to make notes on the main ideas and/or highlight key points in the passage.

In France I live near a little village called Sadillac. It's no more than a cluster of houses, an old chateau, a church and a graveyard surrounded by a few farms and vineyards. The village probably hasn't changed much since the French Revolution; its population hovers around 100. By the graveyard is a simple obelisk with the names of the 30 or so young men from Sadillac
5  who died in the First World War, 1914–18. It's almost impossible to imagine the effect on this tiny community of these fatalities over four years. Every year on November 11th at 11 a.m. — the hour and the day of the 1918 armistice — villagers gather to participate in a short memorial service around the obelisk.

In 2014 it will be a hundred years since the First World War began and yet, by a strange
10  paradox, its presence — in novels, films and television — has never been greater. . . The last old soldier or sailor has died and almost all of the witnesses have gone, but the war exerts a tenacious hold on the imagination.

For us British, the memories, images and stories of 1914–18 seem to have a persistence and a power that eclipse those of the Second World War. I'm symptomatic of this urge to revisit the
15  conflict: my new novel will be my third with the First World War at its centre. When I wrote and directed a movie, 'The Trench', about a group of young soldiers in 1916 waiting for the Battle of the Somme to begin, I was obsessed with getting every detail right: every cap-badge worn and cigarette smoked, every meal eaten. It was as if I wanted the absolute verisimilitude to provide an authentic, vicarious experience so the viewer would be in a position to say, "So
20  this is what it was like, this is what they went through, how they lived — and died".

I think this is the key behind the enduring obsession with that war. To our modern sensibilities it defies credulity that for more than four years European armies faced one another in a 500-mile line of trenches, stretching from the Belgian coast to the border of Switzerland. The war was also fought in other arenas — in Galicia, Italy, the Bosporus, Mesopotamia, East and West
25  Africa, in naval battles on many oceans — but it is the Western Front and trench warfare that define the war in memory. It was a deadly war of attrition in which millions of soldiers on both sides slogged through the mud of No Man's Land to meet their deaths in withering blasts of machine-gun fire and artillery. And at the end of four years and with about nine million troops dead, the two opposing forces were essentially where they were when they started.

30  In France and Germany, the traumas of the Second World War have to a degree erased memories of the First. But in Britain, where almost a million servicemen died, it's still images of the trenches of the Western Front that are shown and that resonate on Remembrance Day. One of the reasons for this is, surely, the power of the poetry. The poets of the First World War . . . are taught in almost all British schools. I can remember Wilfred Owen's terrifying poem

40  And finally, there were family stories.  One hundred years is not so very long ago.  My great-uncle Alexander Boyd was wounded and decorated at the Battle of the Somme.  His brother, my grandfather William Boyd, was wounded a year later at Passchendaele, as the Third Battle of Ypres was known.  Family legend and anecdote fuelled my interest in the war.

But there is another deeper, perhaps more profound reason why the war continues to
45  preoccupy us.  It was a conflict between 19th-century armies equipped with 20th-century weapons — hence the unprecedented carnage. . . The tactics were 19th-century: advance on the enemy.  But the enemy had 20th-century weapons of mass destruction: the battlefield was dominated by tanks, machine guns, howitzers, aircraft and poisonous gas. . .

No society today would accept the horrendous casualty count.  At the beginning of the Battle
50  of the Somme, on July 1, 1916, the British Army suffered 60,000 dead and wounded — in one day.  It was arguably the worst butcher's bill in military history. . . There is a very real sense in which the modern world — our world — was born between 1914 and 1918.  Something changed in human sensibility.  Soldiers wouldn't be willing to engage in such slaughter . . . The days of cannon fodder are over forever as a result of that war. . . After the First World War,
55  nothing in the world would ever be the same.

*Adapted from an article in the New York Times newspaper, January 2012*


**Question**


7.  Both writers express their views about the First World War.  Identify key areas on which they agree.  In your answer, you should refer in detail to both passages.                    5

You may answer this question in continuous prose or in a series of developed bullet points.

### [END OF MODEL QUESTION PAPER]

National
Qualifications
MODEL PAPER 1

# English
# Critical Reading

Date — Not applicable

Duration — 1 hour 30 minutes

**Total marks — 40**

**SECTION 1 — Scottish Text — 20 marks**

Read an extract from a Scottish text you have previously studied and attempt the questions.

Choose ONE text from either

Part A — Drama Pages 2—7

Part B — Prose Pages 8—17

Part C — Poetry Pages 18—28

Attempt ALL the questions for your chosen text.

**SECTION 2 — Critical Essay — 20 marks**

Attempt ONE question from the following genres — Drama, Prose, Poetry, Film and Television Drama, or Language.

Your answer must be on a different genre from that chosen in Section 1.

You should spend approximately 45 minutes on each Section.

Write your answers clearly in the answer booklet provided. In the answer booklet you must clearly identify the question number you are attempting.

Use **blue** or **black** ink.

Before leaving the examination room you must give your answer booklet to the Invigilator; if you do not, you may lose all the marks for this paper.

HODDER
GIBSON
LEARN MORE

## SECTION 1 — SCOTTISH TEXT — 20 marks

Choose ONE text from Drama, Prose or Poetry.

Read the text extract carefully and then attempt ALL the questions for your chosen text.

You should spend about 45 minutes on this Section.

## PART A — SCOTTISH TEXT — DRAMA

### Text 1 — Drama

If you choose this text you may not attempt a question on Drama in Section 2.

Read the extract below and then attempt the following questions.

### *The Slab Boys* by John Byrne

*In this extract, which is from near the end of the play, Lucille surprises everyone with her choice of partner for the Staffie.*

(*Enter LUCILLE dressed for home*)

LUCILLE:     Burton's Corner ... quarter to ... okay?

(PHIL *and* SPANKY *look towards each other*)

ALAN:         Yeh ... right, Lucille.

5   PHIL & SPANKY: (*Together*) Eh??

LUCILLE:     Are you sure you can get your Dad's M.G.?

ALAN:         No problem ...

LUCILLE:     And put some cream on that pimple ... I swear it's twice the size it was this morning.

10   ALAN:         For God's sake ...

LUCILLE:     (*To* PHIL) Sorry ... I couldn't've went through with it even if I had said, yeh ... you can see that, can't you? I mean to say ... look at him ... he's a skelf.

PHIL:         You're looking at a skelf that's branching out, doll ...

LUCILLE:     Aw, go to hell. And if I was you I wouldn't go home via Storey Street ...
15           that's where Bernadette's boyfriend's got his jew-jipsey parlour. He eats smouts like you for his breakfast! (*To* ALAN) If you're not there on the dot I'm going in by myself so be warned! (*Exits*)

ALAN:         Listen, Heck ...

HECTOR:     (*Bravely*) Don't worry about it, Alan ... I'm taking Willie Curry on my ticket.
20           Well, you guys, I better shoot off ... Willie's giving us a lift down the road. You can keep that fitch if you find it, anybody.

(*Changes into overcoat*)

SPANKY:     Heh ... hold on, Hector ... you can't go just like that. What about that money we gave you?

MARKS

25 HECTOR:    Aw, yeh ... a quid, wasn't it?  No ... I'll just hold onto that, if youse don't mind.  Help towards a skin graft for my ear and the down payment on a nylon overall like Jimmy Robertson's got.  'Night all ... (*Exits*)

SPANKY:    The cocky little ...

(HECTOR *re-enters*)

30 HECTOR:    And I'll be expecting some smart grinding from this department in the future.  No palming me off with sub-standard shades, Farrell.  Oh ... sorry to hear you lost your job, Phil.  Not to worry ... you'll not find much difference now you're "officially" out of work.  (*Takes Parker pen from* PHIL'S *pocket and hands it to* ALAN)  See youse at the Staffie.  (*Exits*)

35 ALAN:    I better push off, too ... heavy night ahead.  (*Changes for home*)

SPANKY:    Christ, I even let him into the secrets of gum making ... what happens?  He strolls off into the sunset with the dame hanging from his top lip.  Yeh, I think you better push off, Archie ... go on ... beat it.

(ALAN *crosses to door ... stops*)

40 ALAN:    (*to* PHIL) There's always next year, you know ...

PHIL:    You heard ... beat it!

ALAN:    Fine.  I was going to say "sorry" but I can see you're doing a pretty good job of that on your own.  See you at the Dance ... buy you a small beer perhaps?  And I'll be seeing you on Monday ... Sparky ... so take it easy on the floor ...
45         watch out nobody steps on your fingers ... there's quite a bit of grinding to get through ... That cabinet out there's an embarrassment...

## Questions

1.  By referring to lines 1—17, explain what is revealed about Lucille's character.    2

2.  Explain how Hector's new-found confidence is made clear in lines 19—34.    4

3.  Analyse how Alan's speech in lines 42—46 conveys his attitude to Phil and Spanky.    4

4.  By referring to this extract and elsewhere in the play, discuss the role of Lucille **or** Hector in *The Slab Boys*.    10

OR

**Text 2 — Drama**

If you choose this text you may not attempt a question on Drama in Section 2.

Read the extract below and then attempt the following questions.

***The Cheviot, the Stag and the Black, Black Oil* by John McGrath**

ANDY    The motel — as I see it — is the thing of the future.  That's how we see it, myself and the Board of Directors, and one or two of your local Councillors — come on now, these are the best men money can buy.  So — picture it, if yous will, right there at the top of the glen, beautiful vista — The Crammem Inn, High Rise
5    Motorcroft — all finished in natural, washable, plastic granitette.  Right next door, the "Frying Scotsman" All Night Chipperama — with a wee ethnic bit, Fingal's Caff — serving seaweed-suppers-in-the-basket, and draught Drambuie.  And to cater for the younger set, yous've got your Grouse-a-go-go.  I mean, people very soon won't want your bed and breakfasts, they want everything laid on, they'll
10    be wanting their entertainment and that, and wes've got the know-how to do it and wes have got the money to do it.  So — picture it, if yous will — a drive-in clachan on every hill-top where formerly there was hee-haw but scenery.

*Enter* LORD VAT OF GLENLIVET, *a mad young laird.*

LORD VAT    Get off my land — these are my mountains.

15    ANDY    Who are you, Jimmy?

LORD VAT    Lord Vat of Glenlivet.  I come from an ancient Scotch family and I represent the true spirit of the Highlands.

ANDY    Andy McChuckemup of Crammem Inn Investments Ltd., Govan, pleased for to make your acquaintance Your Worship.  Excuse me, is this your field?

20    LORD VAT    You're invading my privacy.

ANDY    Excuse me, me and wor company's got plans to develop this backward area into a paradise for all the family — improve it, you know, fair enough, eh?

LORD VAT    Look here, I've spent an awful lot of money to keep this place private and peaceful.  I don't want hordes of common people trampling all over the heather,
25    disturbing the birds.

ANDY    Oh no, we weren't planning to do it for nothing, an' that — there'll be plenty in it for you …

LORD VAT    No amount of money could compensate for the disruption of the couthie way of life that has gone on here uninterrupted for yonks.  Your Bantu — I mean
30    your Highlander — is a dignified sort of chap, conservative to the core.  From time immemorial, they have proved excellent servants — the gels in the kitchen, your sherpa — I mean your stalker — marvellously sure-footed on the hills, your ghillie-wallah, tugging the forelock, doing up your flies — you won't find people like that anywhere else in the world.  I wouldn't part with all this even if you
35    were to offer me half a million pounds.

ANDY    A-ha.  How does six hundred thousand suit you?

LORD VAT    My family have lived here for over a century; 800,000.

ANDY    You're getting a slice of the action, Your Honour — 650,000.

*Page four*

MARKS

|   |          |                                                                                          |
|---|----------|------------------------------------------------------------------------------------------|
|   | LORD VAT | I have my tenants to think of.  Where will they go?  750,000.                             |
| 40 | ANDY    | We'll be needing a few lasses for staff and that … 700,000 including the stately home.    |
|   | LORD VAT | You're a hard man, Mr. Chuckemup.                                                         |
|   | ANDY     | Cash.                                                                                     |
|   | LORD VAT | Done (*shake.*)                                                                           |

**Questions**

5.  Look at lines 1–12.

    (i)   Explain what impression is created of Andy's character in these lines.          **2**

    (ii)  Choose **four** specific details of his plan and analyse how each one is made to sound comical.          **4**

6.  By referring to lines 14–44, explain how the dramatist makes Lord Vat a figure of fun to the audience.          **4**

7.  By referring to this extract and elsewhere in the play, discuss McGrath's use of caricatures and/or stereotypes in *The Cheviot, the Stag and the Black, Black Oil*.          **10**

OR

### Text 3 — Drama

If you choose this text you may not attempt a question on Drama in Section 2.

Read the extract below and then attempt the following questions.

### *Men Should Weep* by Ena Lamont Stewart

*In this extract, which is from near the end of Act 1, Jenny arrives home late.*

*[John comes in holding Jenny by the arm. She is about eighteen, made up boldly (for the nineteen-thirties): her lipstick is spread over her mouth, her coat and blouse undone, her hair tousled.]*

JENNY:      Leave me go!

5 *[She shakes herself free and she and John stand glaring at each other. Maggie is watching fearfully.]*

JENNY:      Makin a bloomin fool o me in front o ma friend!

JOHN:      Where hae you been till this time o night?

JENNY:      That's nane o your business. I'm grown up noo.

10 JOHN:      Don't you speak to me like that. I asked ye where ye'd been.

JENNY:      An I tellt ye! Nane o your damned interferin business.

MAGGIE:      Jenny! John!

*[John takes Jenny by the shoulders and shakes her.]*

JOHN:      Where wis ye? Answer me!

15 JENNY:      At the pickshers.

JOHN:      The pickchers comes oot at hauf ten. Where wis ye efter?

JENNY:      [sullen] Wi Nessie Tate an a coupla friends.

*[He lets her go and she flops into a chair, glaringly sullenly at him and rubbing her shoulder.]*

20 JOHN:      I don't approve o yon Nessie Tait.

JENNY:      That's a peety. I dae.

JOHN:      Ye impident little bitch! What I ought tae dae is tak ma belt tae ye.

JENNY:      Jist you try it!

JOHN:      The next time you come in here at this time o night wi yer paint smeared a
25             ower yer face, I wull! Look at yersel!

*[He drags her over to a mirror, then propels her, resisting, to the sink, where, holding her head under his arm, he scrubs off her make-up.]*

JOHN:      There! And in the future, you'll let yer hair grow tae the colour God meant it tae be an leave it that wey.

**MARKS**

**Questions**

8.  By referring to lines 1—11, explain what impressions are created of Jenny's character.     **3**

9.  By referring to lines 13—23, explain how the playwright creates a dramatic conflict between John and Jenny.     **4**

10. By referring to lines 24—29, explain how John's anger is conveyed to the audience.     **3**

11. By referring to this extract and elsewhere in the play, discuss the role of Jenny in *Men Should Weep*.     **10**

### SECTION — SCOTTISH TEXT — 20 marks

**Choose ONE text from Drama, Prose or Poetry.**

**Read the text extract carefully and then attempt ALL the questions for your chosen text.**

**You should spend about 45 minutes on this Section.**

### PART B — SCOTTISH TEXT — PROSE

**Text 1 — Prose**

If you choose this text you may not attempt a question on Prose in Section 2.

Read the extract below and then attempt the following questions.

#### *The Crater* by Iain Crichton Smith

They screamed again, in the sound of the shells, and they seemed to hear an answer. They heard what seemed to be a bubbling. "Are you there?" said Robert, bending down and listening. "Can you get over here?" They could hear splashing and deep below them breathing, frantic breathing as if someone was frightened to death. "It's all right," he said,
5   "if you come over here, I'll send my rifle down. You two hang on to me," he said to the others. He was terrified. That depth, that green depth. Was it Morrison down there, after all? He hadn't spoken. The splashings came closer. The voice was like an animal's repeating endlessly a mixture of curses and prayers. Robert hung over the edge of the crater. "For Christ's sake don't let me go," he said to the other two. It wasn't right that a
10  man should die in green slime.

He hung over the rim holding his rifle down. He felt it being caught, as if there was a great fish at the end of a line. He felt it moving. And the others hung at his heels, like a chain. The moon shone suddenly out between two clouds and in that moment he saw it, a body covered with greenish slime, an obscene mermaid, hanging on to his rifle while the
15  two eyes, white in the green face, shone upward and the mouth, gritted, tried not to let the blood through. It was a monster of the deep, it was a sight so terrible that he nearly fell. He was about to say, "It's no good, he's dying," but something prevented him from saying it, if he said it then he would never forget it. He knew that. The hands clung to the rifle below in the slime. The others pulled behind him. "For Christ's sake hang on to the rifle,"
20  he said to the monster below. "Don't let go." And it seemed to be emerging from the deep, setting its feet against the side of the crater, all green, all mottled, like a disease. It climbed as if up a mountainside in the stench. It hung there against the wall.

"Hold on," he said. "Hold on." His whole body was concentrated. This man must not fall down again into that lake. The death would be too terrible. The face was coming over the
25  side of the crater, the teeth gritted, blood at the mouth. It hung there for a long moment and then the three of them had got him over the side. He felt like cheering, standing up in the light of No Man's Land and cheering. Sergeant Smith was kneeling down beside the body, his ear to the heart. It was like a body which might have come from space, green and illuminated and slimy. And over it poured the merciless moonlight.

30  "Come on," he said to the other two. And at that moment Sergeant Smith said, "He's dead."

MARKS

**Questions**

12. By referring to lines 1—10, analyse how the writer uses sound to intensify the atmosphere.

4

13. By referring to lines 11—22, explain how the writer creates a nightmarish atmosphere.

4

14. By referring to lines 23—31, discuss what the sentence "And over it poured the merciless moonlight." (line 29) contributes to the conclusion of the extract.

2

15. By referring to the extract and to at least one other story by Iain Crichton Smith, discuss how he creates tension his stories.

10

OR

### Text 2 — Prose

If you choose this text you may not attempt a question on Prose in Section 2.

Read the extract below and then attempt the following questions.

### *The Bright Spade* by George Mackay Brown

One night there was a meeting in the ale-house.  All the men of the island were there.  They took counsel together about the impending famine.  That same morning the old man of Cornquoy who lived alone, the fiddler, had been found dead in his chair, after he had been missed for a week.  They broke down his door.  The young dog was gnawing at the
5  corpse's thigh.  Jacob got his fiddle the night he shrouded him, though he knew nothing about music.  The fiddle, once a sweet brimming shell, hung at Jacob's wall like a shrivelled chrysalis.  The old fiddler was as light as a bird to handle.  He needed a narrow grave.

"The meal and the meat are done in the island," said Harald of Ness at the meeting.  "I've
10  eaten nothing myself but a handful of cold potatoes every day for the past week.  My suggestion is this, that seven of the strongest men among us cross between the hills to the shore and get a large supply of limpets and dulse from the rocks at low tide."

The men agreed that it would be necessary to do that.

The seven men chosen set off at dawn the next day.  They were Harald of Ness, Adam of
15  Skarataing, Ezekiel of the Burn, Thomas and Philip of Graystones, Simon the blacksmith, and Walter of Muce.  That same morning the worst blizzard of winter descended, great swirling blankets of snow out of the east.  Tinkers saw the seven men between the hills going towards the shore, like a troop of spectres.  They were never seen again until their bodies were dug from the drifts a week later.

20  For the second time that winter Jacob laid seven men together in the kirkyard.  This time he would accept no payment at all for his services — "for," said he, "it seems I have done better this winter than anyone else in the island ...".

In March Francis Halcrow the coughing sailor who had been with John Paul Jones in the American Wars died at Braebuster.  Jacob buried him for his set of Nantucket harpoons.

25  And then men brought out ploughs, harness, harrows.  The implements were dull and rusty after the hard winter.  Jacob's spade, on the other hand, was thin and bright with much employment.  "God grant," he said to the spade, putting it away in his shed, "that I won't be needing you again till after the shearing and the lobster fishing and the harvest."

MARKS

**Questions**

16. By referring to lines 1—8, identify the narrator's tone and explain how it is created.    3

17. By referring to lines 9—13, explain what impressions the narrator creates of Harald Ness as a person.    2

18. Discuss the effect achieved by naming each one of the men who set off on the journey (lines 14—19).    2

19. By referring to lines 20—28, explain what is revealed about Jacob as a person.    3

20. By referring to the extract and to at least one other story by George Mackay Brown, discuss his use of symbolism in his stories.    10

**OR**

**Text 3 — Prose**

If you choose this text you may not attempt a question on Prose in Section 2.

Read the extract below and then attempt the following questions.

### *The Trick is to Keep Breathing* by Janice Galloway

*In this extract, Tony takes Joy out for the evening.*

There I am in the mirror, inoffensive in a dress with a thick belt to show what remains of the curves. New stockings and slingbacks despite the time of year. Lack of practicality is sexy in women's clothes. The gravel and the crunch of brakes outside makes me stare harder. I try not to hear the different size of shoe thudding on the boards.

5       Hello? Anybody home?

I see Tony from the top of the stairs, holding up a bottle in white paper, green glass and a foil neck pushing up from the tissue like a clumsy orchid.

        Anticipation, he says. Always take it for granted I'm going to win.

The lips disappear into his beard and the teeth appear, very white and straight. It's
10   definitely Tony. He tells me I look lovely, a real picture. I want to tell him it's not me but I smile instead. He reaches out his hand and says it again.

        You look lovely. You really do.

The car is the wrong colour. It plays Country and Western Music as we ease onto the main road.

15      She's on form, he says. Should have seen her this afternoon.

The seat creaks with his weight: now we're round the corner, he relaxes.

        Called round on the off chance you were home but no such luck. Thought you weren't well? Anyway, she's looking good. Nearly as good as you.

He pats my leg.

20      Expect a treat tonight.

I know we're talking about a dog and try to think of something appropriate to say. In the pause, he sings along with the tape.

        *When you're in love with a beautiful woman, it's hard*

He looks sidelong to see my reaction, encouraging me to be cute. He keeps doing it
25   between the sentences.

        Maybe after the race we could go somewhere. On the town. Assume you haven't eaten. Could do with some more even if you have. Few more pounds and you'd be a stunner. How are things by the way? I always forget to ask. You never look ill to me so I forget to ask.

30      *Then somebody hangs up when you answer the phone*

        Just relax and listen to the music. This one's my favourite. Dr Hook. Classic. You don't mind if I run it again. You look great. Should wear a dress more often. Hiding your best assets.

He looks over again, his face melting on the double-take.

35      Christ what did you do to your hands?

I look and see the knuckles bruised and oozy. This is not feminine.

        A dopey voice says Oops. I tripped. Silly me.

I tell myself I am with Tony in his car. I tell myself all the way to Glasgow.

MARKS

**Questions**

21. By referring to lines 1—12, explain how Tony is portrayed as an unpleasant character.          4

22. By referring to lines 13—25, explain how the writer creates an uneasy atmosphere in the car.          2

23. Analyse how aspects of Tony's character are revealed in lines 26—38.          4

24. By referring to the extract and elsewhere in the novel, discuss Joy's relationships with men.          10

HIGHER FOR CfE ENGLISH 2014　72　HODDER GIBSON MODEL PAPERS

OR

### Text 4 — Prose

If you choose this text you may not attempt a question on Prose in Section 2.

Read the extract below and then attempt the following questions.

#### *Sunset Song* by Lewis Grassic Gibbon

*In this extract, which is from Part III (Seed-time), a disagreement arises at the wedding celebration.*

Up at Rob's table an argument rose, Chris hoped that it wasn't religion, she saw Mr Gordon's wee face pecked up to counter Rob. But Rob was just saying what a shame it was that folk should be shamed nowadays to speak Scotch — or they called it Scots if they did, the split-tongued sourocks! Every damned little narrow dowped rat that you met put
5　on the English if he thought he'd impress you — as though Scotch wasn't good enough now, it had words in it that the thin bit scraichs of the English could never come at. And Rob said *You can tell me, man, what's the English for sotter, or greip, or smore, or pleiter, gloaming or glunching or well-kenspeckled? And if you said gloaming was sunset you'd fair be a liar; and you're hardly that, Mr Gordon.*

10　But Gordon was real decent and reasonable, *You can't help it, Rob. If folk are to get on in the world nowadays, away from the ploughshafts and out of the pleiter, they must use the English, orra though it be.* And Chae cried out that was right enough, and God! who could you blame? And a fair bit breeze got up about it all, every soul in the parlour seemed speaking at once; and as aye when they spoke of the thing they agreed that the
15　land was a coarse, coarse life, you'd do better at almost anything else, folks that could send their lads to learn a trade were right wise, no doubt of that, there was nothing on the land but work, work, work, and chave, chave, chave, from the blink of day till the fall of night, no thanks from the soss and sotter, and hardly a living to be made.

Syne Cuddiestoun said that he'd heard of a childe up Laurencekirk way, a banker's son
20　from the town he was, and he'd come to do farming in a scientific way. So he'd said at first, had the childe, but God! by now you could hardly get into the place for the clutter of machines that lay in the yard; and he wouldn't store the kiln long. But Chae wouldn't have that, he swore *Damn't, no, the machine's the best friend of man, or it would be so in a socialist state. It's coming and the chaving'll end, you'll see, the machine'll do all the*
25　*dirty work.* And Long Rob called out that he'd like right well to see the damned machine that would muck you a pigsty even though they all turned socialist tomorrow.

MARKS

Questions

25. By referring to lines 1—9, explain how the writer conveys the strength of Rob's feelings about language.    **4**

26. By referring to lines 10—18, explain how the writer conveys the harshness of life working the land.    **2**

27. By referring to lines 19—26, explain how the writer's use of language conveys the conflicting views about "scientific" farming methods.  You should refer to at least two techniques, such as sentence structure, tone, word choice.    **4**

28. By referring to this extract and elsewhere in the novel, discuss to what extent *Sunset Song* is a celebration of a traditional way of life or an illustration of the inevitability of change.    **10**

OR

### Text 5 — Prose

If you choose this text you may not attempt a question on Prose in Section 2.

Read the extract below and then attempt the following questions.

### *The Cone-Gatherers* by Robin Jenkins

*In this extract from Chapter One, Duror is secretly watching the cone-gatherers.*

Hidden among the spruces at the edge of the ride, near enough to catch the smell of larch off the cones and to be struck by some of those thrown, stood Duror the gamekeeper, in an icy sweat of hatred, with his gun aimed all the time at the feebleminded hunchback grovelling over the rabbit.  To pull the trigger, requiring far less force than to break a
5 rabbit's neck, and then to hear simultaneously the clean report of the gun and the last obscene squeal of the killed dwarf would have been for him, he thought, release too, from the noose of disgust and despair drawn, these past few days, so much tighter.

He had waited over an hour there to see them pass.  Every minute had been a purgatory of humiliation: it was as if he was in their service, forced to wait upon them as upon his
10 masters.  Yet he hated and despised them far more powerfully than ever he had liked and respected Sir Colin and Lady Runcie-Campbell.  While waiting, he had imagined them in the darkness missing their footing in the tall tree and coming crashing down through the sea of branches to lie dead on the ground.  So passionate had been his visualising of that scene, he seemed himself to be standing on the floor of a fantastic sea, with an owl and a
15 herd of roe-deer flitting by quiet as fish, while the yellow ferns and bronzen brackens at his feet gleamed like seaweed, and the spruce trees swayed above him like submarine monsters.

He could have named, item by item, leaf and fruit and branch, the overspreading tree of revulsion in him; but he could not tell the force which made it grow, any more than he
20 could have explained the life in himself, or in the dying rabbit, or in any of the trees about him.

This wood had always been his stronghold and sanctuary; there were many places secret to him where he had been able to fortify his sanity and hope.  But now the wood was invaded and defiled; its cleansing and reviving virtues were gone.  Into it had crept this
25 hunchback, himself one of nature's freaks, whose abject acceptance of nature, like the whining prostrations of a heathen in front of an idol, had made acceptance no longer possible for Duror himself.  He was humpbacked, with one shoulder higher than the other; he had no neck, and on the misshapen lump of his body sat a face so beautiful and guileless as to be a diabolical joke.

MARKS

## Questions

29. Analyse how the word choice in lines 1—7 conveys Duror's loathing for Calum.   **2**

30. By referring to lines 8—17, explain how the writer makes the reader aware of Duror's disturbed state of mind.   **4**

31. Analyse how the imagery in lines 18—29 gives insight into Duror's feelings.   **4**

32. By referring to this extract and elsewhere in the novel, discuss the importance of the conflict between Duror and Calum.   **10**

## SECTION 1 — SCOTTISH TEXT — 20 marks

Choose ONE text from Drama, Prose or Poetry.

Read the text extract carefully and then attempt ALL the questions for your chosen text.

You should spend about 45 minutes on this Section.

## PART C — SCOTTISH TEXT — POETRY

### Text 1 — Poetry

If you choose this text you may not attempt a question on Poetry in Section 2.

Read the extract below and then attempt the following questions.

### *To a Mouse* by Robert Burns

Thy wee-bit housie, too, in ruin!
It's silly wa's the win's are strewin!
An' naething, now, to big a new ane,
O' foggage green!
5  An' bleak December's winds ensuin,
Baith snell an' keen!

Thou saw the fields laid bare an' waste,
An' weary winter comin fast,
An' cozie here, beneath the blast,
10  Thou thought to dwell,
Till crash! the cruel coulter past
Out thro' thy cell.

That wee-bit heap o' leaves an' stibble,
Has cost thee mony a weary nibble!
15  Now thou's turn'd out, for a' thy trouble,
But house or hald,
To thole the winter's sleety dribble,
An' cranreuch cauld!

But Mousie, thou art no thy lane,
20  In proving foresight may be vain;
The best-laid schemes o' mice an' men
Gang aft agley,
An' lea'e us nought but grief an' pain,
For promis'd joy!

25  Still thou art blest, compar'd wi' me!
The present only toucheth thee:
But och! I backward cast my e'e,
On prospects drear!
An' forward, tho' I canna see,
30  I guess an' fear!

MARKS

**Questions**

33. By referring closely to lines 1—6, analyse the use of poetic technique to create sympathy for the mouse's situation.

    2

34. Identify **two** key themes of the poem which are developed in lines 7—18 and explain how each is clarified by the poet's technique.

    4

35. Discuss the mood created in lines 19—30. You should explain the key ideas of these lines and analyse the use of poetic technique to create mood.

    4

36. By referring to this poem and at least one other by Burns, discuss his use of verse form.

    10

OR

### Text 2 — Poetry

If you choose this text you may not attempt a question on Poetry in Section 2.

Read the extract below and then attempt the following questions.

### *Mrs Midas* by Carol Ann Duffy

It was late September.  I'd just poured a glass of wine, begun
to unwind, while the vegetables cooked.  The kitchen
filled with the smell of itself, relaxed, its steamy breath
gently blanching the windows.  So I opened one,
5   then with my fingers wiped the other's glass like a brow.
He was standing under the pear tree snapping a twig.

Now the garden was long and the visibility poor, the way
the dark of the ground seems to drink the light of the sky,
but that twig in his hand was gold.  And then he plucked
10  a pear from a branch — we grew Fondante d'Automne —
and it sat in his palm like a light bulb.  On.
I thought to myself, Is he putting fairy lights in the tree?

He came into the house.  The doorknobs gleamed.
He drew the blinds. You know the mind; I thought of
15  the Field of the Cloth of Gold and of Miss Macready.
He sat in that chair like a king on a burnished throne.
The look on his face was strange, wild, vain.  I said,
What in the name of God is going on?  He started to laugh.

I served up the meal. For starters, corn on the cob.
20  Within seconds he was spitting out the teeth of the rich.
He toyed with his spoon, then mine, then with the knives, the forks.
He asked where was the wine.  I poured with a shaking hand,
a fragrant, bone-dry white from Italy, then watched
as he picked up the glass, goblet, golden chalice, drank.

MARKS

**Questions**

37. By referring to lines 1—6, analyse the use of poetic techniques to create an ordinary, everyday atmosphere.

    **4**

38. By referring to lines 7—12, analyse the use of poetic techniques to convey the confusion beginning to arise in the speaker's mind.

    **2**

39. Explain how, in lines 13—24, the poet conveys the strangeness of the husband's behaviour.

    **4**

40. By referring to this poem and at least one other by Carol Ann Duffy, discuss how she creates and develops ideas and/or situations which are unusual or surprising.

    **10**

OR

### Text 3 — Poetry

If you choose this text you may not attempt a question on Poetry in Section 2.

Read the extract below and then attempt the following questions.

### *Last Supper* by Liz Lochhead

Already she was imagining it done with, this feast, and
exactly
what kind of leftover hash she'd make of it
among friends, when it was just
5   The Girls, when those three met again.
What very good soup
she could render from the bones,
then something substantial, something extra
tasty if not elegant.

10   Yes, there they'd be, cackling around the cauldron,
spitting out the gristlier bits
of his giblets;
gnawing on the knucklebone of some
intricate irony;
15   getting grave and dainty at the
petit-gout mouthfuls of reported speech.

"That's rich!" they'd splutter,
munching the lies, fat and sizzling as sausages.
Then they'd sink back
20   gorged on truth
and their own savage integrity,
sleek on it all, preening
like corbies, their bright eyes blinking
satisfied
25   till somebody would get hungry
and go hunting again.

MARKS

Questions

41. By referring to lines 1–9, explain how the poet develops the metaphor of "this feast".

2

42. Analyse the use of sound in lines 10–16 to create a negative impression of "The Girls".

4

43. Analyse the use of poetic techniques in lines 17–26 to describe the people at the Supper.

4

44. By referring to this poem and at least one other by Liz Lochhead, discuss her ability to describe characters in a precise way.

10

OR

### Text 4 — Poetry

If you choose this text you may not attempt a question on Poetry in Section 2.

Read the poem below and then attempt the following questions.

### *Assisi* by Norman MacCaig

The dwarf with his hands on backwards
sat, slumped like a half-filled sack
on tiny twisted legs from which
sawdust might run,
5  outside the three tiers of churches built
in honour of St Francis, brother
of the poor, talker with birds, over whom
he had the advantage
of not being dead yet.

10  A priest explained
how clever it was of Giotto
to make his frescoes tell stories
that would reveal to the illiterate the goodness
of God and the suffering
15  of His Son.  I understood
the explanation and
the cleverness.

A rush of tourists, clucking contentedly,
fluttered after him as he scattered
20  the grain of the Word.  It was they who had passed
the ruined temple outside, whose eyes
wept pus, whose back was higher
than his head, whose lopsided mouth
said *Grazie* in a voice as sweet
25  as a child's when she speaks to her mother
or a bird's when it spoke
to St Francis.

MARKS

**Questions**

45. Analyse how the use of sound in lines 1—4 enhances the description of the dwarf.

2

46. Explain how the poet creates an ironic tone in lines 5—9.

2

47. Discuss what the speaker's statement "I understood/the explanation and/the cleverness." (lines 15—17) suggests about his feelings at that moment.

2

48. By referring closely to lines 20—27, explain what the poet means by describing the dwarf as a "ruined temple".

4

49. By referring to this poem and at least one other by Norman MacCaig, discuss his use of wry humour in his poetry.

10

OR

### Text 5 — Poetry

If you choose this text you may not attempt a question on Poetry in Section 2.

Read the extract below and then attempt the following questions.

### *Hallaig* by Sorley MacLean

In Screapadal of my people
where Norman and Big Hector were,
their daughters and their sons are a wood
going up beside the stream.

5   Proud tonight the pine cocks
crowing on the top of Cnoc an Ra,
straight their backs in the moonlight –
they are not the wood I love.

I will wait for the birch wood
10  until it comes up by the cairn,
until the whole ridge from Beinn na Lice
will be under its shade.

If it does not, I will go down to Hallaig,
to the Sabbath of the dead,
15  where the people are frequenting,
every single generation gone.

They are still in Hallaig,
MacLeans and MacLeods,
all who were there in the time of Mac Gille Chaluim:
20  the dead have been seen alive.

The men lying on the green
at the end of every house that was,
the girls a wood of birches,
straight their backs, bent their heads.

**MARKS**

**Questions**

**50.** Look at lines 1—12.

    (i)   Identify **two** central concerns of the poem which are introduced in these lines.    **2**

    (ii)  Analyse how the poet's use of symbolism develops either or both of these concerns.    **4**

**51.** By referring closely to lines 13—24, explain how the poet creates a fusion of past and present.    **4**

**52.** By referring to this poem and at least one other by Sorley MacLean, discuss how he explores ideas of tradition and/or heritage in his poetry.    **10**

MARKS

OR

### Text 6 — Poetry

If you choose this text you may not attempt a question on Poetry in Section 2.

Read the poem below and then attempt the following questions.

#### The Thread by Don Paterson

Jamie made his landing in the world
so hard he ploughed straight back into the earth.
They caught him by the thread of his one breath
and pulled him up.  They don't know how it held.
5   And so today I thank what higher will
brought us to here, to you and me and Russ,
the great twin-engined swaying wingspan of us
roaring down the back of Kirrie Hill

and your two-year-old lungs somehow out-revving
10   every engine in the universe.
*All that trouble just to turn up dead*
was all I thought that long week.  Now the thread
is holding all of us: look at our tiny house,
son, the white dot of your mother waving.

### Questions

53.  Analyse the poet's use of imagery in lines 1—4 to describe his feelings about Jamie at the time of his birth.    2

54.  By referring to lines 5—10, explain how the poet expresses his feelings now.    4

55.  Evaluate the effectiveness of the last sentence ("Now … waving.") as a conclusion to the poem.    4

56.  By referring to this poem and at least one other by Don Paterson, discuss his use of verse form to explore important themes.    10

### [END OF SECTION 1]

## SECTION 2 — CRITICAL ESSAY — 20 marks

Attempt ONE question from the following genres — Drama, Prose, Poetry, Film and Television Drama, or Language.

You may use a Scottish text but **NOT** the one used in Section 1.

Your answer must be on a different genre from that chosen in Section 1.

You should spend approximately 45 minutes on this Section.

### DRAMA

> Answers to questions on **drama** should refer to the text and to such relevant features as characterisation, key scene(s), structure, climax, theme, plot, conflict, setting ...

1. Choose a play in which a central character is slow to understand fully the seriousness of his or her behaviour.

   Explain how this situation has developed and discuss how the character's behaviour influences your overall assessment of him or her.

2. Choose a play which explores one of the following: the nature of heroism, the impact of self-delusion, the burden of responsibility.

   Discuss how the dramatist explores this central concern through her or his presentation of one or more than character.

3. Choose from a play a scene in which you consider a character makes a significant error of judgement.

   Briefly explain the nature of this error of judgement and discuss how this error and its consequences influence your understanding of character and/or theme in the play as a whole.

## PROSE — FICTION

> Answers to questions on **prose fiction** should refer to the text and to such relevant features as characterisation, setting, language, key incident(s), climax, turning point, plot, structure, narrative technique, theme, ideas, description ...

4. Choose from a novel or short story an incident in which a character makes a decision which you consider unexpected or unwise or unworthy.

   Explain the circumstances surrounding the decision and discuss its importance to your understanding of character and them in the text as a whole.

5. Choose a novel or short story in which loyalty or trust plays an important part.

   Discuss how the writer explores this idea in a way which adds to your understanding of the central concern(s) of the text as a whole.

6. Choose a novel or short story in which the vulnerability of a central character is apparent at one or more than one key point in the text.

   Explain the situation(s) in which the character's vulnerability emerges and discuss the importance of the vulnerability to your understanding of character and/or theme in the text as a whole.

## PROSE — NON-FICTION

> Answers to questions on **prose non-fiction** should refer to the text and to such relevant features as ideas, use of evidence, stance, style, selection of material, narrative voice ...

7. Choose a piece of **travel writing** which engages you not only intellectually but also emotionally.

   Explain how the writer successfully engages both your mind and your emotions.

8. Choose a work of **biography** or **autobiography** in which the writer brings more than one key incident vividly to life.

   Explain how the writer brings the incidents vividly to life and how they contribute to your understanding of the person involved.

9. Choose a work of **non-fiction** in which the writer expresses outrage or shock about an issue which you feel is important.

   Explain how the writer conveys the emotion hand discuss to what extent this emotional approach enhances your understanding of the issue.

## POETRY

> Answers to questions on **poetry** should refer to the text and to such relevant features as word choice, tone, imagery, structure, content, rhythm, rhyme, theme, sound, ideas ...

10. Choose a poem in which the poet presents an apparently ordinary situation or event in an extraordinary way.

    Discuss how the poet gives impact and meaning to an apparently ordinary situation or event.

11. Choose a poem which you find emotionally unsettling or intellectually challenging.

    Explain how the poem elicits this response from you and discuss how this contributes to your understanding of the central concern(s) of the poem.

12. Choose a poem in which **two or more** of the following techniques significantly enhance the impact of the poem: rhyme, rhythm, sound, imagery.

    Explain how the poet's use of your chosen techniques enhances your understanding of the poem as a whole.

## FILM AND TELEVISION DRAMA

> Answers to questions on **film and television drama**\* should refer to the text and to such relevant features as use of camera, key sequence, characterisation, mise-en-scène, editing, setting, music/sound, special effects, plot, dialogue, ...

13. Choose a film or television drama in which a central character's principles are put to the test.

    Explain how the character's principles are put to the test and discuss how her or his response illuminates a central concern of the text.

14. Choose a film or television drama in which a particular atmosphere is an important feature.

    Show how the film or programme makers create this atmosphere and discuss how it contributes to your appreciation of the text as a whole.

15. Choose a film or television drama which explores a crisis in a relationship or the break-up of a family.

    Discuss how the film or programme makers' exploration of the crisis or break-up contributes to your understanding of character and/or theme.

    \* "television drama" includes a single play, a series or a serial.

## LANGUAGE

> Answers to questions on **language** should refer to the text and to such relevant features as register, accent, dialect, slang, jargon, vocabulary, tone, abbreviation ...

16. Choose some of the rhetorical devices which underpin success in speechmaking.

    By referring to one or more than one important speech, discuss the effectiveness of your chosen rhetorical devices.

17. Choose the language of live broadcasting, e.g. live news coverage, sports commentaries, award ceremonies.

    Identify some of the characteristics of this language and discuss to what extent it is effective in communicating the event to its target audience.

18. Choose aspects of language associated with a particular vocational group such as lawyers, doctors or engineers.

    Identify some examples of the language used within the group and discuss to what extent this shared language contributes to the effectiveness of the group's vocational activities.

**[END OF SECTION 2]**

**[END OF MODEL QUESTION PAPER]**

# Model Paper 2

Whilst this Model Practice Paper has been specially commissioned by Hodder Gibson for use as practice for the Higher (for Curriculum for Excellence) exams, the key reference document remains the SQA Specimen Paper 2014.

> Please note that in the Reading for Understanding, Analysis and Evaluation sections, these model papers use passages from previous Official SQA Papers, but with different questions in line with assessment criteria for the new Higher. There are three Model Papers, but for reasons of space, the third Model Paper does not cover the Scottish Text element.

HODDER
GIBSON
LEARN MORE

National
Qualifications
MODEL PAPER 2

# English
# Reading for Understanding, Analysis and Evaluation

Date — Not applicable

Duration — 1 hour 30 minutes

**Total marks — 30**

Attempt ALL questions.

Write your answers clearly in the answer booklet provided.  In the answer booklet you must clearly identify the question number you are attempting.

Use **blue** or **black** ink.

Before leaving the examination room you must give your answer booklet to the Invigilator; if you do not, you may lose all the marks for this paper.

HODDER
GIBSON
LEARN MORE

The following two passages focus on shopping and consumerism.

**Passage 1**

*In the first passage Carol Midgley, writing in "The Times" newspaper, considers the attraction of shopping and the power of "consumerism".*

Read the passage below and attempt the questions which follow.

This is a story about modern consumerism; it is being written inside a mall.  From my vantage point on a wooden bench purposely designed to be uncomfortable and placed alongside a digital screen pulsing ever-changing adverts selling other outlets, other products, other ways here to spend, spend, spend, I can watch shoals of people hurrying in and out of stores
5   honouring the creed of the turbo-consumer: live to shop.

How did we get here?  How did we get to a point where shopping became the premier leisure activity, where we gladly boarded the work-to-spend treadmill, the insatiable pursuit of "more", which resulted in there being, for example, 121 mobile phones for every 100 people in the UK? Does it even matter?  Shopping doesn't kill anyone, it keeps the economy going and
10   provides one in six jobs.  If it makes people happy, why not leave them to it?

Well, that's just it.   Turbo-consumerism – the age of instant gratification and voracious appetite for "stuff" – cannot make us happy and it never will.  Every time we are seduced into buying one product, another appears that is "new", "improved", better than the one you have. Turbo-consumerism is the heroin of human happiness, reliant on the fact that our needs are
15   never satisfied.  A consumer society can't allow us to stop shopping and be content because then the whole system would die.  Instead it has to sell us just enough to keep us going but never enough that our wants are satisfied.  The brief high we feel is compensation for not having a richer, fuller life.

For years, shops, retail centres, giant malls have been taking over public spaces worldwide,
20   creating a mainstream monoculture.  The pedestrianisation of city centres, though largely regarded as pro-citizen, is in fact primarily to maximise "footfall" and shoppers' "grazing time".  This retail creep has ensured that, increasingly, there's not much else to do but shop. The more we consume, the less space there is to be anything other than consumers.  The space to be citizens and make decisions equally and collectively about the world around us is
25   diminished.  It may be a free country, but we simply have the freedom to shop.  Kings as consumers, pawns as citizens.

Am I over-catastrophising the consumer phenomenon?   In the Liverpool One shopping "experience", where I am sitting, a place teeming with shoppers despite the credit crunch, and punctuated by *Massive Reductions*! signs, people don't look particularly disempowered or
30   depressed.  Purposeful, I suppose, but also strangely distracted, as if they do not notice the environment around them, merely the magnetic shop signs.  I understand the siren call of TK Maxx and how a £3 top can mend a bad day.  But the question is, why does it?

We can answer this question from the basis of evolutionary psychology.  The human body is a practical tool for reproduction and survival, but it is  also the advertising and packaging for our
35   genes and our "fitness indicators".  When a modern woman buys a new dress or a man a Rolex watch they are really self-marketing, saying: "Look at me, I'm attractive, successful, fertile, healthy – mate with me."  It isn't that we are materialistic; in a marketing-dominated culture we just don't know any other way to do it.

But here's the thing: much of this is simply not true.  In reality, consumerism is a poor means
of self-advertising because the vast majority of people don't notice or care what you are
wearing.  The fundamental consumerist delusion is that branded goods are the most effective
way of signalling to others our "fitness".  But even in a turbo-consumer world it's a fallacy that
we care more about the artificial products displayed by people than their conversation, their
wit, or their affection. Yet when mineral water advertised with a photo of a nearly nude
Jennifer Aniston sells for 870 times the price of tap water, then marketing dominates life on
Earth.  Marketers understand that they are selling the sizzle not the steak.

Back at the mall, I speak to two young shoppers staggering under the weight of their carrier
bags.  Will they go home now and put their feet up?  "No, we're taking these bags home in a
taxi," says one.  "Then we're coming back to do another hour before the shops close."

*Adapted from an article in The Times newspaper, July 2009*

MARKS

Questions

1. Re-read lines 1–5.

   (a) Identify **two** ways the mall seems to encourage consumerism.     2

   (b) Analyse how the writer's use of language in these lines emphasises the intensity of consumerism in the mall.     2

2. Re-read lines 6–18.

   (a) Explain why, according to the writer, consumerism might be considered harmless but also unable to make us happy?     4

   (b) Analyse how the writer's use of imagery in lines 11–18 emphasises her criticism of consumerism.     3

3. By referring to **at least two** features of language in lines 19–26, analyse how the writer's use of language conveys her disapproval of the large amount of space that is now devoted to shopping. You should refer in your answer to such features as word choice, sentence structure, tone, imagery …     4

4. To what extent does the writer's description of the shoppers in lines 27–32 suggest that the she believes she is "over-catastrophising the consumer phenomenon" (line 27)?     3

5. Re-read lines 33–46.

   Explain how, according to the writer, "evolutionary psychology" can explain our need for material goods, but why she thinks "much of this is simply not true".     4

6. Evaluate the final paragraph's effectiveness as a conclusion to the ideas of the passage as a whole.     3

**Passage 2**

*In the second passage below, Will Hutton, writing in "The Guardian" newspaper, considers the same topic from a different point of view.*

Read the passage and attempt the question which follows. While reading, you may wish to make notes on the main ideas and/or highlight key points in the passage.

My two daughters have been addicted to shopping for years. From big city luxurious shopping mall to idiosyncratic old clothes shop, they fall upon it greedily. They are fully paid-up members of the allegedly futile and empty materialist culture: rootless, obsessive shoppers for whom filling up their shopping bags is a substitute for politics, community
5    participation, family or faith. Critics of this culture indulge in a collective mass tut-tutting: shopping and everything that goes with it are apparently symbolic of what is wrong with the modern age. Serious shoppers are "slaves to the market", enemies of collective action whose individualistic appetite is helping to homogenise our high streets while destroying our moral wellbeing.

10    Critics also deplore the outcome — industrialised shopping malls, mass advertising, the manipulation of desire by producers and retailers — as if the consumers at the other end of all this effort were just brainwashed dolts colluding unwittingly in the destruction of their spiritual life and the interpersonal relationships which are central to their happiness. Shopping on this scale and with this degree of commitment, critics believe, is a form of psychosis.

15    There is a partial truth in this condemnation, but it too quickly casts the individual shopper as an empty vessel morally corroded by the dark forces of anonymous markets. Critics of shopping are so busy delivering their views that they rarely have the time to surrender to savouring that moment when they might unexpectedly enhance their lives by finding another diverting item on which to spend money – in short, by shopping.

20    My experience of shopping in Hong Kong recently has made me realise that shopping is enormous fun and profoundly satisfying. I'd dashed in to buy cheap gifts for my family and had intended to spend no more than 30 minutes. Instead, I found myself drawn into the heady delights of shopping. Choosing between a cornucopia of famous watch brands, not one of which costs more than £4, is an experience I defy anybody not to enjoy. And on top of that,
25    you can pick and mix every detail: case, colour, buckle, strap. I was shopping as my daughters shop — giving myself over to the minutiae of the experience.

On three floors almost every shop you pass excites another taste or way you might express yourself. Binoculars and telescopes; pocket DVD players; walking sticks; silk wall hangings; leather belts; mirrors; porcelain figurines — it was endless. The bargain prices were an
30    invitation to the recognition that individuals have an infinity of wants, some of which we don't even know about or have forgotten; I fell upon the binoculars with all the delight of a child. Much of the pleasure is not even the buying; it is acquiring the knowledge of the immense range of goods that exist that might satiate your possible wants. Shopping, as my daughters tell me, is life-affirming.

35    I would even extend the argument to the shopping mall – the quintessential expression of the alleged degradation of shopping. Hong Kong proclaims itself the shopping capital of the world; its malls are marble-floored temples to consumption that make their British counterparts look tawdry. But instead of recoiling from the excess, I found it attractive. The effort made to present the goods well is an act of creativity in its own right. The collective impact throbs with
40    vitality.

To condemn shopping as somehow degrading to those who take it seriously as a cultural expression of themselves is to obscure an important dimension of our lives.  True happiness may be about the quality of our interpersonal relationships and wanting to belong to a just society; but it is also about the opportunity to express how we want to live through what we
45    buy.  The genius of shopping is that it offers ordinary people the chance both to generate and to satisfy their multiple wants – as well as propelling our economy.  Instead of the denigration of shopping culture it is time to recognise that the millions who love it are not stupid, being manipulated or slaves of markets – they are doing something important.

*Adapted from an article in The Guardian newspaper, September 2005*

**Question**

7.  Both writers express their views about shopping.  Identify key areas on which they disagree.  In your answer, you should refer in detail to both passages.                    5

You may answer this question in continuous prose or in a series of developed bullet points.

**[END OF MODEL QUESTION PAPER]**

National
Qualifications
MODEL PAPER 2

# English
# Critical Reading

Date — Not applicable

Duration — 1 hour 30 minutes

**Total marks — 40**

## SECTION 1 — Scottish Text — 20 marks

Read an extract from a Scottish text you have previously studied and attempt the questions.

Choose ONE text from either

Part A — Drama Pages 2–7

Part B — Prose Pages 8–17

Part C — Poetry Pages 18–29

Attempt ALL the questions for your chosen text.

## SECTION 2 — Critical Essay — 20 marks

Attempt ONE question from the following genres — Drama, Prose, Poetry, Film and Television Drama, or Language.

Your answer must be on a different genre from that chosen in Section 1.

You should spend approximately 45 minutes on each Section.

Write your answers clearly in the answer booklet provided. In the answer booklet you must clearly identify the question number you are attempting.

Use **blue** or **black** ink.

Before leaving the examination room you must give your answer booklet to the Invigilator; if you do not, you may lose all the marks for this paper.

**SECTION 1 — SCOTTISH TEXT — 20 marks**

Choose ONE text from Drama, Prose or Poetry.

Read the text extract carefully and then attempt ALL the questions for your chosen text.

You should spend about 45 minutes on this Section.

**PART A — SCOTTISH TEXT — DRAMA**

Text 1 — Drama

If you choose this text you may not attempt a question on Drama in Section 2.

Read the extract below and then attempt the following questions.

*The Slab Boys* by John Byrne

*In this extract, Alan intervenes on Hector's behalf.*

|   |   |   |
|---|---|---|
| | HECTOR: | D'you like it, Alan? |
| | ALAN: | It's … er … (PHIL *threatens to snap pen*) … really gadgey, Heck. |
| | HECTOR: | Will I go now and ask her? Will I? (*Heads for door*) |
| 5 | SPANKY: | (*Cutting him off*) Not just yet, Hector … Remember you've still got to go and see Willie. |
| | HECTOR: | Yeh, but I can do that after I've asked Lucille … |
| | PHIL: | No, Spanky's right, kiddo … better go and see Willie first. It's important. Lucille'll not go off the boil. Here, I'll give you my coat to put on … (*Takes off coat*) |
| 10 | HECTOR: | What do I want that for? I don't mind doing a bit of swanking now that my clothes are up to date. |
| | PHIL: | Yeh, but you don't want anybody else to get a preview, do you? Lessen the impact … know what I mean? Get the coat on. (*Forces* HECTOR's *arms into sleeves*) |
| | SPANKY: | (*Pulling balaclava helmet from cupboard*) You better put this on and all … it's draughty in Willie's room. (*Pulls helmet over* HECTOR's *head*) Cosy, eh? |
| 15 | HECTOR: | (*Slightly bamboozled*) Yeh, but will he not think I'm a bit happed up? |
| | PHIL: | That's just it. You've been down at Nurse. Influenza verging on pleurisy. She ordered you home but you decided to soldier on. He'll like that. Maybe not give you your … (*Stops*) |
| | SPANKY: | (*Quickly*) Wireless back. |
| 20 | HECTOR: | I'm not expecting my wireless back. You know what he's like. |
| | SPANKY: | Well, you can't just expect it back cos you've got the flu, Heck … |
| | PHIL: | Triple pneumonia, Spanks. |
| | HECTOR: | I'm all mixed up … what've I got again? |
| | SPANKY: | Triple pneumonia … |
| 25 | PHIL: | Double rupture … |
| | HECTOR: | I'll away along then. |

*Page two*

MARKS

| | | |
|---|---|---|
| SPANKY: | Good man.  All the best. | |

PHIL: Good luck, son … (*They shove* HECTOR *out the door*)  You'll need it.

(*They hold onto each other laughing*)

30 ALAN: Well, I hope you're proud of yourselves … that was a pretty lousy trick to play!

SPANKY: Oh, was it, by jove?

PHIL: A trick, you cad!  Take that!  (*Bops* ALAN's *head a smack*)

ALAN: Hey, watch it!  That was sore … Chuckit!  Okay, so I'm speaking out of turn but that poor little bastard's gone off to Willie Curry's office thinking that underneath
35 that dustcoat and helmet he really does cut a dash … and he'll probably stop off on the way back to have a word with Lucille … doff the coat and hat and you know what'll happen then … she'll wet herself.  Which will probably give you and your crummy friend a big laugh, won't it?

PHIL: Gosh and All Serene … the Fifth Form at St Dominic's.  Listen, Steerforth Minor,
40 if it wasn't for me and Spanks there that 'poor little bastard' wouldn't have any pals. Yeh, that's right.  So, we do take the piss … set him up a bit …

ALAN: More than a bit.

## Questions

1. By referring to lines 1—29, explain how the audience is made to feel sorry for Hector.  **4**

2. Explain how the playwright's use of language in lines 30—32 allows Phil and Spanky to make fun of Alan.  **2**

3. By referring to lines 33—42, explain how the playwright emphasises the animosity between Alan and Phil.  **4**

4. By referring to the extract and elsewhere in the play, discuss the importance of the conflict between Phil and Alan in exploring at least one theme in the play.  **10**

OR

**Text 2 — Drama**

If you choose this text you may not attempt a question on Drama in Section 2.

Read the extract below and then attempt the following questions.

**The Cheviot, the Stag and the Black, Black Oil** by John McGrath

*In this extract, the roots of the Highland Clearances are explained.*

(GAELIC SINGER *is singing a quiet Jacobite song in Gaelic*)

M.C.         It begins, I suppose, with 1746 – Culloden and all that.  The Highlands were in a bit of a mess.  Speaking — or singing — the Gaelic language was forbidden.  (*Singing stops.*)  Wearing the plaid was forbidden.  (SINGER *takes off her plaid, sits.*)  Things
5               were all set for a change.  So Scene One — Strathnaver 1813.

*Drum roll.  Page of book turned, a cottage pops up from in between the next two pages.*

*Enter two Strahnaver girls, singing.*

GIRLS:        Hé mandu's truagh nach tigeadh
                  Hé mandu siod 'gam iarraidh
10              Hé mandu gille's litir
                  He ri oro each is diollaid
                  Heman dubh hi ri oro
                  Hó ró hù ó

*As they sing, a* YOUNG HIGHLANDER *comes on, watches them, talks to audience.*

15   Y.H.         The women were great at making it all seem fine.  But it was no easy time to be alive in.  Sir John Sinclair of Caithness had invented the Great Sheep; that is to say, he had introduced the Cheviot to the North.  Already in Assynt the Sutherland family had cleared the people off their land – and the people were not too pleased about it.

FIRST
WOMAN:     Ach blethers —

SECOND
20   WOMAN:    Cha chuir iad dragh oirnne co diubh.  (They won't bother us here).

FIRST
WOMAN:     The Countess has always been very kind to us.

Y.H.         Aye, and she's away in England.

FIRST
WOMAN.     Why wouldn't she be?

Y.H.         With her fancy palaces and feasts for Kings and fine French wines – and it's our rent
25             she's spending.

FIRST
WOMAN:     Rent!  You never pay any rent –

MARKS

| | | |
|---|---|---|
| Y.H. | | Where would I get the money to pay rent? (*To audience.*) If it's not bad weather flattening the barley, it's mildew on the potatoes, and last year it was both together ... And now they're talking about bringing in soldiers to clear us off the land completely ... |

30

| | |
|---|---|
| SECOND WOMAN: | Saighdearan? De mu dheidhinn saighdearan? (Soldiers — what do you mean, soldiers?) |
| Y.H. | There were one hundred and fifty of them arrived in a boat off Lochinver. |
| FIRST WOMAN: | Would you get on with some work? |

35

| | |
|---|---|
| SECOND WOMAN: | Seo-lion an cogan. (Here fill up the bucket) |

*They sing on, as Y.H. goes to a corner of the cottage to pee in the bucket. They watch him and laugh. Suddenly he panics, does up his trousers and rushes over.*

| | |
|---|---|
| Y.H. | Here — there's a couple of gentlemen coming up the strath. |
| FIRST WOMAN: | Gentlemen? |

40

| | |
|---|---|
| Y.H. | (*to audience*). The two gentlemen were James Loch and Patrick Sellar, factor and under-factor to the Sutherland estates. |
| FIRST WOMAN: | Oh, look at the style of me ... |
| Y.H. | (*handing them the bucket*). You might find a good use for this. (*Goes.*) |

## Questions

5. By referring to lines 1—18, explain how the playwright creates a relaxed mood.  4

6. By referring to lines 19—34, explain how the playwright conveys the difference in outlook between the Young Highlander and the Two Women.  4

7. Explain how the extract ends on a humorous note.  2

8. The staging of *The Cheviot, the Stag and the Black, Black Oil* is very different from that of a conventional play. By referring to the extract and to elsewhere in the play, discuss how effective you find this unconventional staging in exploring at least one key idea in the play.  10

OR

### Text 3 — Drama

If you choose this text you may not attempt a question on Drama in Section 2.

Read the extract below and then attempt the following questions.

### *Men Should Weep* by Ena Lamont Stewart

*In this extract, which is from near beginning of the play, Lily questions some of Maggie's assumptions.*

| | | |
|---|---|---|
| | LILY: | Dae you think you're happy? |
| | MAGGIE: | Aye! I'm happy! |
| | LILY: | In this midden? |
| 5 | MAGGIE: | Ye canna help havin a midden o a hoose when there's kids under yer feet a day. I dae the best I can. |
| | LILY: | I ken ye do. I'd gie it up as hopeless. Nae hot water. Nae place tae dry the weans' clothes ... nae money. If John wad gie hissel a shake ... |
| | MAGGIE: | You leave John alane! He does his best for us. |
| 10 | LILY: | No much o a best. O.K. O.K. Keep yer wig on! Ye're that touchy ye'd think ye wis jist new merriet. I believe you still love him! |
| | MAGGIE: | Aye. I still love John. And whit's more, he loves me. |
| | LILY: | Ye ought to get yer photies took and send them tae the Sunday papers! "Twenty-five years merriet and I still love ma husband. Is this a record?" |
| | MAGGIE: | I'm sorry for you, Lily. I'm right sorry for you. |
| 15 | LILY: | We're quits then. |
| | MAGGIE: | Servin dirty hulkin brutes o men in a Coocaddens pub. |
| | LILY: | Livin in a slum and slavin efter a useless man an his greetin weans. |
| | MAGGIE: | They're *my* weans! I'm workin for ma ain. |
| | LILY: | I'm *paid* for my work. |
| 20 | MAGGIE: | So'm I! No in wages ... I'm paid wi love. [*pause*] And when did you last have a man's airms roon ye? |
| | LILY: | *Men!* I'm wantin nae man's airms roon me. They're a dirty beasts. |
| | MAGGIE: | Lily, yer mind's twisted. You canna see a man as a man. Ye've got them a lumped thegither. Ye're daft! |
| 25 | LILY: | You're *saft*! You think yer man's wonderful and yer weans is a angels. Look at Jenny ... |
| | MAGGIE: | [*instantly on the defensive*] There's naethin wrang wi Jenny! |
| | LILY: | No yet. |

MARKS

**Questions**

9.  Look at lines 1—15.

    (i)  Explain what important aspects of Maggie's character are revealed in these lines.    **4**

    (ii)  Explain one important aspect of Lily's character which is revealed in these lines.    **2**

10.  Analyse how lines 16—28 are structured in such a way as to provide a lively dramatic exchange between Maggie and Lily.    **4**

11.  By referring to the extract and to elsewhere in the play, discuss to what extent men in the play are presented as weak.    **10**

## SECTION 1 — SCOTTISH TEXT — 20 marks

Choose ONE text from Drama, Prose or Poetry.

Read the text extract carefully and then attempt ALL the questions for your chosen text.

You should spend about 45 minutes on this Section.

## PART B — SCOTTISH TEXT — PROSE

### Text 1 — Prose

If you choose this text you may not attempt a question on Prose in Section 2.

Read the extract below and then attempt the following questions.

### *The Painter* by Iain Crichton Smith

*In this extract, the narrator describes the fight between Red Roderick and his father-in-law.*

As Red Roderick was drunk perhaps the advantage given him by relative youth was to a certain extent cancelled. There was however no doubt that he wished to kill the old man, so enraged was he, so frustrated by the life that tortured him. As they swung their scythes towards each other ponderously, it looked at first as if they could do little harm, and
5   indeed it was odd to see them, as if each was trying to cut corn. However, after some time — while the face of the old man gradually grew more demoniac in a renewal of his youth – he succeeded at last in cutting his son-in-law's left leg so that he fell to the ground, his wife running towards him like an old hen, her skirts trailing the ground like broken wings.

But that was not what I meant to tell since the fight in itself, though unpleasant, was not
10   evil. No, as I stood in the ring with the others, excited and horrified, I saw on the edge of the ring young William with his paint-brush and canvas and easel painting the fight. He was sitting comfortably on a chair which he had taken with him and there was no expression on his face at all but a cold clear intensity which bothered me. It seemed in a strange way as if he were asleep. As the scythes swung to and fro, as the faces of the
15   antagonists became more and more contorted in the fury of battle, as their cheeks were suffused with blood and rage, and their teeth were drawn back in a snarl, he sat there painting the battle, nor at any time did he make any attempt to pull his chair back from the arena where they were engaged.

I cannot explain to you the feelings that seethed through me as I watched him. One
20   feeling was partly admiration that he should be able to concentrate with such intensity that he didn't seem able to notice the danger he was in. The other feeling was one of the most bitter disgust as if I were watching a gaze that had gone beyond the human and which was as indifferent to the outcome as a hawk's might be. You may think I was wrong in what I did next. I deliberately came up behind him and upset the chair so that he fell down head
25   over heels in the middle of a brush-stroke. He turned on me such a gaze of blind fury that I was reminded of a rat which had once leaped at me from a river bank, and he would have struck me but that I pinioned his arms behind his back. I would have beaten him if his mother hadn't come and taken him away, still snarling and weeping tears of rage. In spite of my almost religious fear at that moment, I tore the painting into small pieces and

MARKS

30 scattered them about the earth. Some people have since said that what I wanted to do was to protect the good name of the village but I must in all honesty say that that was not in my mind when I pushed the chair over. All that was in my mind was fury and disgust that this painter should have watched this fight with such cold concentration that he seemed to think that the fight had been set up for him to paint, much as a house exists or an old wall.

**Questions**

12. By referring to lines 1—8, explain how the narrator's account creates an ambiguous impression of how serious the fight is.  4

13. By referring to lines 9—18, analyse how the writer makes clear the contrast between William and the two fighters.  4

14. By referring to lines 19—34, describe in your own words why the narrator is so incensed at William.  2

15. By referring to the extract and to at least one other story by Iain Crichton Smith, discuss the impressions he creates of life in a small community.  10

OR

### Text 2 — Prose

If you choose this text you may not attempt a question on Prose in Section 2.

Read the extract below and then attempt the following questions.

**The Eye of the Hurricane** by George Mackay Brown

*In this extract, Captain Stevens tries to convince the narrator to buy him alcohol.*

"Now, Barclay, about this cold of mine."

"Miriam says you haven't got a cold at all," I said.

"The little bitch," he said. "Did she go into your room? She had no right to be disturbing you. I'll speak to her about that. I expect she told you also that I have drinking bouts."

5  "She did," I said.

"Well," he said, "everybody knows. Can't do a thing about it, Barclay. It's a natural thing, like a storm, you just have to let it blow itself out, keep the ship headed into it. Do you understand that, Barclay?"

"I know nothing about it," I said.

10  "I thought writers are supposed to understand things," he said, "the quirks of human nature. That's what they're for. Don't take hard what I say, Barclay. I like you. I'm very glad you're living in this house. I'm just explaining the situation to you, setting the course through the storm, so that you can take your turn at navigating if the need arises. The best way you can help the voyage, Barclay, is just do what I say. I'm the skipper of this ship.

15  And the first thing I want you to do is open that drawer and you'll see a wallet."

"No," I said, and got to my feet.

"There should be four five-pound notes in it. Take one of them out."

"No," I said.

"Two bottles of navy rum from Wilson's, as quick as you can."

20  Charity is no hard-minted currency to be distributed according to whim, a shilling here and a sovereign there – it is the oil and wine that drop uncertainly through the fingers upon the wounds of the world, wherever the roads of pity and suffering cross. It might help this old man, as he said, if I stood close beside him on the bridge till this particular hurricane blew itself out. But I trusted the older wisdom of women. I had made a

25  promise to Miriam.

"No," I said.

"Very well, Mr Barclay," he said after a pause. "Let me see. At the moment you are paying me a rent of two pounds a week, I think. As from Monday next you will pay me four pounds a week. In fact, I think you should make arrangements to leave this house

30  before the end of the month. I find you an unsatisfactory tenant. Now get out."

All night, till I fell into a drowse around three o'clock in the morning, I heard him pacing back and fore, back and fore in his room, an ancient mariner in a ship of dark enchantment.

MARKS

**Questions**

16. By referring to the whole extract, explain the various methods the Captain uses to convince the narrator to buy him alcohol.  4

17. Analyse how the narrator uses imagery in lines 20–25 to explain his views on charity.  4

18. Explain what the last three lines suggest about the narrator's feelings for the Captain.  2

19. By referring to the extract and to at least one other story by George Mackay Brown, discuss how he creates confrontations between characters.  10

OR

### Text 3 — Prose

If you choose this text you may not attempt a question on Prose in Section 2.

Read the extract below and then attempt the following questions.

**The Trick is to Keep Breathing** by Janice Galloway

*In this extract, Joy meets 'Dr Three'.*

The doctor is over an hour late. An entirely different man to Dr Two. But questions involve risk and I don't want to look picky. I follow him down the sea-coloured corridor to a room with no pictures and all the curtains closed. It smells like dog in the rain. Dr Three doesn't waste any time.

5 DR THREE   [Sitting]  Well?

Leather elbow patches on his horrible jacket glint in the gloom. Behind the specs his eyes are all iris.

PATIENT     [Mesmerised]  Well what?  I thought you would start.

DR THREE   Start what?  Start what?  You asked to see me.  You are the one who knows
10            what this is about.

PATIENT     I've been here nearly a week.

DR THREE   Yes.  So what can I do for you?

PATIENT     [Confused.  Has forgotten and is trying to remember.]  Treatment.  I want
           to know about treatment.

15 DR THREE   [Leans back with an ominous creak]  I don't know what sort of thing you
           expected.  There's no set procedure for these things.  You ask to see one of
           us when you feel you need to.  So.  Any other questions?

PATIENT     I have to think.  [Silence]

DR THREE   Well?

20 PATIENT     [Nothing.  Eyes filling up.]

DR THREE   [Draw a long breath through the nose, leaning back on the chair]  How long
           have you been here did you say?

PATIENT     Nearly a week.  I haven't seen anyone.

DR THREE   [Sighing]   I suppose you want a pass.  [Silence]   To go home for the
25            weekend?  You should be going home on pass.  Getting out of here and
           facing up to things on the outside.  You can go out on pass any time you like,
           all right?

PATIENT     No.  I don't understand any of this.

DR THREE   I don't know what that's supposed to mean.

30 PATIENT     It's too fast.  You're rushing me.

DR THREE   All right.  Take your time.  [Silence]  Right then.  Good day.

He taps the bundle of papers on his desk, then folds his arms. The interview is finished. PATIENT stands thinking maybe this is some kind of therapy.

DR THREE   The interview is over.   [Opens a drawer.  The stack of papers flake
35            dangerously.  He pretends not to notice.]

MARKS

**Questions**

20. By referring to lines 1—7, explain how the writer establishes an unwelcoming atmosphere at the start of the extract.

3

21. By referring to lines 8—23, analyse how the exchange between the Patient and Dr Three highlights the lack of communication between them.

4

22. By referring to lines 24—35, explain how the Doctor's uncaring approach is made clear.

3

23. By referring to the extract and elsewhere in the novel, discuss how *The Trick Is To Keep Breathing* explores the way the individual is treated within the Mental Health system.

10

OR

### Text 4 — Prose

If you choose this text you may not attempt a question on Prose in Section 2.

Read the extract below and then attempt the following questions.

**Sunset Song by Lewis Grassic Gibbon**

*In this extract, which is from Part IV (Harvest), Ewan has returned on leave from the army.*

Drunk he had come from the station and more than two hours late.  Standing at last in the kitchen in his kilts he'd looked round and sneered *Hell, Chris, what a bloody place!* as she ran to him.  And he'd flung his pack one way and his hat the other and kissed her as though she were a tink, his hands on her as quickly as that, hot and questing and wise as
5   his hands had never been.  She saw the hot smoulder fire in his eyes then, but no blush on his face, it was red with other things.  But she smothered her horror and laughed, and kissed him and struggled from him, and cried *Ewan, who's this?*

Young Ewan held back, shy-like, staring, and just said *It's father*. At that the strange, swaying figure in the tartan kilts laughed, coarse-like, *Well, we'll hope so, eh Chris? Any*
10   *supper left – unless you're too bloody stand-offish even to have that?*

She couldn't believe her own ears.  *Stand-offish? Oh, Ewan!* and ran to him again, but he shook her away, *Och, all right, I'm wearied. For Christ's sake let a man sit down.*  He staggered to the chair she'd made ready for him, a picture-book of young Ewan's lay there, he picked the thing up and flung it to the other side of the room, and slumped down
15   into the chair. *Hell, what a blasted climb to a blasted place.  Here, give us some tea.*

She sat beside him to serve him, she knew her face had gone white.  But she poured the tea and spread the fine supper she'd been proud to make, it might hardly have been there for the notice he paid it, drinking cup after cup of the tea like a beast at a trough.  She saw him clearer then, the coarse hair that sprang like short bristles all over his head, the neck
20   with its red and angry circle about the collar of the khaki jacket, a great half-healed scar across the back of his hand glinted putrescent blue.  Suddenly his eyes came on her, *Well, damn't, is that all you've to say to me now I've come home?  I'd have done better to spend the night with a tart in the town.*

She didn't say anything, she couldn't, the tears were choking in her throat and smarting
25   and biting at her eyelids, pressing to come, the tears that she'd sworn she'd never shed all the time he was home on leave.  And she didn't dare look at him lest he should see, but he saw and pushed back his chair and got up in a rage, *God Almighy, what are you snivelling about now? You always were snivelling, I mind*.  And out he went, young Ewan ran to her side and flung his arms round her, *Mother, don't cry, I don't like him, he's a tink, that*
30   *soldier!*

MARKS

Questions

24. Analyse how the writer's use of language in lines 1–15 emphasises the offensiveness of Ewan's behaviour.    **4**

25. By referring to lines 16–23, analyse how the writer makes the reader aware of Chris's perception of Ewan.    **4**

26. By referring to the whole extract, identify the change in young Ewan's reaction to his father.    **2**

27. By referring to the extract and elsewhere in the novel, discuss the development of the relationship between Chris and Ewan.    **10**

OR

### Text 5 — Prose

If you choose this text you may not attempt a question on Prose in Section 2.

Read the extract below and then attempt the following questions.

### *The Cone-Gatherers* by Robin Jenkins

*In this extract, Calum witnesses the killing of a deer.*

Calum no longer was one of the beaters; he too was a deer hunted by remorseless men. Moaning and gasping, he fled after them, with no hope of saving them from slaughter but with the impulse to share it with them.  He could not, however, be so swift or sure of foot. He fell and rose again; he avoided one tree only to collide with another close to it; and all

5   the time he felt, as the deer must have, the indifference of all nature; of the trees, of tall withered stalks of willowherb, of the patches of blue sky, of bushes, of piles of cut scrubwood, of birds lurking in branches, and of the sunlight: presences which might have been expected to help or at least sympathise.

The dogs barked fiercely.  Duror fired his gun in warning to those waiting in the ride.

10   Neil, seeing his brother rush into the danger, roared to him to come back.  All the beaters, except Charlie in the rear, joined in the commotion; the wood resounded with their exultant shouts.  Realising this must be the finish or kill, Graham, recuperating on the road, hopped back over the fence into the wood and bellowed loudest of all.

As Duror bawled to his dogs to stop lest they interfere with the shooting, and as the deer

15   hesitated before making the dash across the ride, Calum was quite close to them as, silent, desperate, and heroic, they sprang forward to die or escape.  When the guns banged he did not, as Neil had vehemently warned him to do, fall flat on the ground and put his fingers in his ears.  Instead, with wails of lament, he dashed on at demented speed and shot out onto the broad green ride to hear a deer screaming and see it, wounded in the breast and

20   forelegs, scrabbling about on its hindquarters.  Captain Forgan was feverishly reloading his gun to fire again.  Calum saw no one else, not even the lady or Mr. Tulloch, who was standing by himself about twenty yards away.

Screaming in sympathy, heedless of the danger of being shot, Calum flung himself upon the deer, clasped it round the neck, and tried to comfort it.  Terrified more than ever, it

25   dragged him about with it in its mortal agony.  Its blood came off onto his face and hands.

While Captain Forgan, young Roderick, and Lady Runcie-Campbell stood petrified by this sight, Duror followed by his dogs came leaping out of the wood.  He seemed to be laughing in some kind of berserk joy.  There was a knife in his hand.  His mistress shouted to him: what it was she did not know herself, and he never heard.  Rushing upon the

30   stricken deer and the frantic hunchback, he threw the latter off with furious force, and then, seizing the former's head with one hand cut its throat savagely with the other.  Blood spouted.  Lady Runice-Campbell closed her eyes.  Captain Forgan shook his head slightly in some kind of denial.  Roderick screamed at Duror.  Tulloch had gone running over to Calum.

35   The deer was dead, but Duror did not rise triumphant; he crouched beside it, on his knees, as if he was mourning over it.  His hands were red with blood; in one of them he still held the knife.

**MARKS**

Questions

28. Analyse how the sentence structure in lines 1—8 helps to convey how Calum is feeling.

2

29. By referring to lines 9—25, analyse how the writer's use of language creates a sense of "commotion" (line 11).

4

30. By referring to lines 26—37, explain how the reader is made aware of Duror's state of mind at this point.

4

31. By referring to the extract and elsewhere in the novel, discuss how the writer explores the theme of death in *The Cone-Gatherers*.

10

## SECTION 1 — SCOTTISH TEXT — 20 marks

Choose ONE text from Drama, Prose or Poetry.

Read the text extract carefully and then attempt ALL the questions for your chosen text.

You should spend about 45 minutes on this Section.

## PART C — SCOTTISH TEXT — POETRY

### Text 1 — Poetry

If you choose this text you may not attempt a question on Poetry in Section 2.

Read the extract below and then attempt the following questions.

### *Tam o' Shanter* by Robert Burns

*In this extract, Tam manages to outrun the witches.*

As bees bizz out wi' angry fyke,
When plundering herds assail their byke;
As open pussie's mortal foes,
When, pop! she starts before their nose;
5   As eager runs the market-crowd,
When 'Catch the thief!' resounds aloud;
So Maggie runs, the witches follow,
Wi' mony an eldritch skriech and hollo.

Ah, Tam! ah, Tam! thou'll get thy fairin!
10  In hell they'll roast thee like a herrin!
In vain thy Kate awaits thy comin!
Kate soon will be a woefu' woman!
Now, do thy speedy utmost, Meg,
And win the key-stane o' the brig;
15  There at them thou thy tail may toss,
A running stream they dare na cross.
But ere the key-stane she could make,
The fient a tail she had to shake!
For Nannie far before the rest,
20  Hard upon noble Maggie prest,
And flew at Tam wi' furious ettle;
But little wist she Maggie's mettle —
Ae spring brought aff her master hale,
But left behind her ain grey tail:
25  The carlin claught her by the rump,
And left poor Maggie scarce a stump.

Now, wha this tale o' truth shall read,
Ilk man and mother's son, take heed;
Whene'er to drink you are inclin'd,
30  Or cutty-sarks run in your mind,
Think! ye may buy the joys o'er dear —
Remember Tam o' Shanter's mare.

MARKS

**Questions**

32. Analyse how the extended simile in lines 1—8 creates a vivid picture of what is happening.    **3**

33. By referring to lines 9—26, explain how Burns makes this part of the poem dramatic.    **4**

34. Discuss to what extent you think lines 27—32 are meant as a serious warning to the reader.    **3**

35. Referring to Tam o' Shanter and at least one other poem by Burns, discuss to what extent he passes judgements in his poetry.    **10**

OR

**Text 2 — Poetry**

If you choose this text you may not attempt a question on Poetry in Section 2.

Read the extract below and then attempt the following questions.

*Anne Hathaway* **by Carol Ann Duffy**

The bed we loved in was a spinning world
of forests, castles, torchlight, clifftops, seas
where he would dive for pearls.  My lover's words
were shooting stars which fell to earth as kisses
5  on these lips; my body now a softer rhyme
to his, now echo, assonance; his touch
a verb dancing in the centre of a noun.
Some nights, I dreamed he'd written me, the bed
a page beneath his writer's hands.  Romance
10  and drama played by touch, by scent, by taste.
In the other bed, the best, our guests dozed on,
dribbling their prose.  My living laughing love –
I hold him in the casket of my widow's head
as he held me upon that next best bed.

MARKS

**Questions**

36. By referring to two techniques of poetry, analyse how the first sentence (lines 1—3) establishes the speaker's passion.  2

37. Explain how the poet uses references to writing in lines 3—10 to convey the speaker's feelings .  4

38. Evaluate the effectiveness of lines 11—14 as a conclusion to the poem.  4

39. Love is a common theme in Carol Ann Duffy's poetry.  By referring to this poem and to at least one other by her, discuss how she explores the theme of love.  3

OR

### Text 3 — Poetry

If you choose this text you may not attempt a question on Poetry in Section 2.

Read the extract below and then attempt the following questions.

### *Some Old Photographs* by Liz Lochhead

weather evocative as scent
the romance of dark stormclouds
in big skies over the low wide river
       of long shadows and longer shafts of light

5    of smoke
fabulous film-noir stills of Central Station
of freezing fog silvering the chilled, stilled parks
    of the glamorous past
    where drops on a rainmate are sequins
10    in the lamplight, in the black-and-white

your young, still-lovely mother laughs, the
hem of her sundress whipped up
by a wind on a beach before you were even born

all the Dads in hats
15   are making for Central at five past five
in the snow, in the rain, in the sudden what-a-scorcher,
in the smog, their
belted dark overcoats white-spattered by the starlings

starlings swarming
20   in that perfect and permanent cloud
above what was
never really this photograph
but always all the passing now
and noise and stink and smoky breath of George Square

25   wee boays, a duchess, bunting, there's a
big launch on the Clyde
and that boat is yet to sail

MARKS

Questions

40. By referring to more than one technique of poetry, explain how the poet creates a dream-like atmosphere in lines 1—10.    **4**

41. By referring to lines 11—18, explain how the poet reminds the reader that these photographs are old.    **2**

42. By referring to lines 19—24, explain what impression the poet creates of George Square.    **2**

43. Explain how the poet creates a sense of excitement in the last three lines of the poem.    **2**

44. Liz Lochhead's poems have sometimes been criticised for being overly nostalgic.  By referring to this poem and to at least one other, discuss whether you think this is a fair criticism.    **10**

OR

Text 4 — Poetry

If you choose this text you may not attempt a question on Poetry in Section 2.

Read the extract below and then attempt the following questions.

### *Memorial* by Norman MacCaig

Everywhere she dies.  Everywhere I go she dies.
No sunrise, no city square, no lurking beautiful mountain
but has her death in it.
The silence of her dying sounds through
5  the carousel of language.  It's a web
on which laughter stitches itself.  How can my hand
clasp another's when between them
is that thick death, that intolerable distance?

She grieves for my grief.  Dying, she tells me
10  that bird dives from the sun, that fish
leaps into it.  No crocus is carved more gently
than the way her dying
shapes my mind. — But I hear, too,
the other words,
15  black words that make the sound
of soundlessness, that name the nowhere
she is continuously going into.

Ever since she died
she can't stop dying.  She makes me
20  her elegy.  I am a walking masterpiece,
a true fiction
of the ugliness of death.
I am her sad music.

MARKS

## Questions

45.    "The silence of her dying sounds through
the carousel of language. It's a web
on which laughter stitches itself." (lines 4—6)

     Analyse how any **one** of these images conveys how the speaker has been affected by the death.     3

46.    By referring to lines 9—17, explain how the poet uses contrast to reveal the persona's feelings.     4

47.    By referring to lines 18—23, explain how the persona makes clear the impact the death has had on him.     3

48.    By referring to this poem and to at least one other by Norman MacCaig, discuss his exploration of deeply emotional situations.     10

**OR**

**Text 5 — Poetry**

If you choose this text you may not attempt a question on Poetry in Section 2.

Read the poem below and then attempt the following questions.

***Shores* by Sorley MacLean**

If we were in Talisker on the shore
where the great white mouth
opens between two hard jaws,
Rubha nan Clach and the Bioda Ruadh,
5   I would stand beside the sea
renewing love in my spirit
while the ocean was filling
Talisker bay forever:
I would stand there on the bareness of the shore
10  until Prishal bowed his stallion head.

And if we were together
on Calgary shore in Mull,
between Scotland and Tiree,
between the world and eternity,
15  I would stay there till doom
measuring sand, grain by grain,
and in Uist, on the shore of Homhsta
in presence of that wide solitude,
I would wait there forever,
20  for the sea draining drop by drop.

And if I were on the shore of Moidart
with you, for whom my care is new,
I would put up in a synthesis of love for you
the ocean and the sand, drop and grain.
25  And if we were on Mol Stenscholl Staffin
when the unhappy surging sea dragged
the boulders and threw them over us,
I would build the rampart wall
against an alien eternity grinding (its teeth).

MARKS

Questions

49. By referring to lines 1—10, analyse how the poet conveys the power of natural features.    **3**

50. By referring to lines 11—20, explain how the poet conveys his commitment to the person he is addressing.    **3**

51. The last verse (lines 21—29) is structurally similar to the other two verses, but there are differences.  By referring to both the similarities and the differences, evaluate the last verse as a conclusion to the poem as a whole.    **4**

52. By referring to this poem and to at least one other by Sorley MacLean, discuss the importance of landscape in his poetry.    **10**

OR

## Text 6 — Poetry

If you choose this text you may not attempt a question on Poetry in Section 2.

Read the poem below and then attempt the following questions.

### *Two Trees* by Don Paterson

One morning, Don Miguel got out of bed
with one idea rooted in his head:
to graft his orange to his lemon tree.
It took him the whole day to work them free,
5   lay open their sides, and lash them tight.
For twelve months, from the shame or from the fright
they put forth nothing; but one day there appeared
two lights in the dark leaves.  Over the years
the limbs would get themselves so tangled up
10  each bough looked like it gave a double crop,
and not one kid in the village didn't know
the magic tree in Miguel's patio.

The man who bought the house had had no dream
so who can say what dark malicious whim
15  led him to take his axe and split the bole
along its fused seam, then dig two holes.
And no, they did not die from solitude;
nor did their branches bear a sterile fruit;
nor did their unhealed flanks weep every spring
20  for those four yards that lost them everything,
as each strained on its shackled root to face
the other's empty, intricate embrace.
They were trees, and trees don't weep or ache or shout.
And trees are all this poem is about.

MARKS

**Questions**

53.  Explain how the poet makes the first verse (lines 1–12) sound like the start of a simple folk tale or parable.    4

54.  Explain how lines 13–16 act as a link or turning point in the poem as a whole.    2

55.  By referring to lines 17–24, explain how the poet subverts the idea that the poem is a parable or a tale with a message.    4

56.  By referring to this poem and to at least one other by Don Paterson, discuss his use of symbolism to explore important themes.    10

**[END OF SECTION 1]**

## SECTION 2 — CRITICAL ESSAY — 20 marks

Attempt ONE question from the following genres — Drama, Prose, Poetry, Film and Television Drama, or Language.

You may use a Scottish text but <u>NOT</u> the one used in Section 1.

Your answer must be on a different genre from that chosen in Section 1.

You should spend approximately 45 minutes on this Section.

### DRAMA

> Answers to questions on **drama** should refer to the text and to such relevant features as characterisation, key scene(s), structure, climax, theme, plot, conflict, setting ...

1. Choose a play in which a character shows signs of instability at one or more than one key point in the play.

   Explain the reason(s) for the character's instability and discuss how this feature adds to your understanding of the central concern(s) of the text.

2. Choose a play in which an important part is played by one of the following: crime, punishment, retribution.

   Explain how the dramatist explores the issue and discuss its importance to your understanding of character and/or theme in the play as a whole.

3. Choose from a play a scene which you find amusing or moving or disturbing.

   Explain how the scene provokes this response and discuss how this aspect of the scene contributes to your understanding of the play as a whole.

## PROSE — FICTION

> Answers to questions on **prose fiction** should refer to the text and to such relevant features as characterisation, setting, language, key incident(s), climax, turning point, plot, structure, narrative technique, theme, ideas, description ...

4.  Choose a novel or short story in which envy or malice or cruelty plays a significant part.

    Explain how the writer makes you aware of this aspect of the text and discuss how the writer's exploration of it enhances your understanding of the text as a whole.

5.  Choose a novel or short story in which a character is influenced by a particular location or setting.

    Explain how the character is influenced by the location or setting and discuss how this enhances your understanding of the text as a whole.

6.  Choose a novel or short story in which the death of a character clarifies an important theme in the text.

    Explain how this theme is explored in the text and discuss how the death of the character clarifies the theme.

## PROSE — NON-FICTION

> Answers to questions on **prose non-fiction** should refer to the text and to such relevant features as ideas, use of evidence, stance, style, selection of material, narrative voice ...

7.  Choose a piece of **travel writing** in which the writer's own personality emerges as a significant feature.

    Explain how the style of writing conveys a sense of the writer's personality and discuss to what extent this is important to your understanding of the key idea(s) of the text.

8.  Choose a **non-fiction text** which is written in the specific form of a diary or a journal or a letter.

    Discuss to what extent the writer's exploitation of specific features of the chosen form is important in conveying key idea(s) of the text.

9.  Choose a piece of **journalism** which, in your opinion, deals with a fundamental truth about human nature.

    Explain how the writer's presentation of key ideas enhances your understanding of this fundamental truth.

## POETRY

Answers to questions on **poetry** should refer to the text and to such relevant features as word choice, tone, imagery, structure, content, rhythm, rhyme, theme, sound, ideas ...

10. Choose a poem which explores the pain of love or the pleasure of love or the power of love.

    Discuss how the poet's exploration deepens your understanding of the pain or the power or the pleasure of love.

11. Choose a poem in which there is a powerful evocation of place.

    Discuss how the poet powerfully explores a specific place to explore an important theme.

12. Choose a poem in which humour is used to convey a serious message.

    Discuss how the poet uses humour to convey the underlying seriousness of the poem.

## FILM AND TELEVISION DRAMA

Answers to questions on **film and television drama*** should refer to the text and to such relevant features as use of camera, key sequence, characterisation, mise-en-scène, editing, setting, music/sound, special effects, plot, dialogue, ...

13. Choose a film or television drama which presents a mainly bleak vision of life.

    Explain how the film or programme makers convey the bleakness and discuss to what extent you feel the text offers any optimism.

14. Choose a film or television drama in which the true nature of a major character is gradually revealed.

    Explain how the film or programme makers present the gradual revelation and discuss how this added to your appreciation of the text as a whole.

15. Choose from a film or television drama a sequence in which a tense mood is created through at least two key filmic techniques such as mise-en-scène, montage, soundtrack ...

    Explain how the film or programme makers use these techniques to create a tense mood in the sequence and discuss the importance of the sequence to your appreciation of the text as a whole.

    * "television drama" includes a single play, a series or a serial.

## LANGUAGE

Answers to questions on **language** should refer to the text and to such relevant features as register, accent, dialect, slang, jargon, vocabulary, tone, abbreviation ...

16. Choose some of the ways language is evolving as a result of advances in communication technology.

    By referring to specific examples, discuss to what extent these advances are improving or impeding communication.

17. Choose the language of persuasion used in advertising or in politics.

    Discuss several ways in which the language you have chosen attempts to be persuasive.

18. Choose aspects of language associated with a particular group in society which shares a professional or leisure activity.

    Identify some examples of the language used and discuss how these examples facilitate communication within the group.


[END OF SECTION 2]


[END OF MODEL QUESTION PAPER]

# Model Paper 3

Whilst this Model Practice Paper has been specially commissioned by Hodder Gibson for use as practice for the Higher (for Curriculum for Excellence) exams, the key reference document remains the SQA Specimen Paper 2014.

Please note that, for reasons of space, this Model Paper offers practice in Reading for Understanding, Analysis and Evaluation, and in Critical Essay but does not offer further Scottish Set Text questions.

National
Qualifications
MODEL PAPER 3

# English
# Reading for Understanding, Analysis and Evaluation

Date — Not applicable

Duration — 1 hour 30 minutes

**Total marks — 30**

Attempt ALL questions.

Write your answers clearly in the answer booklet provided.  In the answer booklet you must clearly identify the question number you are attempting.

Use **blue** or **black** ink.

Before leaving the examination room you must give your answer booklet to the Invigilator; if you do not, you may lose all the marks for this paper.

The following two passages focus on video games.

**Passage 1**

*In the first passage Steven Johnson, writing in The Times newspaper, considers whether video games are as bad for young people as is often claimed.*

Read the passage below and attempt the questions which follow.

Reading books enriches the mind; playing video games deadens it — you can't get much more conventional than the conventional wisdom that kids today would be better off spending more time reading books, and less time zoning out in front of their video games.

5 For the record, I think that the virtues of reading books are great. We should all encourage our kids to read more. But even the most avid reader is inevitably going to spend his or her time with other media — games, television, movies, the internet. Yet the question is whether these other forms of culture have intellectual virtues in their own right — different from, but comparable to, reading. Where most critics allege a dumbing down, I see a progressive story: popular culture steadily, but almost imperceptibly, making our brains sharper as we soak in
10 entertainment usually dismissed as so much lowbrow fluff. I hope to persuade you that increasingly the non-literary popular culture is honing different mental skills that are just as important as the ones exercised by reading books.

The most powerful example of this trend is found in the world of video games. And the first and last thing that should be said about the experience of playing today's video games, the
15 thing you almost never hear, is that games are fiendishly, sometimes maddeningly, hard. The dirty little secret of gaming is how much time you spend not having fun. You may be frustrated; you may be confused or disorientated; you may be stuck. But when you put the game down and move back into the real world, you may find yourself mentally working through the problem you have been wrestling with, as though you were worrying a loose tooth.

20 So why does anyone bother playing these things? And why does a seven-year-old soak up, for instance, the intricacies of industrial economics in the game form of SimCity 2000, when the same subject would send him screaming for the exits in a classroom? To date, there has been little direct research into the question of how games get children to learn without realising that they are learning. But I believe a strong case can be made that the power of games to captivate
25 largely involves their ability to tap into the brain's natural reward circuitry. If you create a system in which rewards are both clearly defined and achieved by exploring an environment, you will find human brains drawn to those systems, even if they are made up of virtual characters and simulated sidewalks. In the game world, reward is everywhere. The gaming universe is literally teeming with objects that deliver very clearly articulated rewards: more
30 life, access to new levels, new equipment, new spells. Most of the crucial work in game design focuses on keeping players notified of potential rewards available to them, and how much these rewards are currently needed. Most games offer a fictional world where rewards are larger, and more vivid, and more clearly defined than life.

You may just want to win the game, of course, or perhaps you want to see the game's narrative
35 completed, or in the initial stages of play, you may just be dazzled by the game's graphics. But most of the time, when you're hooked on a game, what draws you in is an elemental form of desire: the desire to see the Next Thing. After all, with the occasional exception, the actual content of the game is often childish or gratuitously menacing. Much of the role play inside the gaming world alternates between drive-by shooting and princess-rescuing. It is not the
40 subject matter that attracts; it is the reward system that draws those players in, and keeps their famously short attention spans locked on the screen.

*Page two*

Playing down the content of video games shouldn't be seen as a cop-out. We ignore the content of many other activities that are widely considered to be good for the brain. No one complains about the simplistic, militaristic plot of chess games. We teach algebra to children 45 knowing full well that the day they leave the classroom 99 per cent of those kids will never again directly employ their algebraic skills. Learning algebra isn't about acquiring a specific tool; it's about building up a mental muscle that will come in handy elsewhere.

So it is with games. It's not what you're thinking about when you're playing a game, it's the way you're thinking that matters. Novels may activate our imagination and may conjure up 50 powerful emotions, but games force you to analyse, to choose, to prioritise, to decide. From the outside, the primary activity of a gamer looks like a fury of clicking and shooting. But if you peer inside the gamer's mind, the primary activity turns out to be another creature altogether: making decisions, some of them snap judgements, some of them long-term strategies.

*Adapted from an article in The Times newspaper, May 2005*

**MARKS**

Questions

1. Re-read lines 1–12.

   (a) Analyse how the writer's word choice in lines 1–3 emphasises the "conventional wisdom" that reading books is better than playing video games.     2

   (b) Explain in your own words "the question" the writer asks in line 6 about "other forms of culture".     2

   (c) **By referring to at least two features of language in lines 8–12** ("Where ... books"), analyse how the writer emphasises the contrast between his positive view of "other forms of culture" and the negative view held by "most critics". You should refer in your answer to such features as word choice, imagery, sentence structure ...     4

2. By referring to lines 13–19, analyse how the writer conveys the difficulty of playing video games by his use of sentence structure **and** imagery.     4

3. Re-read lines 20–33.

   Identify **three** reasons why "reward" is so important to the learning process involved in playing video games. Use your own words as far as possible.     3

4. Re-read lines 34–47.

   Identify **two** criticisms and **two** defences the writer makes of video games.     4

5. Re-read lines 48–54.

   (a) Explain in your own words the key distinction the writer makes between reading a novel and playing a video game.     2

   (b) Analyse how the writer's use of language in lines 50–54 ("From ... strategies") conveys the contrast between what a gamer looks like from "the outside" and what is happening "inside the gamer's mind".     4

## Passage 2

*In the second passage below, the politician and journalist Boris Johnson, writing on his own website, takes a different view about video games.*

Read the passage and attempt the question which follows. While reading, you may wish to make notes on the main ideas and/or highlight key points in the passage.

It's the snarl that gives the game away. It's the sobbing and the shrieking and the horrible pleading — that's how you know your children are undergoing a sudden narcotic withdrawal. As the strobing colours die away and the screen goes black, you listen to the wail of protest from the offspring and you know that you have just turned off their drug, and you know that
5   they are, to a greater or lesser extent, addicts.

Millions of seven-to-fifteen-year olds are hooked, especially boys, and it is time someone had the guts to stand up, cross the room and just say no to Nintendo. It is time to garrotte the Game Boy and paralyse the PlayStation, and it is about time, as a society, that we admitted the catastrophic effect these blasted gizmos are having on the literacy and the prospects of young
10   males.

We demand that teachers provide our children with reading skills; we expect the schools to fill them with a love of books; and yet at home we let them slump in front of the consoles. We get on with our hedonistic 21st-century lives while in some other room the nippers are bleeping and zapping in speechless rapture, their passive faces washed in explosions and gore. They sit
15   for so long that their souls seem to have been sucked down the cathode ray tube.

They become like blinking lizards, motionless, absorbed, only the twitching of their hands showing that they are still conscious. These machines teach them nothing. They stimulate no ratiocination, discovery or feat of memory — though some of them may cunningly pretend to be educational. I have just watched an eleven-year-old play a game that looked fairly historical,
20   on the packet. Your average guilt-ridden parent might assume that it taught the child something about the Vikings and medieval siege warfare. Phooey! The red soldiers robotically slaughtered the white soldiers, and then they did it again, that was it. Everything was programmed, spoon-fed, immediate — and endlessly showering the player with undeserved praise, richly congratulating him for his bogus massacres.

25   The more addictive these games are to the male mind, the more difficult it is to persuade boys to read books. It's not that these young people lack the brains; the raw circuitry is better than ever. It's the software that's the problem. They have not been properly programmed, because they have not read enough. The only way to learn to write is to be forced time and again to articulate your own thoughts in your own words, and you haven't a hope of doing this if you
30   haven't read enough to absorb the basic elements of vocabulary, grammar, rhythm, style and structure; and young males in particular won't read enough if we continually capitulate and let them fritter their lives away in front of these drivelling machines.

So I say now: go to where your children are sitting in auto-lobotomy in front of the console. Summon up all your strength, all your courage. Steel yourself for the screams and yank out
35   that plug. And if they still kick up a fuss, then get out the sledgehammer and strike a blow for literacy.

*Adapted from an article published on Boris Johnson's website in June 2006*

*Page five*

MARKS

Question

6. Both writers express their views about video games. Identify key areas on which they disagree. In your answer, you should refer in detail to both passages.

  5

You may answer this question in continuous prose or in a series of developed bullet points.

**[END OF MODEL QUESTION PAPER]**

National
Qualifications
MODEL PAPER 3

# English Paper 2
# Critical Reading

Date — Not applicable

Duration — 1 hour 30 minutes

**For reasons of space, this Model Paper contains Section 2 — Critical Essay only.**

**SECTION 2 — Critical Essay — 20 marks**

Attempt ONE question from the following genres — Drama, Prose, Poetry, Film and Television Drama, or Language.

You should spend approximately 45 minutes this Section.

Write your answers clearly in the answer booklet provided. In the answer booklet you must clearly identify the question number you are attempting.

Use **blue** or **black** ink.

Before leaving the examination room you must give your answer booklet to the Invigilator; if you do not, you may lose all the marks for this paper.

HODDER
GIBSON
LEARN MORE

## SECTION 2 — CRITICAL ESSAY — 20 marks

Attempt ONE question from the following genres — Drama, Prose, Poetry, Film and Television Drama, or Language.

You may use a Scottish text but **NOT** the one used in Section 1.

Your answer must be on a different genre from that chosen in Section 1.

You should spend approximately 45 minutes on this Section.

## DRAMA

> Answers to questions on **drama** should refer to the text and to such relevant features as characterisation, key scene(s), structure, climax, theme, plot, conflict, setting ...

1.  Choose a play in which a central character experiences rejection or isolation or loneliness.

    Explain how the dramatist makes you aware of the character's situation and discuss how it adds to your understanding of character and/or theme in the play as a whole.

2.  Choose a play which features one of the following conflicts: traditional values versus modern thinking; duty versus self-interest; delusion versus self awareness.

    Explain how the dramatist presents this conflict and discuss how this contributes to your understanding of the play as a whole.

3.  Choose a play in which the setting in time and/or place is an important feature.

    Explain how the dramatist exploits aspects of the setting in a way which enhances your understanding of the central concern(s) of the play as a whole.

## PROSE — FICTION

> Answers to questions on **prose fiction** should refer to the text and to such relevant features as characterisation, setting, language, key incident(s), climax, turning point, plot, structure, narrative technique, theme, ideas, description ...

4. Choose a novel or short story which explores loss or futility or failure.

   Discuss how the writer explores one of these ideas in a way you find effective.

5. Choose a novel or short story in which a particular mood is dominant.

   Explain how the writer creates this mood and discuss how it contributes to your understanding of the text as a whole.

6. Choose a novel or short story in which there is a character who is not only realistic as a person but who has symbolic significance in the text as a whole.

   Explain how the writer makes you aware of both aspects of the character.

## PROSE — NON-FICTION

> Answers to questions on **prose non-fiction** should refer to the text and to such relevant features as ideas, use of evidence, stance, style, selection of material, narrative voice ...

7. Choose a work of **non-fiction** in which vivid description is an important feature.

   Explain in detail how the vivid impression is created and discuss how it contributes to your appreciation of the text as a whole.

8. Choose a work of **biography** or **autobiography** which you feel is inspirational or moving.

   Explain how the writer evokes this response and discuss why you find the text inspirational or moving.

9. Choose a piece of **journalism** which presents difficult or challenging ideas in an accessible way.

   Explain what is difficult or challenging about the writer's ideas and discuss how she or he presents them in an accessible way.

## POETRY

> Answers to questions on **poetry** should refer to the text and to such relevant features as word choice, tone, imagery, structure, content, rhythm, rhyme, theme, sound, ideas ...

10. Choose a poem which features a complex character.

    Explain how the complexity of the character is presented and discuss how significant this aspect of characterisation is to the impact of the poem.

11. Choose **two** poems which approach a similar theme in different ways.

    Explain the nature of these different approaches and discuss which approach leads, in your opinion, to the more pleasing poem.

12. Choose a poem which explores either the problems of growing older or the joys of being young.

    Explain how the poet presents these aspects and discuss to what extent she/he succeeds in deepening your understanding of them.

## FILM AND TELEVISION DRAMA

> Answers to questions on **film and television drama**\* should refer to the text and to such relevant features as use of camera, key sequence, characterisation, mise-en-scène, editing, setting, music/sound, special effects, plot, dialogue, ...

13. Choose a film or television drama in which a character overcomes or gives way to temptation.

    Discuss how the film or programme makers use this situation to influence your response to the text as a whole.

14. Choose a film or television drama which contains a sequence you find disturbing or unsettling.

    Explain how the film or programme makers achieve this response and go on to discuss the importance of the sequence to your appreciation of the text as a whole.

15. Choose a film or television drama in which setting has a significant influence on mood and theme.

    Explain how the film or programme makers reveal this setting and discuss why it is so influential in terms of mood and theme.

    \* "television drama" includes a single play, a series or a serial.

## LANGUAGE

Answers to questions on **language** should refer to the text and to such relevant features as register, accent, dialect, slang, jargon, vocabulary, tone, abbreviation ...

16. Choose some of the ways language differs across generations.

    Identify some of these differences and the factors which cause them.  Go on to discuss to what extent this is advantageous to those involved.


17. Choose the spoken and/or written language used by people who exercise power effectively.

    Identify what is distinctive about the language and discuss why it is effective in influencing its audience.


18. Choose the technical language associated with a sport, a craft, a profession or one of the arts.

    By referring to specific examples, discuss to what extent you feel such language leads to clearer communication.


**[END OF SECTION 2]**


**[END OF MODEL QUESTION PAPER]**

# SQA AND HODDER GIBSON HIGHER FOR CfE ENGLISH 2014

## HIGHER FOR CfE ENGLISH
## SPECIMEN QUESTION PAPER

### PAPER 1 — READING FOR UNDERSTANDING, ANALYSIS AND EVALUATION

Marking Instructions for each question

**Passage 1**

| Question | | Expected Response | Max mark | Additional Guidance |
|---|---|---|---|---|
| 1. | (a) | Candidates should identify two of the writer's feelings in the first paragraph.<br><br>Candidates must use their own words. No marks are awarded for verbatim quotations from the passage.<br><br>*1 mark for each point from the "Additional Guidance" column.* | 2 | Possible answers include:<br><br>• she felt troubled, as though watching an illegal/senseless act<br>• she felt responsible/guilty for a terrible act<br>• she felt morally uncertain; questioned whether or not she was justified in doing this<br><br>or any other acceptable answer |
| | (b) | Candidates should analyse how the language emphasises the importance of trees.<br><br>Marks will depend on the quality of comment on appropriate language feature(s).<br><br>2 marks may be awarded for reference plus detailed/insightful comment; 1 mark for reference plus more basic comment; 0 marks for reference alone.<br><br>*Possible answers shown in the "Additional Guidance" column.* | 4 | Possible answers include:<br><br>*Word choice*<br>• "ever more (precious)" suggests trees' increasing value<br>• "precious" suggests trees are valuable, to be cherished<br>• "a rebuke to built-in obsolescence": trees effectively criticise/stand in opposition to a world where products are designed to have only a limited life<br>• "remnants" suggests precious remains from the past<br>• "mammoth (limb)" suggests something on a massively impressive scale<br>• "reassuring" suggests they offer comfort<br>• "they will endure" suggests permanence, continuity, resilience<br>• "the ancients" suggests trees have been considered valuable throughout the ages<br>• "gods" suggests their almost religious significance<br>• "ring by ring" suggests trees' natural, organic, unhurried growth<br>• "worship" suggests our attitude should be respectful, reverent, devotional<br>• "worse...worship": candidates might argue that the use of alliteration adds to the impact of the concluding statement<br>• use in general of "religious" language ("God's arm", "cathedrals", "gods", "worship") heightens trees' spiritual significance<br>• "our living past": trees connect us to our heritage |

| Question | | Expected Response | Max mark | Additional Guidance |
|---|---|---|---|---|
| 1. | (b) | *(continued)* | | *Imagery*<br>• "a steady point in a churning world": trees offer steadfast permanence in a fast-changing, impermanent, turbulent world<br>• (personification of) "reaches out", "mammoth limb" suggests a majestic living creature<br>• "like God's arm...Rome": simile suggests majesty, beauty, spiritual significance, awesome impact<br>• "calming like cathedrals": simile suggests their scale, majesty, spiritual quality, that they should be treated with reverence, that they are good for our inner well-being<br><br>*Punctuation/sentence structure*<br>• structure of opening sentence "I'm...world": the two phrases at the end of the sentence (heightened by the parallel structure) serve as a powerful development of the "precious" idea<br>• balanced nature of final sentence: the artful juxtaposition of the near-reverent tone of the first part of the sentence, followed by the more matter-of-fact, modern tone of the second half brings the paragraph to a quietly effective conclusion<br><br>or any other acceptable answer |
| 2. | | Candidates should demonstrate understanding of how the protesters differ from what might have been expected.<br><br>Candidates must use their own words. No marks are awarded for verbatim quotations from the passage.<br><br>*1 mark for each point from the "Additional Guidance" column.* | 2 | Possible answers include:<br><br>• we might have expected the protesters to be (over)zealous environmental activists/(ultra) dedicated conservationists (explanation of "eco-warriors")/people who have rejected the conventional values of society (explanation of "hippies")<br>• instead they are just normal people/a typical cross-section of the community/ people of all ages and from all walks of life<br><br>or any other acceptable answer |
| 3. | | Candidates should analyse how the writer's use of language conveys her feelings of unhappiness.<br><br>Marks will depend on the quality of comment. For full marks there must be comment on at least two features. 2 marks may be awarded for reference plus detailed/insightful comment; 1 mark for reference plus more basic comment; 0 marks for reference alone.<br><br>*Possible answers shown in the "Additional Guidance" column.* | 3 | Possible answers include:<br><br>*Sentence structure*<br>• series of three short, simple, matter-of-fact sentences at start of paragraph suggest the inevitable fate that awaits the trees and the irresistible march of the developers<br>• positioning of "By March" at start of sentence suggests fixed, immovable timeline to destruction<br>• structure of fourth sentence ("Local... benefits."): initial praise for efforts of local community is offset immediately by pessimistic recognition of government power; the sentence then reaches a climax with her attack on government policy<br>• use of parenthesis "as new roads do" to emphasise the inevitable futility of government transport policy |

| Question | | Expected Response | Max mark | Additional Guidance |
|---|---|---|---|---|
| 3. | | *(continued)* | | *Word choice:*<br>• "last stand" (could be dealt with as imagery) suggests a defensive position facing inevitable defeat against insuperable odds<br>• "only" suggests defeat itself is inevitable<br>• "determined" suggests inflexible, unyielding nature of government policy<br>• "market" suggests her scepticism about government policy: they are "selling" it as progress but "market" suggests this is more image than reality; suggests government is being unscrupulous, deceitful, conniving<br>• "short-term" suggests transient, limited nature (of benefits)<br>• "dubious" suggests deep uncertainty, unreliability (of benefits)<br>• "fill up" suggests saturation, full to overflowing<br>• "spanking new": hyperbole of her apparent enthusiasm could be argued to betoken her fundamental antipathy<br>• "boarded-up" suggests the development will be to the continued detriment of an already rundown Hastings; suggests that Hastings itself needs attention<br><br>*Contrast*<br>• "spanking new" versus "boarded-up" emphasises the pointlessness of building new premises when existing ones lie empty and abandoned<br><br>*Tone*<br>• some candidates may recognise and discuss the changing tone of this paragraph, in particular the somewhat defeated, hopeless tone of the first three sentences which changes to an angry, scathing, sceptical tone in the rest of the paragraph.<br><br>or any other acceptable answer |
| 4. | (a) | Candidates should identify two claims the government makes about the protesters.<br><br>For full marks there must be understanding demonstrated of two claims.<br><br>Any two points from the "Additional Guidance" column for 1 mark each. | 2 | Possible answers include:<br><br>the government claims the protesters:<br>• are not interested in protecting the environment<br>• are only interested in looking after their own (advantaged) interests<br>• have no interest in the fate of people less well-off/less fortunate than themselves<br><br>or any other acceptable answer |

| Question | | Expected Response | Max mark | Additional Guidance |
|---|---|---|---|---|
| 4. | (b) | Candidates should analyse how at least two features of language convey the strength of the writer's belief in tree conservation.<br><br>Marks will depend on the quality of understanding shown of key ideas and the quality of comment on appropriate language features. 2 marks may be awarded for detailed/insightful comments; one mark for more basic comments; 0 marks for reference alone.<br><br>*Possible answers shown in the "Additional Guidance" column.* | 4 | Possible answers include:<br>*Word choice*<br>• "special kind" suggests people who don't care about trees are particularly awful<br>• "arrogance" suggests the insufferable conceit of those who don't care about trees<br>• "bigger than history" suggests arrogance on a grand scale<br>• (repeated) use of violent language when describing trees — felling (ie "cutting down" suggests something akin to an act of murder; "slicing into" suggests a savage, violent attack; "brutal" suggests a ruthless, crude, cruel, vicious attack; "grotesque" suggests a strange, distorted, unnatural, outrageous act; "chopping down" suggests a categorical, definitive act).<br>• "fine" suggests the majesty, worthiness of the tree<br>• "aching (poignancy)" suggests how deeply hurt she is when trees are cut down<br>• writer's use of "shock tactics" in making a developed, quite visceral comparison between killing living creatures and cutting down trees: some candidates may recognise that the writer shows the strength of her feeling by developing an argument that many readers will find shocking or extreme<br><br>*Imagery*<br>• by comparing (in a very visual way) the fate of trees to the fate of whales and elephants ("mightiest mammal") the writer is associating trees with elevated concepts such as the awesome wonder of the natural world, beauty, majesty, conservation…<br>• "enormous creature" suggests epic scale of what is being destroyed<br><br>*Punctuation/sentence structure*<br>• use of colon (line 31) introduces explanation of what this "special kind of arrogance" involves<br>• punchy conclusion to paragraph ("Not so a tree") emphasises just how different the trees' situation is to even the most impressive or endangered of our natural creatures<br><br>or any other acceptable answer |
| 5. | (a) | Candidates should identify any four reasons given for cutting down trees.<br><br>Candidates should use their own words as far as possible. No marks are awarded for verbatim quotations from the passage.<br><br>*Any four points from the "Additional Guidance" column for 1 mark each.* | 4 | Possible answers include:<br><br>• they may contribute to land sinking (which would affect buildings on that land)<br>• they are regarded as potentially damaging to vehicles<br>• they are regarded as potentially a danger to young people<br>• they shed (twigs and leaves) and that leaves things (public spaces, houses or vehicles) looking dirty and untidy<br>• some trees are considered unfashionable (and people want to replace them with something more popular)<br>• selling trees makes money, can boost a country's economy<br>• they are converted into timber for commercial purposes<br><br>or any other acceptable answer |

| Question | | Expected Response | Max mark | Additional Guidance |
|---|---|---|---|---|
| | (b) | Candidates should analyse how their chosen image emphasises the writer's opposition to cutting down trees.<br><br>Marks will depend on the quality of comment. A detailed/insightful comment will be worth 2 marks; a more basic comment will be worth 1 mark. Mere identification of an image will be 0 marks.<br><br>When dealing with imagery, answers must show recognition of the literal root of the image and then explore how the writer is extending it figuratively.<br><br>*Possible answers shown in the "Additional Guidance" column.* | 2 | Possible answers include:<br><br>• "butchers": just as a butcher is involved in carving up animals into large-scale pieces, so the writer is suggesting that municipal workers are cutting back the trees to a significant degree. It also suggests that the nature of the work performed is rather brutal and indiscriminate<br>• "embarrassed stumps": just as an embarrassed person feels self-conscious and exposed, so the writer is suggesting that trees look vulnerable after the work has been carried out on them<br>• "autumnal hell": just as hell is seen as a place of eternal damnation, so the writer is using this hyperbolic term to ridicule the wild over-reaction of those who find trees a problem at particular times of the year<br>• "like a beautiful girl being forced to sell her hair": just as the girl exchanges a personal asset, an attractive feature for financial gain, so the writer suggests Burma gave away part of the country's natural beauty for money<br><br>or any other acceptable answer |
| 6. | | Candidates should evaluate the final paragraph's effectiveness as a conclusion to the passage as a whole.<br><br>Marks will depend on the quality of comment. For full marks there must be appropriate attention to the idea of a conclusion. A more basic comment may be awarded 1 mark.<br><br>Possible answers shown in the "Additional Guidance" column. | 2 | Possible answers include:<br><br>• the writer concedes that inevitably trees will be cut down to make way for developments, a point she has already made in relation to the Hastings development and government policy in general<br>• the writer returns to an argument which she has discussed throughout the passage: economic growth versus the innate value of trees. The Hastings development is an example of economic growth (very short-term in the writer's opinion), while the writer stresses at several points the value of preserving trees (for example, establishing the majesty and wonder of trees in the opening paragraphs; showing how much they mean to ordinary people protesting against the Hasting development; suggesting they are more important than creatures great and small)<br>• the writer concludes by re-asserting how important a part of our heritage trees are: they are a link to our past ("they are our history inscribed in the natural world") and a means by which people leave their mark on society ("which rich men, planting beautiful orchards to their own glorious memory"). The link to the past idea has already been developed, for example in lines 10-11, while the idea of planting trees for posterity is explicitly discussed in lines 38-39 ("planting...loved ones").<br>• some candidates will recognise the elevated quality of the writing in the final paragraph (quite different in tone to some of the almost brutally graphic sections of the passage) and link it to the persuasively idealistic message the writer has been trying to convey in much of the passage<br><br>or any other acceptable answer |

Passage 2

| Question | | Expected Response | Max Mark | Additional Guidance |
|---|---|---|---|---|
| 7. | | Candidates should identify key areas of agreement in the two passages by referring in detail to both passages.<br><br>There may be some overlap among the areas of agreement. Markers will have to judge the extent to which a candidate has covered two points or one.<br><br>Candidates can use bullet points in this final question, or write a number of linked statements.<br><br>Evidence from the passage may include quotations, but these should be supported by explanations.<br><br>*Approach to marking shown in the "Additional Guidance" column.*<br><br>*Key areas of agreement shown in grid below. Other answers are possible.* | 5 | The mark for this question should reflect the quality of response in two areas:<br><br>• identification of the key areas of agreement in attitude/ideas<br>• level of detail given in support<br><br>The following guidelines should be used:<br><br>**Five marks** — comprehensive identification of three or more key areas of agreement with full use of supporting evidence<br>**Four marks** — clear identification of three or more key areas of agreement with relevant use of supporting evidence<br>**Three marks** — identification of three or more key areas of agreement with supporting evidence<br>**Two marks** — identification of two key areas of agreement with supporting evidence<br>**One mark** — identification of one key area of agreement with supporting evidence<br>**Zero marks** — failure to identify any key area of agreement and/or total misunderstanding of task |

| | Area of Agreement | Janice Turner | Colin Tudge |
|---|---|---|---|
| 1 | awe/wonder/majesty | spiritual, almost religious significance; comparison to whales, elephants | magnificence of the kauri |
| 2 | heritage/permanence | link to previous centuries; certain feature in an uncertain world; will outlive us all | have outlasted the moa; now treated with reverence in New Zealand |
| 3 | trees as teachers | we should question our assumption of superiority | we can learn from trees |
| 4 | ordinary people see trees' importance | Hastings protesters; gift to posterity | New Zealand conservationists; Kenyan women (impact on quality of life) |
| 5 | government and businesses' misguided economic priorities | government short-termism (Britain, Burma, Iceland, etc); trees considered expendable in the interests of "progress" | opposition to tree-based farming; profit-driven outlook of big businesses |
| 6 | lack of respect | councils, officialdom, some homeowners | historical clearing; governments; companies; western desire to control nature |
| 7 | brutality | trees are cut down or cut back quite brutally | hacking and racking continues |

**[END OF SPECIMEN MARKING INSTRUCTIONS]**

# HIGHER FOR CfE ENGLISH
# SPECIMEN QUESTION PAPER

**PAPER 2 — CRITICAL READING**

**SECTION 1 — Scottish Text**

**SCOTTISH TEXT (DRAMA)**

**Text 1 — Drama — *The Slab Boys* by John Byrne**

| Question | Expected Response | Max Mark | Additional Guidance |
|---|---|---|---|
| 1. | Candidates should make reference to two appropriate examples of dialogue with appropriate comment on what is suggested about Phil.<br><br>1 mark for each appropriate reference with comment.<br><br>0 marks for reference/quotation alone. | 2 | Possible answers include:<br><br>**Aggressive personality** — reference and comment on:<br>*"If he catches you going through his stuff, he'll break your jaw"*,<br>*"Shut the folder or I'll get the blame. I get the blame for everything around here…" "Which is exactly how your features are going to look if Phil comes back"*<br><br>**He doesn't accept responsibility** — reference and comment on:<br>*"I get the blame for everything around here…"*<br><br>**Artistic talents** — reference and comment on:<br>*"God, they are good, aren't they? There's one of Elvis…'s dead like him, isn't it?"*<br><br>**Difficult relationship with mother:**<br>*"And there's one of his maw. Christ, you can tell, can't you?"* |
| 2. | Candidates should make reference to two appropriate examples of dialogue with appropriate comment on what is suggested about Curry.<br><br>1 mark for each appropriate reference with comment.<br><br>0 marks for reference/quotation alone. | 2 | Possible answers include:<br><br>*"I remember when Bob Downie used to work here he was always…"* suggests a fondness for telling stories<br><br>*"Jimmy Robertson and I used to go up to Saturday morning classes together…"* suggests he is keen to learn/is sociable.<br><br>*"I showed Bob Downie a few tricks while he was with us. Expect he told you, eh?"* suggests he enjoys being looked up to/can be overbearing/is looking for approval. |
| 3. | Candidates should identify the contrasting attitudes which Curry shows.<br><br>1 mark for each side of the contrast.<br><br>1 additional mark will be awarded for comment on appropriate textual evidence which supports each side of the contrast.<br><br>0 marks for reference/quotation alone. | 4 | Possible answers include:<br><br>**Curry to the Slab Boys**<br>Curry's attitude is negative, eg, dismissive, unsympathetic, severe, intolerant…<br><br>Comment could be made on:<br>*"They aren't yours, Farrell, that's for sure. You've got trouble trying to draw water from that tap over there."*<br><br>*"And they can't be Hector's. Too bold for him…"*<br><br>*"You're not going to tell me they're McCann's"*<br><br>Curry refers to Phil in derogatory terms — *"loafer"*, *"flyman"*, *"crony"*, *"miserable carcase"*<br><br>There is an implication of challenge/conflict in *"Well, we'll soon see about this…"*<br><br>Commanding tone used in *"…Farrell!"*<br><br>Use of imperatives — *"Get a move on!"*, *"Tell him…"*, *"Get those…"*, *"Will you gee yourself up a bit!"* |

| Question | Expected Response | Max Mark | Additional Guidance |
|---|---|---|---|
| **3.** | *(continued)* | 4 | Refers to Spanky as *"Bloody corner boy."* |
| | | | Mockery implied by *"You'd think it was a damned bath you were having!"* |
| | | | Aggressive questioning of Spanky. |
| | | | **Curry to Alan** Curry's attitude is positive, eg ingratiating, sycophantic, obsequious |
| | | | Comment could be made on: *"You never let on Bob Downie was your father… see you young fellows…Chief Designer at Templars…Some of your artwork…Let's have a butcher's."* Curry is now interested in the artwork, mistaking it for Alan's. |
| | | | *"A right talented pair of buggers."* Use of derogatory term in an attempt at humour/familiarity. |
| | | | *"Now Alan, where were we…I dare say your dad's covered some of this ground with you…I showed Bob Downie a few tricks…Right. Alan…what's the first thing we do when we're starting a charcoal sketch?"* Curry is now taking an interest, keen to engage with Alan. |
| | | | Reference could be made to the use of Alan's first name rather than the surnames with which Curry addresses the Slab Boys. |
| **4.** | Candidates should include an acceptable piece of humorous dialogue and should then show how this evokes sympathy for Spanky. 0 marks for quotation/reference alone. A detailed/insightful comment plus reference will score 2 marks; a more basic comment plus reference will be worth 1 mark. Quotation is likely but not necessary. Candidates can illustrate their understanding by referring to the content of the extract. | 2 | Possible answers include: *"Yeh, you have a word with him, kiddo…I'm sure he'll appreciate it."* Spanky's use of sarcasm following Alan's rather derogatory comment on the Slab Room (*"He's wasting his time in here."*) *"And just leave the rest of his body down there?"* Spanky's joke shows that he is able to retaliate with wit in the face of Curry's anger. *"They aren't yours Farrell, that's for sure. You've got trouble trying to draw water from that tap over there."* Curry's sneering joke seems particularly nasty in contrast to the fawning treatment of Alan — unequal treatment makes us sympathetic to Spanky. |
| **5.** | Candidates should discuss how the theme of frustrated ambition is developed in the text and should refer to appropriate textual evidence to support their discussion. 0 marks for reference/quotation alone. Candidates can answer in bullet points in this final question, or write a number of linked statements. | 10 | Up to 2 marks can be achieved for identifying elements of commonality as identified in the question, ie the theme of frustrated ambition. A further 2 marks can be achieved for reference to the extract given. 6 additional marks can be awarded for discussion of similar references to at least one other part of the text by the writer. <u>In practice this means:</u> Identification of commonality (2) (eg: theme, characterisation, use of imagery, setting, or any other key element…) from the extract: 1 × relevant reference to technique/idea/feature (1) 1 × appropriate comment (1) (maximum of 2 marks only for discussion of extract) |

| Question | Expected Response | Max Mark | Additional Guidance |
|---|---|---|---|
| 5. | *(continued)* | 10 | from at least one other text/part of the text:<br><br>as above (×3) for up to 6 marks<br>**OR**<br>more detailed comment ×2 for up to 6 marks<br><br>Thus, the final 6 marks can be gained by a combination of 3, 2 and 1 marks depending on the level of depth/detail/insight. The aim would be to encourage quality of comment, rather than quantity of references.<br><br>In comments on the rest of the play, possible references include:<br>• The Art School's rejection of Phil's application for entry<br>• Hector's failed attempts to take Lucille to the staff dance<br>• The length of time which Slab Boys have to wait before getting a desk<br><br>Many other references are possible. |

**Text 2 — Drama — *The Cheviot, the Stag and the Black, Black Oil* by John McGrath**

| Question | Additional Guidance | Max Mark | Additional Guidance |
|---|---|---|---|
| 6. | Candidates should explain how the minister's speech reveals that he regards himself as a force of authority and control.<br><br>Marks can be awarded for three appropriate references or quotations with suitable commentary (1+1+1).<br><br>OR a reference with more detailed/insightful comment may be awarded 2 marks, plus reference with more basic comment can receive 1 mark (2+1).<br><br>0 marks for reference/quotation alone. | 3 | Candidates should show how the language used reveals that, rather than attending to his congregation's pastoral needs or speaking up as a spokesman or teacher for his community, the minister represents the powers of authority and control, reprimanding and criticizing those resistant to change.<br><br>Possible references include:<br><br>Repeated warnings of "wickedness" suggest that immorality in this life shall not go unpunished in the next one.<br><br>"the wrath of the Almighty" suggests that because of their wrong-doing , they should fear what awaits them.<br><br>"For I will repay, saith the Lord" suggests that vengeance awaits those who are seen to have been wrongdoers in their current life.<br><br>"the troubles that are visiting you are a judgement")/"a warning of the final judgement that is to come" infers a conflation between the secular authorities (landlords) and divine authority, and that this is a foretaste of what is still to come<br><br>"some of you ... are so far from the fold" suggests the wickedness of this life shall not go unpunished in the next one.<br><br>"wailing and gnashing of teeth" suggests the divine torment that is awaiting for offences committed in this life.<br><br>"dignity of your womanhood" suggests that their actions are an attack on women in general and therefore worse because they have been committed by women.<br><br>"risen up to curse your masters"/"violate the laws of the land"/"burning of the writs" all suggest revolting acts or rebellion against their betters or the accepted order or status quo. |

| Question | Additional Guidance | Max Mark | Additional Guidance |
|---|---|---|---|
| 7. | Candidates should include one example of humorous dialogue or stage direction and analyse how it is used.<br><br>1 mark should be awarded for the reference or quotation plus appropriate analysis (1+1).<br><br>0 marks for quotation/reference alone.<br><br>A detailed/insightful comment plus reference will score 2 marks; a more basic comment plus reference will be worth 1 mark.<br><br>Quotation is likely but not necessary. Candidates can illustrate their understanding by referring to the content of the extract. | 2 | Through the use of bracketed directions (Big cheer), (Groan) and (More groans), the rest of the cast act as a chorus, reminiscent of humorous, pantomime-like responses. The cast substitute for the audience's reactions producing a dialogue with the First Girl, similar to audience participation between performers and audience, integral to the light-hearted manner of a ceilidh.<br><br>Humour is evident in the ridiculing and deflating of the figures of authority by ducking the law officers "in a neighbouring pool".<br><br>These farcical methods (as above) involve role reversal in that it was men, historically, who meted this punishment on women.<br><br>Humour is also evident in the First Girl's speech when she refers to "the people made a stout resistance." It is in fact "the women" who carried out the action with the men forming "a second line of defence". This is humorously described in ironic terms by stating this defensive line was "in case the women should receive any ill-treatment." |
| 8. | Candidates should explain what two examples of music contribute to the scene.<br><br>2 marks shall be awarded for the two examples with appropriate comments (1+1)<br><br>0 marks for reference/quotation alone. | 2 | Possible answers include:<br><br>A fiddle and the quiet humming of a hymn set the sombre atmosphere for John to perform his role as the minister. It is ironic in these circumstances that the hymn is "The Lord is my Shepherd" — he is not acting as an appropriate leader of his flock, particularly as the sheep are displacing the tenants.<br><br>After Liz's/First Girl's monologue, a fiddle "strikes up" and plays something upbeat and rousing to allow the company to dance and celebrate their victory of the women over authority, dancing being an integral part of a ceilidh. It seems appropriate that the women should lead off the dance to celebrate a female-won victory. It is also a further example of role reversal. |
| 9. | Candidates should refer to at least two examples of financial detail, and explain how these details are relevant to the themes of the play.<br><br>Candidates may be awarded 3 marks for three appropriate examples/quotations with basic suitable accompanying comment (1+1+1).<br><br>Alternatively, 2 marks may be awarded for a more detailed/insightful comment (2+1).<br><br>0 marks for reference/quotation alone. | 3 | Possible answers include:<br><br>Reference to the Old Man describing how the growth of the Highland population was outstripping the means to sustain it, and that for some, emigration was the only option.<br><br>As a result of the Industrial Revolution and improved agricultural methods, wealth was expanding.<br><br>Methods of capitalism were used to make further profits around the world as well as in the Scottish Highlands.<br><br>A breed of sheep, the Cheviot, was introduced to make money and displace the inhabitants who were there.<br><br>Narratively, the drama is grounded in the history of economic change in the Scottish Highlands where the people were forced to accept emigration either to poorer land, crowded industrial cities or abroad.<br>The forces of exploitative capitalism were to prove stronger than the organisation of the people. |

| Question | Additional Guidance | Max Mark | Additional Guidance |
|---|---|---|---|
| 10 | Candidates should discuss how the theme of the role of women is developed in the play and should refer to appropriate textual evidence to support their discussion.<br><br>0 marks for reference/quotation alone<br><br>Candidates can answer in bullet points in this final question, or write a number of linked statements. | 10 | Up to 2 marks can be achieved for identifying elements of commonality as identified in the question, ie the role of women.<br>A further 2 marks can be achieved for reference to the extract given.<br>6 additional marks can be awarded for discussion of similar references to at least one other part of the text by the writer.<br><br>In practice this means:<br><br>Identification of commonality (2) (eg: theme, characterisation, use of imagery, setting, or any other key element...)<br><br>from the extract:<br><br>1 × relevant reference to technique/idea/feature (1)<br>1 × appropriate comment (1)<br>(maximum of 2 marks only for discussion of extract)<br><br>from at least one other text/part of the text:<br><br>as above (×3) for up to 6 marks<br>**OR**<br>more detailed comment ×2 for up to 6 marks<br><br>Thus, the final 6 marks can be gained by a combination of 3, 2 and 1 marks depending on the level of depth/detail/insight. The aim would be to encourage quality of comment, rather than quantity of references.<br><br>In comments on the rest of the play, possible references include:<br>• Over the different periods women have taken the initiative and led others.<br>• Women have displayed solidarity as well as community spirit, while their male counterparts have responded with indifference or been absent altogether.<br>• The female players of the drama have been given equal opportunity to express themselves through poem, song and general narration.<br><br>Many other references are possible. |

## Text 3 — Drama — *Men Should Weep* by Ena Lamont Stewart

| Question | Expected Response | Max Mark | Additional Guidance |
|---|---|---|---|
| 11. | Candidates should give a clear explanation of Maggie's differing attitudes to Isa and Alec with appropriate reference to the dialogue.<br><br>1 mark should be awarded for each reference or quotation plus appropriate analysis (1+1).<br><br>0 marks for reference/quotation alone. | 2 | Possible answers include:<br><br>**Attitude to Isa**<br>Resents her/has no respect for her/dislikes her/thinks she's not "good enough" for Alec/thinks she's hard-hearted.<br><br>Possible references include:<br><br>• "An here! You've to leave aff tormentin him" — thinks Isa is too hard on Alec; that Alec doesn't deserve such cruel treatment.<br>• "Threatenin to leave him when ye ken he's that daft aboot ye." — thinks Isa is heartless in the face of Alec's devotion.<br>• "Goad kens why" — thinks Isa isn't worth Alec's devotion.<br>• "...ye're a worthless slut if ever there wis yin" — disrespects Isa; thinks she's 'common', not good enough for Alec.<br>• "I'll learn ye tae ca me a bitch! — sees herself as superior to Isa, is ready to teach her a lesson. |

| Question | Expected Response | Max Mark | Additional Guidance |
|---|---|---|---|
| **11.** | *(continued)* | 2 | **Attitude to Alec**<br>Protective of Alec/loving/loyal/sees him as the victim/blind to Alec's weakness/molly-coddles him/treats him like a child.<br><br>Possible references include:<br><br>• "Alec's shiverin; he can hardly staun on his feet" — Maggie worries about his health/is protective of him.<br><br>**and/or**<br>• "An get a packet o Woodbine tae" — indulges him<br>• "Ye ken he's that daft aboot ye" — has sympathy for Alec's devotion and sees him as the victim of Isa's hard-heartedness. |
| **12.** | Candidates should exemplify and explain one example each of Maggie, John and Isa's attitudes to how a man is expected to behave.<br><br>1 mark should be awarded for each reference or quotation plus appropriate analysis (1+1+1).<br><br>0 marks for reference/quotation alone. | 3 | **Maggie**<br>Maggie believes, to an extent, that a husband and wife are equal partners and therefore a man should pull his weight around the house and respect his wife. Men need to talk less about putting the world to rights and should take more decisive action to find employment. A man should support his wife and present a united front against outsiders.<br><br>Possible references include:<br><br>"Ye couldna even wash up a dish for me. It's me that aye has tae dae twa jobs when you get the sack!"<br><br>"Aye, I've seen yous men lookin for work. Haudin up the street corners, ca'in doon the Government…"<br><br>"(Pause) Whit a meant wis…"<br><br>"And I like a man…tae stand up for his wife."<br><br>**Isa**<br>For all her hard, calculating ways, Isa sees her identity as an extension of her man's. She wants men to be men — to take the traditional dominant role — which is why she finds Alec's personality so disappointing.<br><br>Possible references include:<br><br>"Quite right. A woman disnae respect a man that's *nae* a man."<br><br>"That's the stuff! He's needin somebody tae tak him in haun. He's beyond me. I cannae dae naethin with him."<br><br>"Aye, he's jist a great big baby. If he disnae get whit he wants, he greets…"<br><br>"I like a man tae *be* a man. Staun up for hissel." |

| Question | Expected Response | Max Mark | Additional Guidance |
|---|---|---|---|
| 12. | (continued) | 3 | **John** <br> He believes himself to be the man of the house and, as such, women should submit to his superiority.  His traditional working class male chauvinism means he believes housework is beneath him, he can treat his wife disrespectfully and his word is final. <br> Possible references include: <br> "Aw, shut up harpin on that string." <br> "Tae Hell wi this Jessie business every time I'm oot o a job!" <br> "I'm no turnin masel intae a bloomin skivvy!  I'm a man!" <br> "There's nae drink comin intae this hoose!" <br> "Shut yer mouth or I'll shut it for ye!" |
| 13. | Candidates should make reference to the stage directions to support discussion about John's character. <br><br> A single detailed/insightful comment about John's character, supported by reference to the stage directions, could score 2 marks.  Alternatively, two more basic comments on two examples could score 1 mark each. <br><br> 0 marks for reference/quotation alone. | 3 | Candidates should identify John's utter defeat when reminded of his failure to provide for his family.  His bravado is quickly extinguished in the face of the truth, revealing the vulnerability which lies just under the surface of his macho posturing. <br> Possible references: <br> *"John, as if he had been shot…"* — suggests the instant blow to his pride when reminded that he does not provide for his family. <br> *"…drops Alec…"* — suggests the instant blow to his pride, to the extent that he doesn't feel he has the right to have any authority over even the weakest member of his family. <br> *"…slumps…puts his head in his hands."* — suggests how defeated and hopeless he feels. <br> *"demoralised"* suggests how his identity as a man is based on his pride as head of the house. |
| 14. | Candidates should explain two examples of John's behaviour that Maggie finds disappointing. <br><br> 0 marks for reference/quotation alone. | 2 | Possible answers include: <br> Maggie is disappointed by John blaming her for not keeping the house in order. <br> "Ma Goad!  Whit a hell o a hoose tae come hame tae!" <br> Maggie is disappointed by the aggressive/bullying/disrespectful way John speaks to her. <br> "Aw, shut up harpin on that string" <br> "Shut yer mouth or I'll shut it for ye!" <br> Maggie is disappointed by John's lack of support for her. <br> "Well, ye're certainly actin like yin." (a "bitch") <br> Maggie is disappointed by John's sympathy/understanding for Isa. <br> "Maggie!  That's no fair.  She's upset" <br> "Don't cry, Isa; he's nae worth it." <br> Maggie is disappointed by John blaming her for the way Alec has turned out. <br> "It's *your* fault.  You spoiled him frae the day he wis born." <br> Maggie is disappointed by John's lack of compassion for Alec. <br> "ye're getting nae whisky.  D'ye understan?" <br> Maggie is disappointed by John's betrayal in not taking her side. <br> "And I like a man…tae stand up for his wife." |

| Question | Expected Response | Max Mark | Additional Guidance |
|---|---|---|---|
| **15.** | Candidates should discuss to what extent this scene is important to Maggie's character development and should refer to appropriate textual evidence to support their discussion.<br><br>0 marks for reference/quotation alone.<br><br>Candidates can choose to answer in bullet points in this final question, or write a number of linked statements. | 10 | Up to 2 marks can be achieved for identifying elements of commonality as identified in the question, ie Maggie's development as a character. A further 2 marks can be achieved for reference to the extract given.<br>6 additional marks can be awarded for discussion of similar references to at least one other part of the text by the writer.<br><br><u>In practice this means:</u><br><br>Identification of commonality (2) (eg: theme, characterisation, use of imagery, setting, or any other key element…)<br><br>from the extract:<br><br>1 × relevant reference to technique/idea/feature (1)<br>1 × appropriate comment (1)<br>(maximum of 2 marks only for discussion of extract)<br><br>from at least one other text/part of the text:<br><br>as above (×3) for up to 6 marks<br>OR<br>more detailed comment ×2 for up to 6 marks<br><br>Thus, the final 6 marks can be gained by a combination of 3, 2 and 1 marks depending on the level of depth/detail/insight. The aim would be to encourage quality of comment, rather than quantity of references.<br><br>In comments on the rest of the play, possible references include:<br><br>• Maggie's portrayal in the opening scenes of the play: down-trodden; exhausted; oppressed by poverty and running a chaotic home; accepting of her lot; loyal to John.<br>• Maggie's continued development as the play progresses, eg reaches breaking point with the children and her situation in general.<br>• Maggie is driven by her determination to do what she wants and by what is best for her family; takes control of her life.<br><br>Many other references are possible. |

**Text 1 — Prose — *In Church* by Iain Crichton Smith**

| Question | Expected Response | Max Mark | Additional Guidance |
|---|---|---|---|
| **16.** | Candidates should cover both (i) futility and (ii) cruelty, and both language features of word choice and sentence structure. Points on futility are more likely to be found in the first paragraph; and on cruelty in the second<br>(1+1+1+1).<br><br>0 marks for reference/quotation alone. | 4 | Possible answers include:<br><br>**Futility**<br>Sentence structure<br>• Repetition of "over and over" to little point<br>• Climactic sentence ending emphasising relentlessness<br>Word choice<br>• "continuously revised"<br>• "scribbled over endlessly"<br><br>**Cruelty**<br>Sentence structure<br>• Short, harsh sentences<br>• Mostly climactic sentences, emphasising, eg "the beaks", "going for the head"<br>• Sentence patterning using violent description in participial clauses, eg "probing upwards from below", "pecking and jabbing" |

| Question | Expected Response | Max Mark | Additional Guidance |
|---|---|---|---|
| **16.** | *(continued)* | 4 | Word choice<br>• Emphasis on violent action, eg "attacked… probing"<br>• Emphasis on persistence, eg "synchronise their movements", "zeroing in on it"<br>• The single bird's vulnerability, eg "upwards from below", "was weakening" |
| **17.** | Candidates should explain how the anecdote about the dogfight develops the theme of the futility of war.<br><br>Marks may be awarded for a comment with supporting evidence.  2 marks may be awarded for one detailed/insightful comment; 1 mark for a more basic point.  ( Marks awarded = 2 or 1+1)<br><br>Detailed reference or quotation may be used, plus comment.<br><br>0 marks for reference/quotation alone. | 2 | Candidates may focus on the pointlessness of victory in which the victor is also killed; the noble and human qualities displayed by the German pilot (which do not save him); the parallel of the birds fighting to the death = nature "at war" and the human conflict supposedly about ideals<br><br>Possible references include:<br><br>• "long duel/…in turn/…shot down/…/bullet… penetrated his back…out at the chest"<br>• "pilot seated at the controls", "upright', "disciplined", "aristocratic", "eyes staring straight ahead", and perfectly dead" |
| **18.** | Candidates should discuss how the writer conveys the narrator's unfamiliarity with his surroundings.<br><br>2 marks can be awarded for reference plus detailed/insightful comment; 1 mark for reference plus more basic comment.<br><br>0 marks for reference/quotation alone. | 4 | Possible answers include:<br><br>• "staring" — the verb conveys his focused attention on the church<br>• "never been in a church like this before" — the phrase "like this" conveys his unfamiliarity<br>• "either a helpless or a welcoming gesture" — use of "either" shows his lack of familiarity with the imagery in the stained glass window<br>• "which he thought might be a confessional" — use of "might be" conveys his unfamiliarity<br>• "gazed for a long time at the… cross" — conveys his interest in his surroundings<br>• "silence was oppressive" — conveys his sense of unease in an unfamiliar setting<br>• "not at all like the churches at home" — "not at all" shows that everything is different<br>• "there was more ornament, it was less bare, more decorated" — list of phrases conveys the unfamiliar details he notices |
| **19.** | Candidates should discuss how the writer develops the theme of the destructive nature of war and should refer to appropriate textual evidence to support their discussion.<br><br>0 marks for reference/quotation alone.<br><br>Candidates can answer in bullet points in this final question, or write a number of linked statements. | 10 | Up to 2 marks can be achieved for identifying elements of commonality as identified in the question, ie the destructive nature of war.<br>A further 2 marks can be achieved for reference to the extract given.<br>6 additional marks can be awarded for discussion of similar references to at least one other short story by the writer.<br><br><u>In practice this means:</u><br><br>Identification of commonality (2) (eg:  theme, characterisation, use of imagery, setting, or any other key element…)<br><br>From the extract:<br><br>1 × relevant reference to technique/idea/feature (1)<br>1 × appropriate comment (1)<br>(maximum of 2 marks only for discussion of extract)<br><br>From at least one other text/part of the text:<br><br>As above (x3) for up to 6 marks<br>**OR**<br>More detailed comment x2 for up to 6 marks |

| Question | Expected Response | Max Mark | Additional Guidance |
|---|---|---|---|
| 19. | (continued) | 10 | Thus, the final 6 marks can be gained by a combination of 3, 2 and 1 marks depending on the level of depth/detail/insight. The aim would be to encourage quality of comment, rather than quantity of references. |
| | | | In comments on other texts, possible references include: |
| | | | • The raid in *The Crater* — insignificant in itself but leads to horrifying deaths<br>• Morrison turned into a "monster" in the green slime of the crater<br>• In *The Telegram* — focus on the suffering of those left back home, fearing but not understanding the war |
| | | | Many other references are possible. |

**Text 2 — Prose — *A Time to Keep* by George Mackay Brown**

| Question | Expected Response | Max Mark | Additional Guidance |
|---|---|---|---|
| 20. | For full marks, answers should cover the topics of both "poverty of the land" and "inadequacy as a farmer", using both reference and comment. 2 marks may be awarded for reference plus detailed/insightful comment; 1 mark for reference plus more basic comment.<br><br>0 marks for reference/quotation alone. | 4 | Possible answers include:<br><br>**Poverty of the land**<br>• "Stones and clumps of heather" — simple description illustrating land unsuitable for cultivation<br>• "squelch into a sudden bit of bog" — alliteration emphasising the difficulties faced in tilling the land<br>• "no-one on God's earth could plough such a wilderness" — exaggeration emphasising the narrator's pessimism and feelings of dissatisfaction<br>• "my spade rang against stones" -—onomatopoeia emphasising poor quality of the land<br><br>**Inadequacy as a farmer**<br>• "They lay, red bits of rag …" — impressionistic description/basic symbolism/sentence structure illustrating the consequences of not being up to the job<br>• "What a fool!" — use of internal monologue to give narrative viewpoint |
| 21. | Candidates should analyse how sentence structure is used to develop the narrator's worsening mood.<br><br>2 marks may be awarded for reference plus detailed/insightful comment; 1 mark for reference plus more basic comment.<br><br>0 marks for references alone. | 4 | Possible answers include:<br><br>• "It was Good Friday" — short, terse sentence illustrating the narrator's rationalist unwillingness to accept the religiosity of his neighbours<br>• "There was one stone … tearing the sharp bits out of the ground" — climactic sentences illustrating the difficulty of the task and the increasing ferocity of his response to it<br>• "The house was dead.  The pot sat black …" — sparse, severe sentence structure illustrating the bleakness of his mood<br>• "I closed my eyes" — economy/brevity of sentence structure to suggest the blankness and nihilism of his attitude(s) |

| Question | Expected Response | Max Mark | Additional Guidance |
|---|---|---|---|
| **22.** | Candidates may choose to concentrate on Ingi's attempts to lighten his mood or to show how she worsens it. Either will be acceptable. Reference plus detailed/insightful comment will be awarded 2 marks; 1 mark for reference plus more basic comment.<br><br>0 marks for reference/quotation alone. | 2 | Possible answers include:<br>• "She rose up quickly … put her cold hand on my forehead" — Ingi shows sympathy and solicitude; she attempts to tend to his physical weakness<br>• Ingi tries to cheer him up by telling him about the new lambs "such bonny peedie things!"<br>• "Ingi was at the service with the laird …" — her religiosity, and acceptance of her neighbours' communal worship, worsens his antipathy towards religion and the community |
| **23.** | Candidates should discuss how the writer creates flawed but engaging characters and should refer to appropriate textual evidence to support their discussion.<br><br>0 marks for reference/quotation alone.<br><br>Candidates can answer in bullet points in this final question, or write a number of linked statements. | 10 | Up to 2 marks can be achieved for identifying elements of commonality as identified in the question, ie characters who are flawed but nonetheless engage the reader's sympathy.<br>A further 2 marks can be achieved for reference to the extract given.<br>6 additional marks can be awarded for discussion of similar references to at least one other short story by the writer.<br><br>Underline: In practice this means:<br><br>Identification of commonality (2) (eg: theme, characterisation, use of imagery, setting, or any other key element…)<br><br>from the extract:<br><br>1 × relevant reference to technique/idea/ feature (1)<br>1 × appropriate comment (1)<br>(maximum of 2 marks only for discussion of extract)<br><br>from at least one other text/part of the text:<br><br>as above (×3) for up to 6 marks<br>**OR**<br>more detailed comment ×2 for up to 6 marks<br><br>Thus, the final 6 marks can be gained by a combination of 3, 2 and 1 marks depending on the level of depth/detail/insight. The aim would be to encourage quality of comment, rather than quantity of references.<br><br>In comments on other stories, possible references include:<br>• The character of Flaws in *The Whaler's Return* — well intentioned and compassionate but naïve and easily distracted<br>• In *Tartan the Vikings*, sparing the children while raiding the village (Kol murdered)<br>• In *The Eye of the Hurricane*, Captain Stevens' drunkenness, yet he is respected by comrades for courage and decency<br><br>Many other references are possible. |

Text 3 — Prose — *The Trick is to Keep Breathing* by Janice Galloway

| Question | Expected Response | Max Mark | Additional Guidance |
|---|---|---|---|
| 24. | Candidates should explain how Galloway makes the reader aware of Joy's attitude towards the psychiatrist.<br><br>Attitude should be clear, but may be implicit.<br><br>2 marks may be awarded for reference plus detailed/insightful comment, showing contribution to understanding of attitude.<br><br>1 mark for reference plus more basic comment.<br>2 marks may be awarded (1+1) in this way.<br><br>0 marks for reference/quotation alone. | 2 | Candidates should recognise that Joy is dismissive of the psychiatrist/mocking/expects visit to be a waste of time.<br><br>Possible answers include:<br><br>• Use of humour, eg "Lesson1", "Lesson2" undermines seriousness of her situation/listing her expectations of the visit/as though she has prepared herself for the worthlessness of the visit<br>• Opening line states emphatically that she "knew" it would be a "disappointment".<br>• Dismissive tone in "psychiatrists aren't as smart as you'd think"/"not mind-readers...look as though they are."<br>• Refers to him as "Dr One" — not worthy of a name/suggests they are all the same.<br>• Disappointed in his question "So ... Why ...?" — exactly as predicted in her list. Adds to humour<br>• "He thought I wasn't trying" — suggests she believes he does not understand her |
| 25. | Candidates should analyse how the writer's use of language is effective in conveying Joy's state of mind.<br><br>Candidates' understanding of Joy's mood should be clear but may be implicit.<br><br>Two examples of references plus detailed/insightful explanation awarded 2 marks each = 4.<br><br>Or four examples with more basic explanation (1+1+1+1).<br><br>Marks may be awarded for combinations of above.<br><br>0 marks for reference/quotation alone. | 4 | Candidates should refer to: state of mind: panic/loss of control/confusion/sense of panic.<br><br>Word choice: "my throat was contracting" — difficulty in breathing<br><br>Metaphor: "I was about to short-circuit" — suddenly shut down/break down<br><br>Sentence structure: repetition of "I hadn't" emphasises her sense of panic at what she hadn't prepared for<br><br>Separates parts of herself to emphasise her feeling of disembodiment: brain and body feel separate<br><br>Personification: "My mouth knew more..."/"The voice didn't need me....like me" — as if she has no control over the voice — it is an entity on its own. Reinforces this with "I let...out of harm's way."<br><br>She wants to try to co-operate but sees the whole thing as pointless — emphasised by the voices in italics<br><br>Repetition of "whispered" — makes voices seem alive |
| 26. | Candidates should analyse how the writer highlights the significance of Michael's death.<br><br>For full marks, different techniques should be exemplified and commented on in terms of effectiveness.<br><br>Reference plus detailed/insightful comment = 2 marks.<br><br>Reference plus more basic comment = 1 mark.<br><br>Marks may be awarded for combination of the above.<br><br>0 marks for reference/quotation alone. | 4 | Possible answers include:<br><br>**Structure:**<br>Indented sections represent Joy's spoken words. Contrast between matter of matter of fact tone, achieved by short sentences, and final part of sentence "and he drowned" puts emphasis on this point; short sentences leading up to this summarise the many contributing factors in her breakdown, but emphasis on "he drowned" shows this is the most significant factor; sentence does not end with a full stop suggesting she continues to think about this/puts emphasis on this part of the sentence.<br><br>Repetition of "he drowned" — emphasises significance of this.<br>"He drowned" — short sentence in paragraph of its own — emphasises significance of the point.<br><br>Flashback to Michael's accident: "side of the pool....and the sky" — emphasises the reality of her situation; this is what she fears. |

| Question | Expected Response | Max Mark | Additional Guidance |
|---|---|---|---|
| **26.** | *(continued)* | 4 | **Contrast:**<br>Between inner feelings and what she says "I heard the last bit twisting out of kilter…"<br><br>**Word choice:**<br>"out of kilter" — suggests loss of balance perhaps caused by panic/fear;<br>"eerie" — suggests something sinister/something terrifying<br><br>**Imagery:**<br>Simile: "like the Bates Motel in Psycho" — comparison to horror movie makes her terror about remembering the accident clear;<br>Personification: furniture seems to be alive — "liver-coloured furniture breathing" — nightmarish image emphasises her terror |
| **27.** | Candidates should discuss how the writer develops the theme of loss and should refer to appropriate textual evidence to support their discussion.<br><br>0 marks for reference/quotation alone.<br><br>Candidates may choose to answer in bullet points in this final question, or write a number of linked statements. | 10 | Up to 2 marks can be achieved for identifying elements of commonality as identified in the question, ie the theme of loss.<br>A further 2 marks can be achieved for reference to the extract given.<br>6 additional marks can be awarded for discussion of similar references to at least one other part of the text by the writer.<br><br>In practice this means:<br><br>Identification of commonality (2) (eg: theme, characterisation, use of imagery, setting, or any other key element…)<br><br>from the extract:<br><br>1 × relevant reference to technique/idea/feature (1)<br>1 × appropriate comment (1)<br>(maximum of 2 marks only for discussion of extract)<br><br>from at least one other text/part of the text:<br><br>as above (×3) for up to 6 marks<br>OR<br>more detailed comment ×2 for up to 6 marks<br><br>Thus, the final 6 marks can be gained by a combination of 3, 2 and 1 marks depending on the level of depth/detail/insight. The aim would be to encourage quality of comment, rather than quantity of references.<br><br>In comments on the rest of the novel, possible references include:<br><br>• The loss of Michael — horror of holiday experience<br>• The loss of her mother — devastating effects of bereavement<br>• The loss of self — determination — anorexia/relationships with men<br><br>Many other references are possible. |

**Text 4 — Prose — *Sunset Song* by Lewis Grassic Gibbon**

| Question | Expected Response | Max Mark | Additional Guidance |
|---|---|---|---|
| 28 | Candidates should discuss any two aspects of each character, supported by appropriate textual reference.<br><br>Two aspects of John Guthrie's character with appropriate reference for 2 marks.<br><br>Two aspects of Long Rob's character with appropriate reference for 2 marks.<br><br>0 marks for reference/quotation alone. | 4 | Possible answers include:<br><br>**John Guthrie**<br>Alert/decisive/energetic/persistent, determined/angry, religious fervour<br><br>Possible references include:<br><br>"first down at the … Knapp"<br><br>"ran … banged … cried … smashed in"<br><br>"and when he got no answer he smashed in the window"<br><br>*"Damn't to hell do you want to be roasted?"*<br><br>**Long Rob**<br>Athletic/in tune with nature/brave/compassionate/calm under pressure/kind/unconcerned about his own safety<br><br>Possible references include:<br><br>"louping dykes like a hare"<br><br>"helped Mrs Strachan with the bairns"<br><br>"smoking his pipe as cool as you please"<br><br>"dived in and out", "tore and rived that off a blazing wall" |
| 29. | Candidates should analyse how the writer's use of language creates a sense of urgency.<br><br>Reference and comment to show how sense of urgency is created. 2 marks may be awarded for detailed/insightful comment; 1 mark for more basic comment (2 or 1+1).<br><br>0 marks for reference/quotation alone. | 2 | Possible answers include:<br><br>"blazing" — fire is burning strongly, creating danger<br><br>"lapping" — inescapable presence of the fire which is wrapping, enfolding, surrounding<br><br>"crackling" — onomatopoeic loud rustling<br><br>Many very long sentences which convey the frenzied panic as one event runs on from another, eg "He was first down at the …"<br><br>"the bairns scraiched" shows their inarticulate fear/panic<br><br>"he'd only his breeks on" shows rush — no time to get dressed |
| 30. | Candidates should analyse how the writer's use of language conveys the ferocity of the fire.<br><br>Reference and comment to show how sense of urgency is created. 2 marks may be awarded for detailed/insightful comment; 1 mark for more basic comment (2 or 1+1).<br><br>0 marks for reference/quotation alone. | 4 | Possible answers include:<br><br>"swithered" — suggests frightening spectacle of the barn which moved from side to side as a result of the fire<br><br>"roared" — suggests the fire made a loud, ferocious sound like a wild animal<br><br>"roaring alight" — as above, but again combines sight and sound<br><br>"snarling" — onomatopoeic/personification, suggesting the fire is making a growling sound like an ill-natured beast<br><br>"eating in to" — suggests unstoppable force which is consuming, making inroads into<br><br>"charred" — reduced to carbon<br><br>"screamed and screamed" — repetition emphasises the horse's fear or pain as it cried out shrilly<br><br>"smell and smoke" — alliteration conveys inescapable presence of the fire's effects |

| Question | Expected Response | Max Mark | Additional Guidance |
|---|---|---|---|
| 30. | *(continued)* | 4 | Frequent linking of actions with the repeated use of "and" suggests the continuous, confused activity due to danger caused by fire's ferocity, eg "And at that sound ... and cried ... and she screamed ... and to help ... and the bairns ... and Long Rob ..." |
| | | | Narrative and dialogue combined in the same sentence to indicate there is no time to pause or waste, eg "But pipe and all he dived in ... *Oh my sampler!* and in Rob tore ... " |
| | | | Rare use of a colon to split the viable rescue actions from the impossible — "He it was ... another angle:  but that was no good ..." |
| 31. | Candidates should discuss how the writer conveys positive aspects of the community and should refer to appropriate textual evidence to support their discussion.<br><br>0 marks for reference/quotation alone.<br><br>Candidates can answer in bullet points in this final question, or write a number of linked statements. | 10 | Up to 2 marks can be achieved for identifying elements of commonality as identified in the question, ie positive presentation of the community.<br>A further 2 marks can be achieved for reference to the extract given.<br>6 additional marks can be awarded for discussion of similar references to at least one other part of the text by the writer.<br><br><u>In practice this means:</u><br><br>Identification of commonality (2) (eg: theme, characterisation, use of imagery, setting, or any other key element...)<br><br>from the extract:<br><br>1 × relevant reference to technique/idea/feature (1)<br>1 × appropriate comment (1)<br>(maximum of 2 marks only for discussion of extract)<br><br>from at least one other text/part of the text:<br><br>as above (x3) for up to 6 marks<br>**OR**<br>more detailed comment x2 for up to 6 marks<br><br>Thus, the final 6 marks can be gained by a combination of 3, 2 and 1 marks depending on the level of depth/detail/insight.  The aim would be to encourage quality of comment, rather than quantity of references.<br><br>In comments on the rest of the novel, possible references include:<br><br>• the threshing at Peesie's Knapp;<br>• the visit of Long Rob and Chae to Blawaerie at New Year<br>• the celebration of Chris's wedding<br><br>Many other references are possible. |

**Text 5 — Prose — *The Cone Gatherers* by Robin Jenkins**

| Question | Expected Response | Max Mark | Additional Guidance |
|---|---|---|---|
| 32. | For full marks candidates should make reference to how both sympathy and admiration are evoked, but there is no requirement for equal coverage of the two elements.<br><br>One detailed/insightful comment, supported by reference from lines 1-40, may be awarded 2 marks; a more basic comment plus reference should be awarded 1 mark. Thus marks may be awarded 2+2, 2+1+1 or 1+1+1+1.<br><br>0 marks for reference/quotation alone. | 4 | References could be used to support sympathy and/or admiration.<br><br>**Possible answers include:**<br><br>"Neil appeared like an old man...He would cautiously go down on his haunches, wait, apparently to gather strength and endurance against the pain of that posture..." — Neil's rheumatism, worsened by Lady Runcie's Campbell's thoughtless rejection of the brothers from the beach hut and their subsequent soaking, causes him great pain and yet he is stoical and perseveres with the task in hand. The alliteration in "pain of that posture" emphasises the discomfort<br><br>"...and then would begin to pick up the seed-cases...if it were not." — the detailed nature of Jenkins' description emphasises the painstaking nature of the task /Neil's dogged determination to carry out the task properly despite the pain he is in.<br><br>"...as ninety out of a hundred would be barren." — the statistic demonstrates Neil's perseverance in carrying out so futile a task, which adds to our admiration<br><br>"crippled with rheumatism", "hobbled on his haunches" —Jenkins' detailed description(s) of the severity of Neil's physical problems adds to the sympathy we feel for him<br><br>"Such fidelity to so simple but indispensible a task...magnificent trees." — Neil's stoical commitment to his work evokes the simple goodness of the common man in the face of adversity<br><br>"To praise it...inadequacy of life itself." — Neil's quiet faithfulness to his task is a thing of great nobility and seems to illustrate something fundamental about man's existence<br><br>"Behind him Neil began to sob", "And he began to pour out an account of the expulsion..." — Neil's burden of looking after and protecting Calum is overwhelming when he is faced with the thoughtless cruelty of others. "Sob" has connotations of childish crying, which effectively conveys the distress of Neil<br><br>"I'm responsible for him, Mr. Tulloch..." — Neil's simple declaration of dedication to looking after and protecting Calum provokes great admiration<br><br>"No man on earth has ever...so well." — Mr Tulloch recognises Neil's loyalty to Calum, and admires his selfless commitment to his brother's well-being<br><br>"...how stooped and contorted Neil was then, by rheumatism and despair..." — Neil's problems are both physical and emotional, creating sympathy in the reader<br>"...as if in some terrible penance, he was striving to become in shape like his brother." — the idea of Neil doing "penance" because he feels such guilt for failing to stand up to Lady Runcie Campbell provokes sympathy for the despair he feels and the burden he carries on his own |

| Question | Expected Response | Max Mark | Additional Guidance |
|---|---|---|---|
| 33. | Candidates should explain Neil's attitude to Lady Runcie Cambell.<br><br>This attitude does not have to stated separately; it can be explained through the references given.<br><br>2 marks may be awarded for a detailed/insightful comment plus reference.<br><br>1 mark should be awarded for a more basic comment plus reference.<br><br>0 marks for reference/quotation alone. | 4 | Neil's attitude towards Lady Runcie Campbell: he bitterly resents her superior attitude towards the brothers, in particular Calum, and is angered and insulted by her behaviour towards them<br><br>Possible answers include:<br><br>"Why is it, Mr Tulloch…that the innocent have always to be sacrificed?" — Neil is bitter about the way he and Calum have been treated because they are of low social standing in the eyes of Lady Runcie Campbell; they are not worthy so must be "sacrificed" for her comfort<br><br>He is also referring to the working class man fighting at war to preserve a way of life which gives nothing to him, or people like him (but is much to the benefit of the ruling elite as symbolised by Lady Runcie Campbell)<br><br>"We were driven out like slaves…Her dog was to be saved from the storm but not my brother." — Neil is disgusted by Lady Runcie Campbell's callous treatment of the brothers. She values animals over men, and thinks her superior social standing justifies her actions<br><br>"Did she think we were monkeys that would bite her?" — Neil is angered by Lady Runcie Campbell's ignorant prejudice towards the brothers, thinking that they are little better than uncivilised animals just because they are simple working men<br><br>"Neil shook his head dourly.<br>My brother's the shape…to despise him?" — Neil cannot agree with Mr Tulloch's more measured attitude towards Lady Runcie Campbell. He points out Lady Runcie Campbell's arrogance in believing herself a greater judge than God Himself, but also hints at her hypocrisy as a Christian. |
| 34. | Candidates should explain Mr Tulloch's attitude to Lady Runcie Cambell.<br><br>This attitude does not have to be stated separately; it can be explained through the references given.<br><br>2 marks may be awarded for a detailed/insightful comment plus reference.<br><br>1 mark should be awarded for a more basic comment plus reference.<br><br>0 marks for reference/quotation alone. | 2 | Mr Tulloch's attitude towards Lady Runcie Campbell: he is more measured and sympathetic, recognising the conflict she feels between being seen to do her "duty" as a member of the ruling class and reaching out to all men with Christian compassion<br><br>Possible references include:<br><br>"I think maybe she was taken by surprise…Maybe she got a bit of a shock." — Tulloch recognises the unexpected nature of the brothers' appearance in the beach hut, and is prepared to believe that Lady Runcie Campbell acted out of surprise rather than malice<br><br>"She's a good woman really; but she's got a code to live by." — Tulloch recognises that Lady Runcie Campbell's decisions are driven by her need to be seen to be doing what is expected of a woman in her position. She must uphold the natural division between the classes and preserve the "code" on which society is founded |

| Question | Expected Response | Max Mark | Additional Guidance |
|---|---|---|---|
| 35. | Candidates should discuss the central concern of the innocent being sacrificed, and its development, and should refer to appropriate textual evidence to support their discussion.<br><br>0 marks for reference alone.<br><br>Candidates can answer in bullet points in this final question, or write a number of linked statements. | 10 | Up to 2 marks can be achieved for identifying elements of commonality as identified in the question, ie theme of sacrifice of the innocent.<br>A further 2 marks can be achieved for reference to the extract given.<br>6 additional marks can be awarded for discussion of similar references to at least one other part of the text by the writer.<br><br><u>In practice this means:</u><br><br>Identification of commonality (2) (eg: theme, characterisation, use of imagery, setting, or any other key element…)<br><br>from the extract:<br><br>1 × relevant reference to technique/idea/feature (1)<br>1 × appropriate comment (1)<br>(maximum of 2 marks only for discussion of extract)<br><br>from at least one other text/part of the text:<br><br>as above (×3) for up to 6 marks<br>**OR**<br>more detailed comment x2 for up to 6 marks<br><br>Thus, the final 6 marks can be gained by a combination of 3, 2 and 1 marks depending on the level of depth/detail/insight. The aim would be to encourage quality of comment, rather than quantity of references.<br><br>In comments on the rest of the novel, possible references include:<br>• The conflict involving Duror, Calum and Neil — the weak and vulnerable at the mercy of a more powerful and malevolent force<br>• The world of nature (the wood) mirrors the world of war: Jenkins' use of animal imagery suggests a world of destruction and violence, culminating in the deer hunt<br>• Calum's death: the culmination of Calum's Christ-like associations<br>Many other references are possible. |

**Text 1 – Poetry – *Holy Willie's Prayer* by Robert Burns**

| Question | Expected Response | Max Mark | Additional Guidance |
|---|---|---|---|
| 36. | Candidates should explain what Holy Willie means when he calls himself a "chosen sample". 2 marks may be awarded for detailed/insightful comment plus reference; 1 mark for more basic comment plus reference. | 2 | Possible answers include:<br><br>• A reference to Calvinism/predestination/the Elect<br>• God has chosen Willie to be one of the Elect<br>• Willie claims not to be able to understand why he has been "chosen" and demonstrates mock-modesty |
| 37. | Candidates should comment on the contradiction between Willie's words and actions/feelings for full marks.<br><br>Candidates should focus on two examples; 2 marks may be awarded for detailed/insightful comment plus reference; 1 mark for more basic comment plus reference.<br><br>The contrast/contraction should be clear in the commentary.<br><br>0 marks for reference/quotation alone. | 4 | Possible answers include:<br>**Words**<br>• "a pillar o' thy temple" — "pillar" suggests something strong/steadfast, creating the sense that Willie sees himself as a good (moral) example to others<br>• "Strong as a rock" — simile suggests strength/power of something natural — suggesting Willie sees himself as a natural choice of leader<br>• "A guide, a buckler and example (/To a thy flock.)" — the list of items suggests that Willie sees himself as special and a moral leader/supporter defender of morality/faith |

| Question | Expected Response | Max Mark | Additional Guidance |
|---|---|---|---|
| 37. | *(continued)* | 4 | • "I am keepet by Thy fear/Free frae them a" — reference to "fear" suggests that Willie respects God's power and will live a good life; "free" suggests his life will avoid sin and he will keep the Commandments |
| | | | **Actions/feelings** |
| | | | • "fash'd wi' fleshly lust" — Willie admits giving in to one of the deadly sins, thus proving he is not a good example to others; "fash'd" is informal suggesting he sees his actions as trivial/bothersome rather than morally wrong |
| | | | • "yestreen, Thou kens, wi' Meg" — use of informal "Thou" is disrespectful, suggesting Willie views God as a friend rather than the powerful Creator of his faith; the tone of "Thou kens" suggests Willie is not really ashamed of his actions, his lust; he does not treat women with respect |
| | | | • "I'll ne'er lift a lawless leg/Again upon her" — use of alliteration to emphasise "lawless leg" adds to the triviality of the expression and to Willie's hypocrisy |
| | | | • "Wi Leezie's lass, three times I trow" — tone here is almost boastful, suggesting Willie is anything but reverent and atoning for his sins; use of alliteration again trivializes the comment; informality of the expression emphasises his lack of respect for the (unnamed) girl |
| | | | • "I was fou" — informal expression again suggests he treats God as a friend and is not ashamed of his behaviour |
| | | | • "wad never steer her" — "steer" has animalistic connotations and emphasises his lack of respect for the girl |
| 38. | Candidates should identify the change of tone with two examples for 1 mark each.<br><br>0 marks for reference/quotation alone. | 4 | Possible answers include:<br><br>**Tone**<br>• "Maybe Thou lets this fleshly thorn/Buffet Thy servant e'en and morn/Lest he o'er proud and high should turn" — the tone is reflective, as Holy Willie considers that God might be tormenting him with these humiliating events to stop him becoming arrogant.<br>• "But God confound their stubborn face/ And blast their name" — the tone is of anger as Holy Willie berates his congregation for their behaviour. This emphasises his anger and contradicts his desire to pray; the lines emphasise his desire for vengeance upon his enemies. |
| 39. | Candidates should discuss the contrast between Holy Willie and at least one other character and should refer to appropriate textual evidence to support their discussion.<br><br>0 marks for reference/quotation alone.<br><br>Candidates can answer in bullet points in this final question, or write a number of linked statements. | 10 | Up to 2 marks can be achieved for identifying elements of commonality as identified in the question, ie the contrast between Holy Willie and another character or characters.<br>A further 2 marks can be achieved for reference to the extract given.<br>6 additional marks can be awarded for discussion of similar references to at least one other poem by the poet. |

| Question | Expected Response | Max Mark | Additional Guidance |
|---|---|---|---|
| 39. | *(continued)* | 10 | <u>In practice this means:</u><br><br>Identification of commonality (2) (eg: theme, characterisation, use of imagery, setting, or any other key element...)<br><br>from the extract:<br><br>1 × relevant reference to technique/idea/feature (1)<br>1 × appropriate comment (1)<br>(maximum of 2 marks only for discussion of extract)<br><br>from at least one other text/part of the text:<br><br>as above (×3) for up to 6 marks<br>**OR**<br>more detailed comment (×2) for up to 6 marks<br><br>Thus, the final 6 marks can be gained by a combination of 3, 2 and 1 marks depending on the level of depth/detail/insight. The aim would be to encourage quality of comment, rather than quantity of references.<br><br>In comments on other poems by Burns, possible references include:<br>• *Tam O'Shanter* — relishing life, non-hypocritical<br>• *A Poet's Welcome to his Love-Begotten Daughter* — non-apologetic self-awareness, warm and genuinely loving<br>• *Address to the Deil* — ironic sense of own flaws<br>Many other references are possible. |

## Text 2 – Poetry – Originally by Carol Ann Duffy

| Question | Expected Response | Max Mark | Additional Guidance |
|---|---|---|---|
| 40. | 2 marks can be awarded for two examples which highlight the dramatic impact.<br><br>A detailed/insightful comment on one example may be awarded 2 marks.<br><br>Reference plus basic comment for 1 mark.<br><br>0 marks for reference/quotation alone. | 2 | Possible answers include:<br>• Word choice of "we"/"our" suggests a sense of comforting group identity/defining event in family history<br>• Repetition of "our" suggests the need for group identity in the face of new circumstances<br>• Word choice of "fell" suggests a loss of control over event/helplessness in the face of change<br>• Word choice of "cried"/"bawling" suggests the degree of distress caused by the move.<br>• The sequence "the city .... rooms" suggests a poignant re-tracing of the route/desire to return<br>• Word choice of "vacant" suggests the physical/ emotional emptiness of the place that used to be home<br>• The climactic conclusion to the sequence "city ... any more." suggests the finality of the move<br>• The word choice of "stared" suggests a stunned reaction to the move.<br>• The contrast of the poet's reaction — "stared"— with the reactions of her brothers —"cried"/"bawling" — highlights the poet's shocked reaction<br>• Symbolic use of "blind toy" — like the poet the toy is unfeeling and unaware of what is happening<br>• Word choice of "holding its paw" suggests a desperate need for comfort/reassurance |

| Question | Expected Response | Max Mark | Additional Guidance |
|---|---|---|---|
| **41.** | Candidates should explain fully what Duffy means by the image "all childhood is an emigration." <br><br> Simple comment about journey to adulthood for 1 mark. <br><br> A detailed/insightful comment may be awarded 2 marks. <br><br> Reference to journey alone = 0 marks. | 2 | Possible answers include: <br><br> Childhood is a journey from safety/security/the familiar <br> **OR** <br> Childhood is a journey into the unknown/to independence/potentially risky and dangerous situations. |
| **42.** | Candidates should analyse how the poet's use of poetic technique conveys the distress of the family members. <br><br> 3 marks can be awarded for three examples of language highlighting the distress. <br><br> Reference plus basic comment for 1 mark. (1+1+1). <br><br> Alternatively, 2 marks may be awarded for reference plus more detailed/insightful comment (2+1). <br><br> 0 marks for reference/quotation alone. | 3 | Possible answers include: <br> • The positioning/abruptness of the minor sentence "Your accent wrong" suggests lack of acceptance/sense of exclusion. <br> • The parenthesis/positioning of "which seem familiar" suggest a sense of confusion/disorientation/déjà vu triggered by the new environment. <br> • The word choice of "unimagined" suggests some unspeakable horror. <br> • The word choice of "big boys" suggests the intimidating appearance of the boys/the vulnerability of the poet. <br> • The detail "eating worms" suggests outlandish/disgusting behaviour. <br> • The word choice of "shouting" suggests the intimidating nature of the way the boys are speaking. <br> • The word choice of "you don't understand" suggests confusion/alienation. <br> • The image "anxieties … loose tooth" suggests that a loose tooth causes annoyance but the parents' concerns about the move won't go away. <br> • The word choice of "in my head" suggests that the parents' concerns have made a deep impression on the poet. <br> • The italics/the phrase *"I want … country"* suggests the strength of the desire to return. <br> • The word choice of *"want" "our"/"own"* suggests the depth of her desire for the familiar. |
| **43.** | Candidates should show understanding of the term "conclusion" and show how the content of the last stanza continues — or contrasts with — ideas and/or language from the first two stanzas. <br><br> 3 marks can be awarded for three appropriate, basic comments. <br><br> A detailed/insightful comment on one example may be awarded 2 marks. <br><br> Other examples are acceptable. <br><br> 0 marks for reference/quotation alone. | 3 | Possible answers include: <br> **Ideas** <br> • The poet has moved on in her life, and she has adapted to her new life <br> • This move has created a sense of uncertainty as to her true origins, and sense of belonging <br><br> **Language** <br> • "But" suggests a change from her previous outsider status to becoming assimilated into the new environment. <br> • The sequence "you forget … or change" suggests the gradual/indeterminable process of assimilation. <br> • The idea of "brother swallow a slug" links back to "eating worms" and suggests her brother's acceptance of the local culture. <br> • The use of the dialect word "skelf" suggests a hankering back to previous home or limited influence of previous culture on her. <br> • The image "skelf of shame" suggests that just as a "skelf" is a splinter of wood, so is her sense of shame in betraying her past rather limited. |

| Question | Expected Response | Max Mark | Additional Guidance |
|---|---|---|---|
| 43. | *(continued)* | 3 | • The image "my tongue … snake" suggests that just as a snake sheds its old skin, she is shedding her old life/adapting to suit her new life.<br>• The idea of "my voice … like the rest" links back to "Your accent wrong" suggesting the poet's continuing assimilation into her new culture.<br>• The list "I lost … the right place?" suggests an awareness of the amount she has lost by emigrating.<br>• The use of the question at the end of the previous list introduces uncertainty — has she actually "lost" the items in the list?<br>• The positioning/abruptness of "And I hesitate" suggests the poet's uncertainty about her cultural identity or where she really belongs. |
| 44. | Candidates should discuss the use of contrast in this and other poems by Carol Ann Duffy and should refer to appropriate textual evidence to support their discussion.<br><br>0 marks for reference/quotation alone.<br><br>Candidates can answer in bullet points in this final question, or write a number of linked statements. | 10 | Up to 2 marks can be achieved for identifying elements of commonality as identified in the question, ie use of contrast to highlight main concerns of this and other poems by Duffy.<br>A further 2 marks can be achieved for reference to the extract given.<br>6 additional marks can be awarded for discussion of similar references to at least one other poem by the poet.<br><br><u>In practice this means:</u><br><br>Identification of commonality (2) (eg: theme, characterisation, use of imagery, setting, or any other key element…)<br><br>from the extract:<br><br>1 × relevant reference to technique/idea/feature (1)<br>1 × appropriate comment (1)<br>(maximum of 2 marks only for discussion of extract)<br><br>from at least one other text/part of the text:<br><br>as above (×3) for up to 6 marks<br>**OR**<br>more detailed comment ×2 for up to 6 marks<br><br>Thus, the final 6 marks can be gained by a combination of 3, 2 and 1 marks depending on the level of depth/detail/insight. The aim would be to encourage quality of comment, rather than quantity of references.<br><br>In comments on other poems, possible references include:<br><br>• Conventional romance versus realistic love in "Valentine"<br>• Love and hate/revenge in "Havisham"<br>• Peacefulness of darkroom versus horror of war zone in "War Photographer"<br><br>Many other references are possible. |

**Text 3 — Poetry — *For My Grandmother Knitting* by Liz Lochhead**

| Question | Expected Response | Max Mark | Additional Guidance |
|---|---|---|---|
| **45.** | Candidates should analyse how the poet's use of poetic technique helps to clarify the main ideas of the poem. <br><br>2 marks may be awarded for detailed/insightful comment plus reference; 1 mark for more basic comment plus reference. <br><br>0 marks for reference/quotation alone. | 2 | Possible answers include: <br><br>• "There is no need they say" — the speech makes clear that the grandmother's efforts are unappreciated/misunderstood <br>• "the needles still move" — the present tense makes clear the persistence of the grandmother in continuing to stay busy <br>• "their rhythms in the working of your hands" — the word choice makes clear her skill <br>• "once again ... fisher-girl." — the sibilance of "sure and skilful" makes clear her past, the way that she had to work hard to get by <br>• Alliteration of "master of your movements then" emphasises her skill in the past <br>• Sibilance and onomatopoeia of "slit the still-tickling quick silver fish" recreating the sound of the needles working <br>• Imagery of "silver fish" suggesting that she makes the needles come to life/can control their movement <br>• "Hard work ... of necessity" word choice makes clear the austerity of her life/her need to work |
| **46.** | Candidates should analyse how the poet conveys what the grandmother's life was like as a younger woman. <br><br>3 marks can be awarded for reference plus detailed/insightful comment;1 mark for reference plus more basic comment. <br><br>Thus, marks can be awarded 2+1 or 1+1+1. <br><br>0 marks for reference/quotation alone. | 3 | Possible answers include: <br><br>• Repetition of "once the hands" emphasising the number of tasks, showing stages of married life — wedding day, caring for husband, looking after children/bringing up family <br>• Word choice of "the hand-span waist" uses the word "hand" to refer to the grandmother as slim and fragile <br>• Word choice of "scrubbed his back" shows her performing a task for husband, working hard <br>• Alliteration of "made do and mended" emphasising the repetitive tasks/need to scrimp and save and make the best of what they had <br>• Onomatopoeia and sibilance of "scraped and slaved slapped" emphasising the repetitive nature of her life <br>• Series of verbs "mended scraped ... slaved slapped" emphasising the number of tasks which she had to perform <br>• Word choice of "slapped sometimes" shows that she was capable of being harsh and strict when she felt it was necessary |
| **47.** | Candidates should identify the grandchildren's attitude to their grandmother and explain how it has been conveyed. <br><br>2 marks can be awarded for one example with detailed/insightful comments or two examples with more basic comments. <br><br>0 marks for reference/quotation alone. | 2 | Possible answers include: <br><br>• "But now ..." — conjunction shows that despite all that their grandmother has done, her children seem ungrateful/do not understand her <br>• "there is no need"/"no necessity" shows the children's failure to understand the grandmother's need to be busy and productive <br>• Repetition of "too much ... too many" shows that the children are extremely insistent and constantly ask her to stop <br>• "wave them goodbye Sunday" shows how regularly they visit but that they ultimately leave the grandmother alone <br>• Ellipsis of "there's no necessity ... " suggests that they continue to protest at the amount of knitting, and consider her efforts a waste of time |

| Question | Expected Response | Max Mark | Additional Guidance |
|---|---|---|---|
| 48. | Candidates should show understanding of the term "conclusion" and show how the content of lines 34—45 continues — or contrasts with — ideas and/or language from the previous lines.<br><br>3 marks can be awarded for three appropriate, basic comments.<br><br>A detailed/insightful comment on one example may be awarded 2 marks.<br><br>Other examples are acceptable.<br><br>0 marks for reference/quotation alone. | 3 | Possible answers include:<br>**Ideas**<br>• Grandmother's aged frailty compared to younger, stronger "versions" of her<br>• Her skills remain, though not necessarily understood/appreciated<br><br>**Language**<br>• "big on shrunken wrists" emphasises the physical damage done to the grandmother, contrasts with the "hand-span" waist earlier in the poem<br>• Series of minor sentences/adjectives of "Swollen-jointed. Red. Arthritic. Old" emphasising the accumulated damage to her hands and wrists, climaxing with the simple conclusion that she is "old"<br>• "But" at the beginning of the sentence and line emphasising that despite her ailment the grandmother continues to knit tirelessly<br>• Enjambement of "But ... stop" in contrast to the line "Swollen-jointed ... Old." emphasising that her grandmother is in perpetual motion<br>• Word "rhythms" from earlier in the poem emphasising the regular, faultless nature of the grandmother's knitting<br>• Word choice of "easily" placed on a line of its own emphasises how effortless it is<br>• Repeated structure of "as if ... remembered ... as if ... forgotten" showing that the movement has become almost instinctive<br>• "remembered ... forgotten" refers back to her grandmother's life previously |
| 49. | Candidates should discuss the importance of the theme of memory in Lochhead's work and should refer to appropriate textual evidence to support their discussion.<br><br>0 marks for reference/quotation alone.<br><br>Candidates can answer in bullet points in this final question, or write a number of linked statements. | 10 | Up to 2 marks can be achieved for identifying elements of commonality as identified in the question, ie the theme of memory in other poems by Lochhead.<br>A further 2 marks can be achieved for reference to the extract given.<br>6 additional marks can be awarded for discussion of similar references to at least one other poem by the poet.<br><br>In practice this means:<br><br>Identification of commonality (2) (eg: theme, characterisation, use of imagery, setting, or any other key element...)<br><br>from the extract:<br><br>1 × relevant reference to technique/idea/feature (1)<br>1 × appropriate comment (1)<br>(maximum of 2 marks only for discussion of extract)<br>From at least one other text/part of the text:<br><br>as above (×3) for up to 6 marks<br>**OR**<br>more detailed comment ×2 for up to 6 marks<br><br>Thus, the final 6 marks can be gained by a combination of 3, 2 and 1 marks depending on the level of depth/detail/insight. The aim would be to encourage quality of comment, rather than quantity of references. |

| Question | Expected Response | Max Mark | Additional Guidance |
|---|---|---|---|
| 49. | *(continued)* | 10 | In comments on other poems, possible references include:<br><br>• *The Bargain*: memory of perfect day in love — sense of impermanence<br>• *View of Scotand/Love Song*: contrast and continuum — past rituals and more genuine personal Hogmanays<br>• *Some Old Photographs*: romanticising of past undercut by sense of reality<br><br>Many other references are possible. |

### Text 4 — Poetry — *Sounds of the Day* by Norman MacCaig

| Question | Expected Response | Max Mark | Additional Guidance |
|---|---|---|---|
| 50. | Candidates should demonstrate awareness of how the poet uses poetic technique to create a vivid sense of place. A single detailed/insightful comment may be awarded 2 marks; more basic comments will be worth 1 mark each. Thus, marks may be awarded 2+2, 2+1+1 or 1+1+1+1.<br><br>0 marks for reference/quotation alone. | 4 | Possible answers include:<br><br>• Onomatopoeia of "clatter" illustrates vivid/loud/strident sound of horses' hooves which were a familiar part of everyday life.<br>• Alliteration in "clatter came" emphasises the expected quality/ordinariness of the sound.<br>• Sibilance of "horses crossing" creates a soothing tone to echo his feelings of contentment in this place.<br>• Onomatopoeia of "creaked". The high pitched sound conveys the energy of the location/the variety of sounds surrounding the narrator.<br>• Consonance of "snuffling puff" contrasts with harsher sounds to create a sense of reassurance, establishing the blanket of sounds which were part of the environment.<br>• Repetition of "blocking … unblocking" to echo the cyclical order of the natural world and its continuous, everyday sounds.<br>• Imagery of "black drums rolled". Just as a drum roll is a loud and booming sound, the poet is suggesting that the roar of the sea illustrates the strength and power of nature. Reference could be made to word choice of "black" foreshadowing the difficulty that lies ahead.<br>• Parallel structure of "when……it was" to reinforce the familiar/customary/regular pattern of the place and its inhabitants.<br>• Humorous/ironic reference to the "lapwing" conveys MacCaig's dislike of the attitude of self-interested landowners whose attitudes are mirrored by the bird's territorial instinct |
| 51. | Candidates should demonstrate awareness of the intrinsic nature of the change in circumstance. This may be implicit in comments on how the poet uses poetic technique to convey the change.<br><br>A single detailed/insightful comment may be awarded 2 marks; more basic comments will be awarded 1 mark each.<br><br>Reference alone: 0. Mere identification of feature: 0. | 2 | Possible answers include:<br><br>• Sibilance/onomatopoeia of "scraped shut" mirrors the emotional pain of the narrator as the closing door scratches the hard surface creating a harsh/unnatural/unpleasant sound. Contrasts with previous stanza which highlighted the reassuring sounds of the natural world.<br>• Symbol of a door scraping shut to echo the fundamental nature of the change/finality of the closed door emphasises the cessation of what has gone before. |

| Question | Expected Response | Max Mark | Additional Guidance |
|---|---|---|---|
| **51.** | *(continued)* | 2 | • Positioning of "end" emphatically conveys the absolute/definitive nature of the change (and its implications) on the narrator. <br>• Word choice of "all the sounds" reinforces the dramatic change. All that mattered is gone as the previously comforting effect of "all the sounds" is now lost. <br>• Change in verb tense to present (at end of stanza) makes clear the impact of the change as the immediacy invites the reader to share their distress. <br>• Candidates may also make valid comments on the single sentence, three line stanza contrasting with the previous stanza, to exemplify the change from the free/busy/open environment of the natural world to the confined and enclosed space in which he now finds himself. |
| **52.** | Candidates should demonstrate awareness of how the poet makes clear the impact of this incident on the narrator, through his use of language. <br><br>A detailed/insightful comment may be awarded 2 marks; more basic comments will be awarded 1 mark each. <br><br>0 marks for reference/quotation alone. Mere identification of feature: 0. <br><br>Be alert to answers which make valid points dealing with imagery as word choice. | 4 | Possible answers include: <br><br>**Stanza 3** <br>• Word choice of "You left me" creates a blunt/accusatory tone. Displays narrator's emotional response. Candidates may offer valid comments linked to feelings of shock/anger/resentment. <br>• Reference may also be made to personal pronouns "You…me" to create intimacy and further establish the deep emotional effects of the parting. <br>• Word choice (and positioning) of "beside" demonstrates the lack of the physical presence of the loved one, conveying feelings of isolation. <br>• Word choice of "quietest" stands in stark contrast to life affirming sounds of stanza 1 emphasising the void of meaningful sound now the person has left. <br>• Candidates may also comment on the short, single sentence stanza which is stripped bare to echo/mirror the raw emotions of the narrator. <br><br>**Stanza 4** <br>• Personal pronouns "I … I … my" convey the narrator's immediate reaction as being somewhat naïve/self-indulgent. <br>• Word choice of "pride only" suggests the narrator's reaction to the shock was initially on a superficial level. <br>• Positioning of "forgetting that" signals the dawning realisation that the emotional effects of the loss will be on a much deeper level. <br>• Word choice/onomatopoeia of "plunge" has connotations of depth/immersion suggesting that the impact will be much greater than initially perceived. <br>• Word choice of "freezing" creates a bleak/despairing tone highlighting his pain/distress/anguish. |

| Question | Expected Response | Max Mark | Additional Guidance |
|---|---|---|---|
| 52. | *(continued)* | 4 | • Positioning of "you feel" begins to plot how the narrator's positive emotions have been overtaken and shut down as a consequence of the parting.<br>• Extended metaphor "bangle of ice … numb". Just as a hand thrust into ice-cold water will take a moment to react, so the poet suggests that the impact of the loss moves from an initial, localised shock into a general closing down of all feeling. The blow of the person leaving has overwhelmed the narrator and isolated him from all that was previously meaningful. This clarifies the poet's message about the all-consuming nature of loss. |
| 53. | Candidates should discuss how MacCaig uses contrast to explore theme in his work and should refer to appropriate textual evidence to support their discussion.<br><br>0 marks for reference/quotation alone.<br><br>Candidates can answer in bullet points in this final question, or write a number of linked statements. | 10 | Up to 2 marks can be achieved for identifying elements of commonality as identified in the question, ie MacCaig's use of contrast to develop theme.<br>A further 2 marks can be achieved for reference to the extract given.<br>6 additional marks can be awarded for discussion of similar references to at least one other poem by the poet.<br><br>In practice this means:<br><br>Identification of commonality (2) (eg: theme, characterisation, use of imagery, setting, or any other key element…)<br><br>from the extract:<br><br>1 × relevant reference to technique/idea/feature (1)<br>1 × appropriate comment (1)<br>(maximum of 2 marks only for discussion of extract)<br><br>from at least one other text/part of the text:<br><br>as above (×3) for up to 6 marks<br>**OR**<br>more detailed comment x2 for up to 6 marks<br><br>Thus, the final 6 marks can be gained by a combination of 3, 2 and 1 marks depending on the level of depth/detail/insight. The aim would be to encourage quality of comment, rather than quantity of references.<br><br>In comments on other poems, possible references include:<br><br>• The external grotesqueness contrasting with the inner beauty in Assisi<br>• The noisy life force that is Aunt Julia contrasting with the silence of death<br>• The professionalism contrasting with the raw suffering in Visiting Hour<br><br>Many other references are possible. |

Text 5 — Poetry — *Heroes* by Sorley MacLean

| Question | Expected Response | Max Mark | Additional Guidance |
|---|---|---|---|
| 54. | Candidates should reference the use of poetic technique and explain how this contributes to the effectiveness of the opening stanza.<br><br>2 marks for detailed/insightful comment plus reference; 1 mark for more basic comment plus reference.<br><br>0 marks for reference/quotation alone. | 2 | Possible answers include:<br><br>Repetition of names of legendary heroes effective in establishing theme of heroism in battle<br>**OR**<br>Contrast of specific Scottish names and place-names with anonymous English soldier or "everyman" effective in establishing tone of irony/theme of heroism<br>**OR**<br>"I did not see" effective in establishing poet's feelings about/attitudes towards the English soldier/tone of irony |
| 55. | Candidates should discuss the speaker's attitude towards the English soldier.<br><br>2 marks for reference plus detailed/insightful comment; 1 mark for reference plus more basic comment.<br><br>For full marks, candidates should make reference to both sections of the poem.<br><br>0 marks for reference/quotation alone. | 4 | Possible answers include:<br><br>From lines 5—11<br>• "poor little chap"/"chubby cheeks" or reference — word choice conveys sympathy towards soldier because he is young/inexperienced/childish/to be pitied<br>• "knees grinding" or reference — word choice conveys sympathy for soldier's nervousness/anxiety<br>• "pimply unattractive face" or reference — word choice conveys soldier is not conventionally handsome/heroic/poet is unsympathetic towards soldier/does not admire soldier<br>• "garment of the bravest spirit" or reference — word choice conveys the poet feels the soldier's outward appearance hides/covers his bravery<br>• He was not a hit "in the pub in the time of the fists being closed" or reference — word choice/use of inverted commas for legal jargon/formal language shows that poet dismisses the idea that soldier was typically drunk/violent<br>• "a lion against the breast of battle" or reference — word choice (contrasting with earlier word choice) conveys poet's admiration for soldier's bravery<br><br>From lines 35—38<br>• "a great warrior of England" or reference — tone of irony<br>• "a poor manikin on whom no eye would rest" or reference — metaphor conveys poet's sympathy towards soldier's youth/inexperience/inferiority<br>• "no Alasdair of Glen Garry" or reference — irony of soldier's achievements in comparison with legendary hero<br>• "he took a little weeping to my eyes" or reference — word choice/use of unusual verb construction/irony conveys that poet feels sadness but simultaneously undermines soldier's heroism |

| Question | Expected Response | Max Mark | Additional Guidance |
|---|---|---|---|
| **56.** | Candidates should quote or reference at least two examples of use of poetic technique and explain fully how these convey the horror of war. 2 marks may be awarded for reference plus detailed/ insightful comment; 1 mark for reference plus more basic comment.<br><br>0 marks for reference/quotation alone. | 4 | Possible answers include:<br>• "morose wounding showers" or reference — word choice/personification conveys power/ darkness of attack<br>• "His hour came" or reference — word choice conveys idea that his time for glory/death has arrived/is inevitable<br>• "notched iron splinters" or reference — consonance/word choice conveys brutality of attack<br>• "in the smoke and flame" or reference — word choice conveys poor visibility/darkness/danger<br>• "shaking and terror of the battlefield" or reference — word choice focuses on fear/ anxiety of soldiers in face of attack/lack of heroism<br>• "bullet shower" or reference — metaphor conveys amount and range of shots/attack<br>• "it wasn't much time he got" or reference — structure/blunt word choice conveys speed of attack/death<br>• "He kept his guns to the tanks" or reference — word choice conveys soldier's bravery/ determination in face of attack<br>• "bucking with tearing crashing screech" or reference — repetition of participles/ consonance emphasises violence/speed/extent of attack<br>• "that biff" or reference — informal/slang word/ understatement/irony to describe fatal blow/ shot conveys power of blow/shot |
| **57.** | Candidates should discuss how MacLean develops a theme or themes through his observation of people or places and should refer to appropriate textual evidence to support their discussion.<br><br>0 marks for reference/quotation alone.<br><br>Candidates can answer in bullet points in this final question, or write a number of linked statements. | 10 | Up to 2 marks can be achieved for identifying elements of commonality as identified in the question, ie how MacLean develops theme through observation of people or places.<br>A further 2 marks can be achieved for reference to the extract given.<br>6 additional marks can be awarded for discussion of similar references to at least one other poem by the poet.<br><br><u>In practice this means:</u><br><br>Identification of commonality (2) (eg: theme, characterisation, use of imagery, setting, or any other key element…)<br><br>from the extract:<br><br>1 × relevant reference to technique/idea/feature (1)<br>1 × appropriate comment (1)<br>(maximum of 2 marks only for discussion of extract)<br><br>from at least one other text/part of the text:<br><br>as above (×3) for up to 6 marks<br>**OR**<br>more detailed comment x2 for up to 6 marks<br><br>Thus, the final 6 marks can be gained by a combination of 3, 2 and 1 marks depending on the level of depth/detail/insight. The aim would be to encourage quality of comment, rather than quantity of references. |

| Question | Expected Response | Max Mark | Additional Guidance |
|---|---|---|---|
| 57. | *(continued)* | 10 | In comments on other poems, possible references include:<br>• *Hallaig*: love song to place develops theme of injustice (of clearances)<br>• *Screapadal*: beauty of area used as warning against destructive urge of humanity<br>• *Shores*: love explored in terms of ocean/beach/rocks<br>Many other references are possible. |

**Text 6 — Poetry — *The Ferryman's Arms* by Don Paterson**

| Question | Expected Response | Max Mark | Additional Guidance |
|---|---|---|---|
| 58. | Candidates should discuss how the poet uses poetic technique to introduce theme in the opening.<br><br>1 mark should be awarded for one main theme introduced in the opening.<br><br>2 marks should be awarded for comment on language/literary techniques.<br><br>2 marks may be awarded for one detailed, insightful comment on one example;<br><br>**OR**<br><br>2 marks may be awarded for two more basic comments on two examples (1+1).<br><br>0 marks for reference/quotation alone. | 3 | Possible answers include:<br>**Themes**<br>• Death<br>• The divided self<br>**References**<br>• Symbolism of "Ferryman" — reference to Greek mythology, Charon ferrying souls of dead to Hades<br>• "Arms" — suggests embrace by death<br>• "About to sit down" — sense of life interrupted by suddenness of death/recognition of divided self<br>• References to darkness ("Guinness", "darkened back room") = death<br>• Symbol/simile of moth = soul taking flight/drawn towards the darkness<br>• "ten minutes to kill" — cliché suggests opposite: time is killing us<br>• "hell of it" — horror of life being used up/afterlife<br>• "half-pint of Guinness": incompleteness<br>• "took myself on" — paradox present in any challenge to self<br>• Contrast between passive verb ("was magnetized") and active ("I took") — self as opposing antagonists |
| 59. | For full marks, candidates should provide comments on example(s) showing both "stages" in the change of mood.<br><br>This could be done through 2 marks for a detailed/insightful comment on one example OR more basic comments on two different examples (1+1).<br><br>0 marks for reference/quotation alone. | 4 | Possible answers include:<br>**Examples suggesting alienation/uncertainty**<br>• Symbolism "Slotting/a coin in the tongue" — ancient ritual of preparing dead for final journey: turns game into encounter with mortality<br>• "stood with my back turned" — symbolic of things going on behind his back/not grasping what is happening<br>• "rumble" — symbolic reference to thunder, approach of something ominous<br>• "cowl" — reference to hooded figure (death)<br>• Sound: "abrupt intestinal rumble" — suggests discomfort, lack of control<br>• "clacked on the slate" onomatopoeia suggests alarming, discordant sound<br>• "striplight batted awake" — intermittent sound suggests inefficiency, neglect<br>• "dusty green cowl" creates image of slightly squalid, unnerving "trap" waiting for him<br>• Word choice: "looked around for a cue" — sense of helplessness<br>• "cue" double meaning ("cue" in drama) — need for hint to help in understanding |

| Question | Expected Response | Max Mark | Additional Guidance |
|---|---|---|---|
| **59.** | *(continued)* | 4 | **Examples suggesting confidence**<br>• Word/verb choice: "I went on to make" — dynamic verb suggesting control of world around him<br>• Word choice/connotations: "immaculate clearance" — sense of clean, in control, powerful action<br>• Metaphor: "low punch" suggests confident manipulation of rules<br>• Word choice: "low punch … wee dab of side" suggests speaker confidently practising trickery<br>• "vanishing trick": metaphor —sense of magical accomplishment<br>• Word choice: "stopped/before gently rolling back": sense of poise and control reinforces mood of confidence<br>• Enjambement: "stopped/before … " suggests smooth movement = confidence (as above)<br>• Personification: "shouldering its way" — white ball moving with confidence reflects the speaker's increased confidence |
| **60.** | Candidates should show understanding of the term "conclusion" and show how the content of the second stanza continues — or contrasts with — ideas and/or language from the first stanza.<br><br>3 marks can be awarded for three appropriate, basic comments.<br><br>A detailed/insightful comment on one example may be awarded 2 marks.<br><br>Other examples are acceptable.<br><br>0 marks for reference/quotation alone. | 3 | Possible answers include:<br><br>**Ideas**<br>• The idea of the divided self<br>• Our lack of choice/journey towards death, which we face alone<br><br>**Language**<br>• Visual image of ferry arriving, almost unobtrusively ("without breaking the skin of the water") or 'innocently' ("chugged" is childish, non-threatening word) echoes "drawn, like a moth" and "gently rolling back" but this is the awaited ferry, bringing the idle passing of time (this life?) to an end<br>• "Black as my stout", "somewhere unspeakable" returns us to an ominous, mysterious world (shadowed by death)<br>• "Foaming lip mussitates endlessly … trying to read and re-read the shoreline" is a metaphor for our lifelong, constant attempts to understand life and death ( develops idea of drinking Guinness)<br>• Poem closes on image of "losing opponent" — sense of this part of self being temporarily defeated or left behind emphasised by disrupted rhythm, short, parenthetical phrases ("stuck in his tent of light", "for practice"), enjambement (" sullenly/knocking")<br>• Paradox of ferry possibly taking "my losing opponent" who is also himself. First clear reference to this "opponent" as separate: game can now be seen in this context — theme of divided self falls into place |

| Question | Expected Response | Max Mark | Additional Guidance |
|---|---|---|---|
| 61. | Candidates should discuss how Paterson uses ordinary experiences to explore deeper truths about humanity and should refer to appropriate textual evidence to support their discussion.<br><br>0 marks for reference/quotation alone.<br><br>Candidates can answer in bullet points in this final question, or write a number of linked statements. | 10 | Up to 2 marks can be achieved for identifying elements of commonality as identified in the question, ie Paterson's use of language to explore the deeper truths behind ordinary experiences.<br>A further 2 marks can be achieved for reference to the extract given.<br>6 additional marks can be awarded for discussion of similar references to at least one other poem by the poet.<br><br><u>In practice this means:</u><br><br>Identification of commonality (2) (eg: theme, characterisation, use of imagery, setting, or any other key element…)<br><br>from the extract:<br><br>1 × relevant reference to technique/idea/feature (1)<br>1 × appropriate comment (1)<br>(maximum of 2 marks only for discussion of extract)<br><br>from at least one other text/part of the text:<br><br>as above (×3) for up to 6 marks<br>**OR**<br>more detailed comment ×2 for up to 6 marks<br><br>Thus, the final 6 marks can be gained by a combination of 3, 2 and 1 marks depending on the level of depth/detail/insight. The aim would be to encourage quality of comment, rather than quantity of references.<br><br>In comments on other poems, possible references include:<br>• Use of image of gallstone being kicked by boy; game linked to theme of death in *Nil, Nil*<br>• The central symbol of the thread — fragility of human life in The Thread<br>• Paradox used in *Waking with Russell* to explore nature of (parental) love<br><br>Many other references are possible. |

**SECTION 2 – Critical Essay**

**Supplementary marking grid**

| | Marks 20-19 | Marks 18-16 | Marks 15-13 | Marks 12-10 | Marks 9-6 | Marks 5-1 | Marks 0 |
|---|---|---|---|---|---|---|---|
| **Knowledge and understanding** The critical essay demonstrates: | a comprehensive knowledge and understanding of the text | a very clear knowledge and understanding of the text | a clear knowledge and understanding of the text | an adequate knowledge and understanding of the text | limited evidence of knowledge and understanding of the text | little knowledge and understanding of the text | no knowledge of the text and its central concerns |
| | a comprehensive selection of textual evidence to support a relevant and coherent argument | very clear textual evidence to support an argument which is clearly focused on the demands of the question | clear textual evidence to support the demands of the question | adequate textual evidence to support a line of thought which has some focus on the question | limited textual evidence to support focus on the demands of the question | little textual evidence to support focus on the demands of the question | no attempt to answer the question and no textual evidence |
| **Analysis** The critical essay demonstrates: | a comprehensive analysis of the effect of features of language/filmic techniques | a very clear analysis of the effect of features of language/filmic techniques | a clear analysis of the effect of features of language/filmic techniques | an adequate analysis of the effect of features of language/filmic techniques | limited analysis of the effect of features of language/filmic techniques | little analysis of features of language/filmic techniques | no analysis of features of language/filmic techniques |
| **Evaluation** The critical essay demonstrates: | a committed, very clear evaluative stance with respect to the text and the task | a very clear evaluative stance with respect to the text and the task | a clear evaluative stance with respect to the text and the task | adequate evidence of an evaluative stance with respect to the text and the task | limited evidence of an evaluative stance with respect to the text and the task | little evidence of an evaluative stance with respect to the text and the task | no evidence of evaluation |
| **Technical Accuracy** The critical essay demonstrates: | • few errors in spelling, grammar, sentence construction, punctuation and paragraphing • the ability to be understood at first reading | | | | • errors in spelling, grammar, sentence construction, punctuation and paragraphing which impede understanding | | |

**[END OF SPECIMEN MARKING INSTRUCTIONS]**

## HIGHER FOR CfE ENGLISH
## MODEL PAPER 1

**PAPER 1 — READING FOR UNDERSTANDING, ANALYSIS AND EVALUATION**

Marking Instructions for each question

**Passage 1**

| Question | | Expected Response | Max Mark | Additional Guidance |
|---|---|---|---|---|
| 1. | (a) | Candidates should analyse how the writer conveys the destructive nature of the First World War.<br><br>Marks will depend on the quality of comment on appropriate language feature(s).<br><br>2 marks may be awarded for reference plus detailed/insightful comment; 1 mark for reference plus more basic comment; 0 marks for reference alone.<br><br>*Possible answers are shown in the "Additional Guidance" column.* | 4 | Possible answers include:<br><br>*Word choice*<br>• any of "boomed … screamed … rattled … cracked … cries … echoed" with appropriate comment on connotation of chosen word(s), such as violent, aggressive, disturbing, discordant<br>• "desolate" suggests barren land, no life, isolation<br>• "reduced" suggests deterioration, a negative process of erosion<br>• "piles" suggests random and unsightly nature of the ruins<br>• "smoking rubble" highlights total devastation, nothing remained but debris<br>• "acre upon acre" suggests the vast, endless area affected, all reduced to similar state of devastation<br>• "splintered" suggests broken into small, unrecognisable pieces; the woodland was beyond hope of repair or regeneration<br>• "blackened stumps" suggests trees are broken, fire-damaged remains of what they once were<br><br>*Onomatopoeia*<br>• any of "boomed … screamed … rattled … cracked" emphasises incessant, debilitating noise on the battlefield; conveys the varying pitches of sound (from low and threatening to high and frightening)<br><br>*Sentence Structure*<br>• list ("howitzers … dying") suggests never-ending/frantic activity, the variety of sensory assault<br>• in the first sentence of paragraph one there is a lengthy build up of noise/drama followed the sudden simplicity of "suddenly fell quiet" to contrast the horror of war with the suddenness of peace<br><br>or any other acceptable answer |
| | (b) | Candidates should explain what effects the war had on "those left behind"?<br><br>Candidates must use their own words. No marks are awarded for verbatim quotations from the passage.<br><br>*1 mark for each point from the "Additional Guidance" column.* | 3 | Possible answers include:<br><br>• some could not celebrate the fact, could not feel happy that the war was finally over (explanation of "little cause for rejoicing")<br>• they were exhausted/weakened (explanation of "enervated")<br>• some thought deeply about their experience (explanation of "some were able to remember and reflect on what they had been through")<br>• some soldiers were confused, adrift, numb (explanation of "Others simply felt lost")<br>• their lives were dominated by the experience of war (explanation of "The war had swallowed them up …" /"occupied their every waking moment") |

| Question | | Expected Response | Max Mark | Additional Guidance |
|---|---|---|---|---|
| | (b) | (continued) | | • they would never be free from the nightmare/ could not escape from memories (explanation of "… just as it was to haunt their dreams in the future") |
| | | | | or any other acceptable answer |
| 2. | | Candidates should explain what the writer suggests is surprising about the way people in Britain view the First World War? | 3 | Possible answers include: |
| | | Candidates must use their own words. No marks are awarded for verbatim quotations from the passage. | | • despite Britain's involvement in more recent/ equally terrible conflicts, we still view the First World War as having a greater significance (explanation of "There have been other wars since 1918 … collective imagination.") |
| | | 1 or 2 marks (depending on the quality of the explanation) for each point from the "Additional Guidance" column. | | • despite the losses suffered by many countries involved in the First World War, Britain still considers itself to have suffered more than these other nations (explanation of "The international catastrophe that was the First World War has been adopted as a peculiarly national trauma.") |
| | | | | or any other acceptable answer |
| 3. | | Candidates should identify three important ways the First World War affected Britain. | 3 | Possible answers include: |
| | | Candidates must use their own words. No marks are awarded for verbatim quotations from the passage. | | • enormous numbers of (young) men were killed (as per statistics) |
| | | 1 mark for each point from the "Additional Guidance" column. | | • the talents and/or potential of a generation were destroyed (explanation of "flower of British youth") |
| | | | | • a society which seemed ideal and had no evils or imperfections ceased to exist (explanation of "Eden" and/or "prelapsarian") |
| | | | | • an imagined idyllic world was gone forever (explanation of "somehow always perfect summer weather") |
| | | | | • the loss of hope/optimism (explanation of "yearningly back rather than expectantly forward") |
| | | | | or any other acceptable answer |
| 4. | | Candidates should analyse how the writer's use of language conveys how important the First World War has become to us. | 4 | Possible answers include: |
| | | Marks will depend on the quality of comment on appropriate language feature(s). | | • "tremendously large place" suggests the war occupies an overwhelming space, is of great importance in our thoughts |
| | | 2 marks may be awarded for reference plus detailed/insightful comment; 1 mark for reference plus more basic comment; 0 marks for reference alone. | | • "the world and its history" a somewhat grandiose concept of the War's all-encompassing influence |
| | | Possible answers are shown in the "Additional Guidance" column. | | • "seemingly endless resource" suggests the war is a continuous source of inspiration, has unlimited potential |
| | | | | • list of professions ("novelists … composers") emphasises the vast range of literature and media which is inspired by the history of the First World War |
| | | | | • "engraved" just as "engraved" is to have been permanently marked by cutting into a surface so the images from the First World War are permanently lodged in our minds |
| | | | | • "the national consciousness" suggests the awareness is deeply ingrained in what it means to be British |
| | | | | • "(recognise them) instantly" suggests that images of the war have become like old friends; we are deeply familiar with these images |
| | | | | • list of the "images" emphasises the number/ range of images we have stored in our consciousness |

| Question | Expected Response | Max Mark | Additional Guidance |
|---|---|---|---|
| 4. | *(continued)* | 4 | • sequence/order of list in final sentence: it could be argued that the final list acts rather like a condensed chronology/a series of snapshots of the war, thus reminding us that we are so familiar with these events that they can be summarized in a few powerful phrases<br>• repetitive structure used to describe each image of war ("the foreign place … the lines … the rows… the scarlet poppies..") repetition builds to a climax which reminds us of the power contained within the inevitable image of poppies/shell-holes<br><br>or any other acceptable answer |
| 5. | Candidates should explain in their own words the two opposing views of the First World War.<br><br>Candidates must use their own words. No marks are awarded for verbatim quotations from the passage.<br><br>*1 mark for each point from the "Additional Guidance" column.* | 4 | Possible answers include:<br><br>*Traditional view:*<br>• the leaders did not know what they were doing/made serious mistakes (explanation of "incompetent High Command")<br>• the loss of life was a continual, relentless process (explanation of "repeatedly")<br>• the High Command deliberately, callously sent soldiers to their deaths (explanation of "sacrificed")<br>• the death toll was staggeringly high (explanation of "thousands of men")<br>• there was so little gain (explanation of "a few yards of churned earth")<br>• the conditions were especially squalid (explanation of "mud, blood")<br>• it seemed a pointless waste of life (explanation of "futility")<br><br>*Alternative view:*<br>• the leaders were not all cold-hearted bunglers (explanation of "callous incompetents")<br>• the front line soldiers were not all ill-fated conscripts (explanation of "hapless and unwilling")<br>• some of the battles were extremely well executed (explanation of "brilliantly planned and fought")<br>• we must remember that we did actually emerge victorious (explanation of "we did, after all, win the war")<br><br>or any other acceptable answer |
| 6. | Candidates should evaluate the effectiveness of the last two paragraphs as a thought-provoking and emotional conclusion to the passage as a whole.<br><br>Marks will depend on the quality of evaluative comment.<br><br>2 marks may be awarded for reference plus detailed/insightful comment; 1 mark for reference plus more basic comment; 0 marks for reference alone. For full marks there must be reference to ideas and language, but there is no requirement for a balanced treatment of these elements. There must also be some comment on the effectiveness of these lines as "a thought-provoking and emotional conclusion to the passage".<br><br>*Possible answers are shown in the "Additional Guidance" column.* | 4 | Possible answers include:<br><br>*Ideas:*<br>• the overall poignancy of referring to the very last survivor of the War, the last living link to this momentous event<br>• the opening sentence of the penultimate paragraph stresses our interest in first-hand testimony, "what it was like" — Harry Patch is able to provide this<br>• Harry Patch's experiences give us a view of war which is very different from that of military historians<br>• Harry's lack of knowledge about military strategies reminds us of the writer's earlier point about the difference between ordinary soldiers and High Command |

| Question | Expected Response | Max Mark | Additional Guidance |
|---|---|---|---|
| 6. | *(continued)* | | • the writer has already mentioned the terrible conditions endured by combatants — Harry Patch's memories of "filth ... discomfort ... exhaustion ..." remind us of these conditions<br>• the writer chooses to conclude using direct quotation to highlight the authentic voice of someone directly involved<br>• Harry Patch's comment on the "expendable" nature of ordinary soldiers harks back to the popular view that the war was "conducted by an incompetent High Command"/ war was nothing but "mud, blood and futility"<br>• Harry Patch's comment that the war was "a terrible waste" reinforces the writer's earlier point about the terrible losses sustained during the First World War<br><br>*Language:*<br>• italicization of "like" reminds reader of importance of eyewitness accounts and allows writer to introduce Harry Patch/links to "he knew what a battlefield was like."<br>• "diminished band" — links back to writer's earlier points about loss<br>• "wading around in the filth" — brings us back to the opening view of devastation on the battlefields of France and reminds us that Harry experienced this<br>• "lice-ridden ... discomfort ... exhaustion ... fear" — list of difficult conditions reinforces the writer's earlier point about the nature of warfare<br>• "blown to pieces" — quotation reminds us of devastating nature of First World War<br>• "millions of men" — enormous/indeterminate number is used to remind us of the immense scale of the conflict and the terrible human cost of the war<br>• "expendable" — reminds us of the sacrifices made by Harry and his comrades<br>• "waste ... terrible waste" — repetition is used to highlight the futility of casualties in the First World War<br><br>or any other acceptable answer |

**Passage 2**

| Question | | Expected Response | Max Mark | Additional Guidance |
|---|---|---|---|---|
| 7. | | Candidates should identify key areas of agreement in the two passages by referring in detail to both.<br><br>There may be some overlap among the areas of agreement.  Markers will have to judge the extent to which a candidate has covered two points or one.<br><br>Candidates can use bullet points in this final question, or write a number of linked statements.<br><br>Evidence from the passage may include quotations, but these should be supported by explanations.<br><br>*Approach to marking is shown in the "Additional Guidance" column.*<br><br>*Key areas of agreement are shown in the grid below.  Other answers are possible.* | 5 | The mark for this question should reflect the quality of response in two areas:<br><br>• identification of the key areas of agreement in attitude/ideas<br>• level of detail given in support<br><br>The following guidelines should be used:<br><br>**Five marks** — comprehensive identification of three or more key areas of agreement with full use of supporting evidence<br>**Four marks** — clear identification of three or more key areas of agreement with relevant use of supporting evidence<br>**Three marks** — identification of three or more key areas of agreement with supporting evidence<br>**Two marks** — identification of two key areas of agreement with supporting evidence<br>**One mark** — identification of one key area of agreement with supporting evidence<br>**Zero marks** — failure to identify any key area of agreement and/or total misunderstanding of task |

| | Area of Agreement | Peter Parker | William Boyd |
|---|---|---|---|
| 1. | it has had a profound effect on the British psyche | it still has strong hold on the national consciousness, more so than in any other country involved | a century later, WWI continues to loom large in the nation's consciousness and media |
| 2. | it was a conflict which changed attitudes to war | the scale of the slaughter changed the British mind-set — we tend to look back to a Golden Age before 1914 rather than to the future | casualties were so high that they changed attitudes — no army or nation would accept them today |
| 3. | the scale of casualties — never experienced before or since | British casualties were far greater than in any other war at any time in history | the unprecedented British and Empire casualty figures cannot be forgotten |
| 4. | the horrific nature of warfare — trenches and weapons of mass destruction | the scale of the slaughter meant Britain lost a "generation" — "the flower of British youth" | in the minds of British people it is the mass slaughter of the Western front which dominates |
| 5. | many people believe the conflict was futile (because of the leaders' incompetence) | conventional view that leadership was inept | the 500-mile line of trenches, the war of attrition; the outdated tactics in the face of modern weapons |
| 6. | the enduring impact of war literature, iconography, music, films | the war features in a large body of work — history textbooks, novels, poems, plays, films and musical compositions | in Britain our literature, films and documentaries have kept memories alive |
| 7. | the impact of combatants" personal narratives, memories, recollections | memoirs/memories such as those of Harry Patch inspire deep interest | his family connections with WW1 have ignited/sustained his interest |

**[END OF MODEL MARKING INSTRUCTIONS]**

# HIGHER FOR CfE ENGLISH
# MODEL PAPER 1

**PAPER 2 — CRITICAL READING**

**SECTION 1 — Scottish Text**

For all Scottish Texts, marking of the final question, for 10 marks, should be guided by the following generic instruction in conjunction with the specific advice given for the question on each Scottish Text:

**Candidates can answer in bullet points in this final question, or write a number of linked statements.**

**0 marks for reference/quotation alone.**

Up to 2 marks can be achieved for identifying elements of commonality as identified in the question.
A further 2 marks can be achieved for reference to the extract given.
6 additional marks can be awarded for discussion of similar references to at least one other part of the text (or other story or poem) by the writer.

In practise this means:

Identification of commonality (2) (e.**g**.: theme, characterisation, use of imagery, settng, or any other key element ...)

from the extract:

1 × relevant reference to technique/idea/feature (1)
1 × appropriate comment (1)
(maximum of 2 marks only for discussion of extract)

from at least one other text/part of the text:

as above (×3) for up to 6 marks
OR
more detailed comment ×2 for up to 6 marks.

Thus, the final 6 marks can be gained by a combination of 3, 2 and 1 marks depending on the level of depth/detail/insight. The aim would be to encourage quality of comment, rather than quantity of references.

**SCOTTISH TEXT (DRAMA)**

**Text 1 — Drama — *The Slab Boys* by John Byrne**

| Question | Expected Response | Max Mark | Additional Guidance |
|---|---|---|---|
| 1. | Candidates should identify an aspect of Lucille's character and support this with reference to the text.<br><br>1 mark for an aspect of character; 1 for reference and explanation.  0 marks for reference/quotation alone. | 2 | Possible answers include:<br><br>***Character:***<br>• brash, self-confident, menacing/bullying/ aggressive/threatening<br><br>***Reference to and explanation of:***<br>• "Burton's Corner ... quarter to ... okay?" — laying down the law<br>• "put some cream on that pimple ... I swear it's twice the size it was this morning" — less than diplomatic<br>• "look at him ... he's a skelf" — open insult<br>• "Aw, go to hell" — rudely dismissive<br>• "He eats smouts like you for his breakfast" — relishing possibility of Phil's suffering<br>• "If you're not there on the dot ..." — she's the boss<br>• "so be warned!" — threatening |

| Question | Expected Response | Max Mark | Additional Guidance |
|---|---|---|---|
| 2. | Candidates should explain how Hector's words and actions reveal his new-found confidence.<br><br>1 mark for each appropriate reference with comment. 0 marks for reference/quotation alone. | 4 | Possible answers include:<br>• speaks "Bravely" suggesting he is prepared to stand up for himself<br>• not interested in apology/explanation from Alan<br>• confidence shown in "Well, you guys …"<br>• not ashamed/shy to say getting a lift from the boss<br>• dismissive "keep that fitch" — he's moved on to better things<br>• keeps the money — doesn't give in to Spanky's demand<br>• has the confidence to come back in<br>• issues orders to Spanky — puts him in his place<br>• uses Spanky's surname to sound controlling, dominant<br>• cheeky to Phil about his laziness<br>• restores pen to rightful owner |
| 3. | Candidates should analyse Alan's speech to explain his attitude to Phil and Spanky.<br><br>1 mark for the general tone of superiority, talking down to them, sneering …<br><br>1 mark for each appropriate reference and comment. 0 marks for reference/quotation alone. | 4 | Possible answers include:<br>• sneers at Phil's self-pity ("doing a pretty good job of that on your own")<br>• mock geniality of "buy you a small beer perhaps"<br>• "Sparky" — pay-back for all the wrong names he's been called<br>• reference to stepping on fingers portrays him as Neanderthal<br>• "cabinet's an embarrassment" — repeating Curry's earlier words aligns Alan with bosses |
| 4. | Candidates should discuss the role of Lucille or Hector in the play as a whole and should refer to appropriate textual evidence to support their discussion.<br><br>0 marks for reference/quotation alone. | 10 | The generic marking guide, covering aspects of commonality, can be found on page 193.<br><br>In comments on the rest of the play, possible references include:<br><br>*Lucille*<br>• the complications over who is her date at the Staffie<br>• her sharp-tongued ability to stand up to Phil<br>• her being terrified by appearance of Hector at window<br><br>*Hector*<br>• the hapless butt of Phil and Spanky's mockery<br>• the farcical nature of his make-over<br>• his changed status by the end of the play — gets a desk<br><br>Many other references are possible. |

**Text 2 — Drama — *The Cheviot, the Stag and the Black, Black Oil* by John McGrath**

| Question | | Expected Response | Max Mark | Additional Guidance |
|---|---|---|---|---|
| 5. | (i) | Candidates should identify an aspect of Andy's character and support this with reference to the text.<br><br>1 mark for an aspect of character; 1 for reference and explanation. 0 marks for reference/quotation alone. | 2 | Possible answers include:<br><br>• spiv, on the make, self-seeking — the seemingly endless list of tacky money-making schemes he can reel off<br>• cynical, corrupt ("these are the best men money can buy")<br>• obsessed with modernity ("the thing of the future", "to cater for the younger set")<br>• no sense of traditional beauty, values ("formerly there was hee-haw but scenery")<br>• slovenly of speech: ("yous …wes've … and that … hee-haw") |
| | (ii) | Candidates should identify **four** specific details of Andy's plan and analyse how each one is made to sound comical.<br><br>1 mark for each acceptable explanation. 0 marks for simply identifying an aspect of the plan. | 4 | Possible answers include:<br><br>• "Crammem Inn": "Inn" suggests something welcoming, traditional, but this has idea of cramming in as many as possible<br>• "High Rise Motorcroft": "croft" suggests traditional, homely, but Motorcroft sounds industrial, lots of cars, etc.; also anything high rise would look hideously out of place<br>• "Frying Scotsman" is a pun on Flying Scotsman (an object of pride, beauty); changing to "Frying" is a dig at Scots' penchant for fried food<br>• "All Night Chipperama" — unhealthy food; "Chipperama" suggests on a lavish, garish scale; "all night" would be noisy, disruptive<br>• "Fingal's Caff" — pun on Fingal's Cave; "caff" (as opposed to "café") has overtones of cheap and nasty<br>• "seaweed-suppers-in-the-basket" — "supper" idea is joke from "fish supper" etc.; "in-the-basket" is a dig at the then current fashion for meals such as chicken-in-the-basket<br>• "draught Drambuie" — having a powerful liqueur on draught is ludicrous, suggests Andy either doesn't know what it is or sees no problem in drinking spirits by the pint<br>• "Grouse-a-go-go" — some kind of discotheque, coined with the "a-go-go" tag from current fashion with something/anything remotely Highland<br>• "a drive-in clachan on every hill-top" — "clachan" suggests something old, established, with a sense of community; "drive-in" is the ultimate in modern convenience |
| 6. | | Candidates should explain how Lord Vat is made to be a figure of fun to the audience.<br><br>1 mark for each acceptable reference and comment. 0 marks for reference/quotation alone. | 4 | Possible answers include:<br><br>• his very name: Vat of Glenlivet — meant to sound like a traditional Highland title, but in fact is a joke about whisky and overindulgence<br>• "these are my mountains" ridiculous claim, as if he glibly believes he owns the landscape (+ humorous hint of song of same title)<br>• "ancient Scotch family" — use of "Scotch" ironically shows he is anglified, out of touch<br>• "I represent the spirit of the Highlands" — vain, pompous (perhaps, in an ironic way, true)<br>• "hordes of common people" — shows his unquestioning contempt for "common people", comically condemned out of his own mouth<br>• "No amount of money could" — we rather suspect this won't be true |

| Question | | Expected Response | Max Mark | Additional Guidance |
|---|---|---|---|---|
| 6. | | *(continued)* | | • "the couthie way of life" — cringe-making reference to imaginary lifestyle<br>• confusion of Bantu and Highlander, Sherpa and stalker shows he doesn't even know which continent he's in<br>• approves of Highlanders only because they're good servants<br>• "ghillie-wallah" — again confusing Indian servant with Highland one<br>• unconscious double entendre in "doing up your flies"<br>• "wouldn't part [for] half a million" — yet quickly begins a bartering session which is soon settled<br>• "Cash"/"Done": comic conclusion, like a rehearsed routine |
| 7. | | Candidates should discuss McGrath's use of caricatures and/or stereotypes (there will be an element of overlap, which should be allowed) and should refer to appropriate textual evidence to support their discussion.<br><br>0 marks for reference/quotation alone. | 10 | The generic marking guide, covering aspects of commonality, can be found on page 193.<br>In comments on the rest of the play, possible references include:<br><br>• the compliant Minister who connives with the landlord<br>• Texas Jim with his square dance and love of his "home"<br>• the characters represented by the two Singers (Dr Green of Surrey, Herr Heinrich Harr, etc.)<br><br>Many other references are possible. |

## Text 3 — Drama — *Men Should Weep* by Ena Lamont Stewart

| Question | | Expected Response | Max Mark | Additional Guidance |
|---|---|---|---|---|
| 8. | | Candidates should explain what impressions are created of Jenny's character.<br><br>1 mark for each impression supported by reference. 0 marks for reference/quotation alone. | 3 | Possible answers include:<br><br>• her appearance (make-up, clothing, hair) suggests someone rather brazen, "loose", unconcerned with appearances<br>• "Leave me go" — suggests defiance, aggression, no fear of father<br>• "shakes herself free" — suggests independence, lack of respect for father<br>• "glaring at each other" — suggests she is strong-willed, not intimidated by her father<br>• "... in front o ma friend!" — suggests concern for status, lack of concern for father's point of view, perhaps taunting him with unknown "friend"<br>• " I'm grown up noo" — suggests she is assertive, tired of being treated like a child<br>• "An I tellt ye!" — suggests anger in her voice, standing up for herself<br>• "Nane o your damned interferin business" — suggests prepared to insult, defy her father, use provocative language |

| Question | Expected Response | Max Mark | Additional Guidance |
|---|---|---|---|
| **9.** | Candidates should explain how the playwright creates a dramatic conflict between John and Jenny.<br><br>1 mark for each relevant point supported by reference.  0 marks for reference/quotation alone. | 4 | Possible answers include:<br><br>• the fact that all the speeches in these lines are short and aggressive, frequently indicated by use of exclamation marks<br>• John grabs her — physical hostility<br>• the aggression in "Where wis ye?  Answer me!" — harsh question and command<br>• Jenny's sullen, minimal response "At the pickshers."<br>• John's relentless demand for more information (to begin with he wanted to know where she was, now it's where she was after that)<br>• her behaviour when he lets her go — "flops" suggesting lack of respect; "glaring sullenly" showing her antagonism; "rubbing her shoulder" to remind John (and the audience) of his manhandling of her<br>• John, with both questions answered, presses on with dismissive comment about her friend — "yon" sounds contemptuous<br>• Jenny's provocative response "That's a peety. I dae."<br>• John resorts to insulting language: "Ye impudent little bitch"<br>• the open threat of more violence: "Tak ma belt tae ye."<br>• Jenny's dismissive, sneering, challenging, defiant "Jist you try it!" |
| **10.** | Candidates should explain how John's anger is conveyed to the audience.<br><br>1 mark for each reference and comment.  0 marks for reference/quotation alone. | 3 | Possible answers include:<br><br>• "paint smeared" — he belittles her appearance; "paint" instead of "make-up", "smeared" suggesting something messy, unattractive<br>• "a ower yer face" — as if she has applied it randomly, made herself look hideous<br>• "Look at yersel!" — antagonistic exclamation, implying she looks a mess<br>• "drags ... propels ... holding ... scrubs" — violent, aggressive actions suggesting his temper<br>• "There!" — a sort of triumphant declaration of his victory<br>• "the colour God meant it tae be" — self-righteous, pompous moralising |
| **11.** | Candidates should discuss the role of Jenny in the play and should refer to appropriate textual evidence to support their discussion.<br><br>0 marks for reference/quotation alone. | 10 | The generic marking guide, covering aspects of commonality, can be found on page 193.<br><br>In comments on the rest of the play, possible references include:<br>• Jenny as rebel, independent spirit<br>• prepared to do anything to escape her family and its poverty<br>• the showdown with her father at the end<br><br>Many other references are possible. |

**Text 1 — Prose — *The Crater* by Iain Crichton Smith**

| Question | Expected Response | Max Mark | Additional Guidance |
|---|---|---|---|
| 12. | Candidates should analyse how the writer uses sound to intensify the atmosphere.<br><br>2 marks for an insightful comment and reference. 1 mark for a basic comment and reference. 0 marks for reference/quotation alone. | 4 | Possible answers include:<br><br>• "screamed" suggests uncontrolled, panicky, high-pitched, in pain<br>• "bubbling" suggests feeble, dislocated, connotations of something vaguely supernatural, unworldly<br>• "splashing" suggests frantic activity<br>• "breathing, frantic breathing" suggests someone struggling to stay alive<br>• "splashings came closer" suggests something menacing getting nearer<br>• "voice was like an animal's" suggests inhuman, lack of control<br>• "a mixture of curses and prayers" a surreal, confused combination of anger and invocation |
| 13. | Candidates should explain how the writer creates a nightmarish atmosphere.<br><br>2 marks for an insightful comment and reference. 1 mark for a basic comment and reference. 0 marks for reference/quotation alone. | 4 | Possible answers include:<br><br>• "as if there was a great fish at the end of a line" suggests that he's struggling with some mythical creature<br>• "He felt it moving." — short sentence creates feeling of shock, threat<br>• "moon shone suddenly out" — abrupt, dramatic change in light<br>• "in that moment he saw it" — sudden revelation; use of unspecific "it" reinforces dreamlike effect<br>• "covered with greenish slime" — sickening, disgusting<br>• "an obscene mermaid" — something usually considered attractive, glamorous is distorted<br>• "two eyes, white in the green face" — disembodied, unsettling<br>• "the mouth, gritted, tried not to let the blood through" — suggests the effort, the pain, the suffering<br>• "monster of the deep" — frightening, threatening, aggressive being from another world<br>• "he said to the monster below" — idea of dialogue with a "monster" is disturbing<br>• "emerging from the deep" — suggestion of approaching threat, some sort of prehistoric monster rising from a swamp<br>• "all green, all mottled, like a disease" — horrific description of a slimy, blotchy creature, which is likened to a sickness/virus<br>• "stench" — emphasises the overwhelming unpleasantness and horror of the scene<br>• "It hung there …" — creates picture of something supernatural, defying gravity |
| 14. | Candidates should discuss what the sentence "And over it poured the merciless moonlight." contributes to the conclusion of the extract.<br><br>2 marks for an insightful comment and reference. 1 mark for a basic comment and reference. 0 marks for reference/quotation alone. | 2 | Possible answers include:<br><br>• it creates sense of the cruelty of nature, the moon as observer of the macabre proceedings below<br>• it is as if, while Robert frantically (and heroically) seeks to rescue his comrade, a greater power knows the futility of it<br>• it prepares the reader for the shattering of Robert's elation at his "rescue" |

| Question | Expected Response | Max Mark | Additional Guidance |
|---|---|---|---|
| **15.** | Candidates should discuss how Crichton Smith creates tension in *The Crater* and at least one other story and should refer to appropriate textual evidence to support their discussion. <br><br> 0 marks for reference/quotation alone. | 10 | The generic marking guide, covering aspects of commonality, can be found on page 193. <br><br> In comments on other stories, possible references include: <br> • the elder's approach in *The Telegram* <br> • the ending of *Mother and Son* <br> • the dying man in *The Crater* <br> Many other references are possible. |

### Text 2 – Prose – *The Bright Spade* by George Mackay Brown

| Question | Expected Response | Max Mark | Additional Guidance |
|---|---|---|---|
| **16.** | Candidates should identify the narrator's tone and explain how it is created. <br><br> 1 mark for an appropriate identification of tone + 2 marks for a single insightful explanation; 1 mark for a basic explanation. 0 marks for reference/quotation alone. | 3 | Possible answers include: <br><br> Tone: unemotional, detached, purely factual <br><br> References: <br> • preponderance of simple, flat, sentences, no elaboration <br> • as if simple reportage, statement of fact <br> • absence of comment, reflection – even at a detail as gruesome as the dog gnawing the corpse or a detail as bizarre as Jacob's acceptance of the fiddle <br> • even the imagery ("shell ... chrysalis") sounds more factual than evocative |
| **17.** | Candidates should explain what impressions the narrator creates of Harald Ness as a person. <br><br> 1 mark for each reference and comment. 0 marks for reference/quotation alone. | 2 | Possible answers include: <br><br> • seems to be looked up to, respected – speaks uninterrupted, his plan is accepted without demur <br> • unemotional, absence of self-pity when he describes what he has eaten <br> • realistic, practical, pragmatic plan <br> • includes himself in risky venture – brave, prepared to accept risks on behalf of others, sacrifice for the community |
| **18.** | Candidates should discuss the effect achieved by naming each one of the men who set off on the journey. <br><br> 2 marks for a single insightful comment. 1 mark for a basic point. 0 marks for reference/quotation alone. | 2 | Possible answers include: <br><br> • it humanises them, hence adds to the tragedy of their death <br> • the length of the list emphasises the extent of the loss <br> • it develops the idea that they were all known to everyone, sense of a small, close-knit community <br> • it sustains the "chronicle" style, recording of basic facts (nothing said about their personalities, for instance) |
| **19.** | Candidates should explain what is revealed about Jacob as a person. <br><br> 2 marks for a single insightful comment. 1 mark for a basic point. 0 marks for reference/quotation alone. | 3 | Possible answers include: <br><br> • aware that he is benefitting from others' suffering ("I have done better this winter than anyone") <br> • makes (minor) concession by not accepting payment for the seven men ... <br> • ... but reverts to usual collection of something/anything ("set of Nantucket harpoons") <br> • perhaps some sense of guilt ("God grant ...") ... <br> • ... but more likely a simple acceptance <br> • deeply rooted in cycle of the seasons, knows that winter and death will come round again <br> • accepts his role in the community with a sense of resignation |

| Question | Expected Response | Max Mark | Additional Guidance |
|---|---|---|---|
| 20. | Candidates should discuss George Mackay Brown's use of symbolism in *The Bright Spade* and at least one other story and should refer to appropriate textual evidence to support their discussion. <br><br> 0 marks for reference/quotation alone. | 10 | The generic marking guide, covering aspects of commonality, can be found on page 193. <br><br> In comments on other stories, possible references include: <br><br> • the money in *The Whaler's Return* <br> • the wireless in *The Wireless Set* <br> • the wreck of the Danish ship in *The Eye of the Hurricane* <br><br> Many other references are possible. |

Text 3 — Prose — *The Trick is to Keep Breathing* by Janice Galloway

| Question | Expected Response | Max Mark | Additional Guidance |
|---|---|---|---|
| 21. | Candidates should explain how Tony is portrayed as an unpleasant character. <br><br> 2 marks for a single insightful comment and reference. 1 mark for a basic point and reference. 0 marks for reference/quotation alone. | 4 | Possible answers include: <br><br> • his arrival is announced by "gravel and the crunch of brakes" suggesting something noisy, grating, impatient; he is de-personalised <br> • "stare harder" suggests the thought of his arrival causes her to tense up <br> • his approach is described menacingly in terms of feet getting closer <br> • "thudding" is a harsh, pounding sound, intimidating <br> • his flaunting of the bottle suggests someone rather brash, showy <br> • the "clumsy orchid" description associates him with a distortion of beauty <br> • "Always take it for granted I'm going to win" reeks of over-confidence (and possible double entendre) <br> • the "lips … beard … teeth" references suggest something vaguely animal-like, rather unsettling <br> • the clichéd compliments ("a real picture") are repeated ad nauseam |
| 22. | Candidates should explain how the writer creates an uneasy atmosphere in the car. <br><br> 2 marks for a single insightful comment and reference. 1 mark for a basic point and reference. 0 marks for reference/quotation alone. | 2 | Possible answers include: <br><br> • the fact that it is an entirely one-sided conversation; Joy says nothing <br> • "It plays Country and Western Music" — surreal idea of car as animate object <br> • "The seat creaks with his weight" suggests he is overweight, oppressive <br> • Tony's remarks are laden with innuendo, cheap come-ons ("Nearly as good as you", "Expect a treat tonight") <br> • "He pats my leg" suggests making unwelcome advances <br> • his overtly suggestive pausing at "it's hard …" waiting for a response <br> • his leering way of looking at her, which is repeated after every sentence |

| Question | Expected Response | Max Mark | Additional Guidance |
|---|---|---|---|
| 23. | Candidates should analyse how aspects of Tony's character are revealed.<br><br>2 marks for a single insightful comment and reference. 1 mark for a basic point and reference. 0 marks for reference/quotation alone. | 4 | Possible answers include:<br>• short, clipped sentences suggest not much of a conversationalist, sees everything in simple terms<br>• all one-way — suggests he's not interested in what Joy might have to say, single-mindedly pursuing his simple goal of seducing her<br>• references to her weight, to her illness suggest high level of insensitivity<br>• references to her appearance and potential for being a "stunner" reveal him as sexist, old-fashioned<br>• "Just relax and listen to the music" sounds deeply insincere<br>• "This one's my favourite" suggests he can't avoid self-centredness<br>• "You don't mind If I run it again" is a statement rather than a question, he's going to do it regardless of any opinion Joy might have<br>• "Hiding your best assets" — a lewd comment, which he pretends is a mistake<br>• perhaps genuine shock, concern when he asks about her hands |
| 24. | Candidates should discuss Joy's relationships with men and should refer to appropriate textual evidence to support their discussion<br><br>0 marks for reference/quotation alone. | 10 | The generic marking guide, covering aspects of commonality, can be found on page 193.<br><br>In comments on the rest of the novel, possible references include:<br>• her affair with Michael<br>• her teenage romance with Paul<br>• her relationship with David<br><br>Many other references are possible. |

Text 4 — Prose — *Sunset Song* by Lewis Grassic Gibbon

| Question | Expected Response | Max Mark | Additional Guidance |
|---|---|---|---|
| 25. | Candidates should explain how the writer conveys the strength of Rob's feelings about language.<br><br>2 marks for an insightful comment and reference. 1 mark for a basic comment and reference. 0 marks for reference/quotation alone. | 4 | Possible answers include:<br>• "shame"/ "shamed" suggests that non-users of Scots/Scotch are a source of dishonour, humiliation<br>• "the split-tongued sourocks!" suggests a contemptuous attitude, accusation of hypocrisy<br>• "Every damned little narrow dowped rat" is an all-inclusive condemnation of English-speakers ("Every"); contemptible ("damned"); insubstantial, lacking substance ("little, narrow dowped"); loathsome, to be looked down on ("rat")<br>• "put on the English" suggests use of English forced, affected, pretentious<br>• "thin bit scraichs" suggests he thinks of English as weak, anaemic, shrill, strident<br>• *You can tell me, man ...*" Rob's tone is quite belligerent, challenging Gordon to dare to disagree<br>• the list of words which Rob claims have no English equivalent suggests how extensive he thinks such a category is |

| Question | Expected Response | Max Mark | Additional Guidance |
|---|---|---|---|
| 26. | Candidates should explain how the writer conveys the harshness of life working the land.<br><br>1 mark for each appropriate reference + comment. 0 marks for reference/quotation alone. | 2 | Possible answers include:<br><br>• repetition ("coarse, coarse", "work, work, work, and chave, chave, chave") stresses the amount of effort required, echoes the repetitive nature of the work<br>• "from the blink of day till the fall of night" conveys the extreme length of the working day<br>• "soss and sotter" the alliteration/onomatopoeia emphasises the filth, unpleasantness of the work |
| 27. | Candidates should explain how the writer's use of language conveys the conflicting views about "scientific" farming methods.<br><br>For full marks there should be reference to and comment on at least two features of language. 2 marks for an insightful comment and reference. 1 mark for a basic comment and reference. 0 marks for reference/quotation alone. | 4 | Possible answers include:<br><br>• there are four different (reported) speakers involved: Cuddieston, Banker's son, Chae, Long Rob; shows range of views being put forward<br>• sentence openers ("Syne ... So ... But ... And") indicate different points of view being proposed<br>• "childe" suggests contempt for banker's son, suggests naïve, inexperienced<br>• "clutter of machines" presents machinery as untidy, chaotic, not effective<br>• "the best friend of man" suggests human quality, of extreme usefulness<br><br>• Chae's forceful tone: *"Damn't, no ..."*<br>• Rob's mocking, humorous tone: "damned machine that would muck you a pigsty even though they all turned socialist to-morrow" |
| 28. | Candidates should discuss to what extent *Sunset Song* is a celebration of a traditional way of life or an illustration of the inevitability of change and should refer to appropriate textual evidence to support their discussion.<br><br>0 marks for reference/quotation alone. | 10 | The generic marking guide, covering aspects of commonality, can be found on page 193.<br><br>In comments on the rest of the novel, possible references include:<br><br>• the closeness of the community, e.g. the fire at Peesie's Knapp, the wedding<br>• Chris's decision to stay on the farm<br>• the impact of the War<br>• technological developments in farming<br><br>Many other references are possible. |

## Text 5 — Prose — *The Cone-Gatherers* by Robin Jenkins

| Question | Expected Response | Max Mark | Additional Guidance |
|---|---|---|---|
| 29. | Candidates should analyse how word choice conveys Duror's loathing for Calum.<br><br>2 marks for an insightful comment and reference. 1 mark for a basic comment and reference. 0 marks for reference/quotation alone. | 2 | Possible answers include:<br><br>• "feebleminded" suggests he sees him as stupid, sub-normal<br>• "hunchback" a very belittling, offensive word, suggests he focuses on the deformity<br>• "grovelling" distorts Calum's attempts at mercy into something demeaning, as if he's begging, bowing and scraping<br>• "obscene" suggests any sound from Calum would be seen as something disgusting, lascivious |

| Question | Expected Response | Max Mark | Additional Guidance |
|---|---|---|---|
| 30. | Candidates should explain how the writer makes the reader aware of Duror's disturbed state of mind.<br><br>2 marks for an insightful comment and reference.<br>1 mark for a basic comment and reference.<br>0 marks for reference/quotation alone. | 4 | Possible answers include:<br><br>• that he had "waited over an hour" just to see them suggests it is an obsession<br>• "purgatory of humiliation" is an exaggerated way to describe his feelings, suggests how deeply affected he is<br>• "as if ... forced to wait upon them as upon his masters" — a reversal of the norm, suggests how distorted his view is<br>• his apparent desire to see the cone-gatherers come to harm, a sense of relish in "come crashing down" and "lie dead on the ground"<br>• the extended metaphor in which he imagines himself standing on a sea floor and sees features around him as if they were underwater — bizarre, dreamlike, surreal:<br> • "standing on the floor of a fantastic sea" — acknowledges that it's dreamlike, fanciful<br> • "with an owl and a herd of roe-deer flitting by quiet as fish" — terrestrial creatures transformed in his mind into aquatic ones<br> • "ferns and bronzen bracken ... gleamed like seaweed" — terrestrial flora transformed into aquatic, ironically described in terms of great beauty<br> • "spruce trees ... like submarine monsters" — distorted view of trees as dangerous/threatening underwater beasts |
| 31. | Candidates should analyse how the imagery gives insight into Duror's feelings.<br><br>2 marks for an insightful comment and reference.<br>1 mark for a basic comment and reference. 0 marks for reference/quotation alone. | 4 | Possible answers include:<br><br>• "the overspreading tree of revulsion in him" sees, recognises the hatred within him as organic, taking him over totally<br>• "his stronghold and sanctuary" gives the idea of him being at war, needing to defend himself, being isolated<br>• "fortify his sanity and hope" shows awareness that he is mentally unstable and wishes to fight against this<br>• "invaded and defiled" depicts the cone-gatherers as an enemy, a threat, corrupting, dirty<br>• "its cleansing and reviving virtues" depicts the wood as a place of healing, suggests he views nature as more powerful perhaps than human agency<br>• "like the whining prostrations of a heathen in front of an idol" sees Calum as something alien, primitive, submissive, lacking dignity, entirely different<br>• "diabolical joke" as if dreamed up by the devil, intended to cause him (Duror) suffering; "joke" because of the incongruity of the ugly features and the beautiful face |
| 32. | Candidates should discuss the importance of the conflict between Duror and Calum and should refer to appropriate textual evidence to support their discussion.<br><br>0 marks for reference/quotation alone. | 10 | The generic marking guide, covering aspects of commonality, can be found on page 193.<br><br>In comments on the rest of the novel, possible references include:<br><br>• Duror's lying about Calum exposing himself<br>• the deer drive<br>• the ending<br><br>Many other references are possible. |

**Text 1 — Poetry —** *To a Mouse* **by Robert Burns**

| Question | Expected Response | Max Mark | Additional Guidance |
|---|---|---|---|
| **33.** | Candidates should analyse the use of poetic technique to create sympathy for the mouse's situation.<br><br>1 mark for reference and comment. 0 marks for reference/quotation alone. | 2 | Possible answers include:<br><br>• word choice of "wee-bit housie" suggests something modest, basic, unelaborate<br>• the minor sentence/exclamation suggests the poet feels shocked at the loss<br>• word choice of "silly" suggests something very simple, basic<br>• word choice of "strewin" suggests the relentless destruction caused by the wind<br>• alliteration of "naethin, now" slightly emphasises the mouse's plight<br>• word choice of "bleak December" suggests the depressing, austere situation at the height of winter<br>• word choice of "Baith snell an' keen!" suggests the unpleasantness and suffering the mouse will face |
| **34.** | Candidates should identify two themes of the poem and explain how each is clarified by the poet's technique.<br><br>2 marks for a clear statement of theme, supported by reference and comment. 1 mark for a less clear statement or for weak support. 0 marks for reference/quotation alone. | 4 | Possible answers include:<br><br>• mouse's foresight, preparation, supported by:<br>  • "thou saw ... thou thought" suggesting planning<br>  • contrast of "bare an' waste" and "cozie" to suggest what mouse was trying to guard against<br>  • "dwell" suggests the safety, protection the mouse had hoped for<br>  • "cost thee mony a weary nibble" — emphasises the effort that has been expended on the nest<br>• man's destruction of his plans, supported by:<br>  • "crash!" — onomatopoeic representation of the sudden destruction<br>  • "thou's turn'd out" — idea of him being rejected<br>  • "cruel coulter" — alliteration emphasises the harshness of the plough<br>  • "cranreuch cauld" — alliteration emphasises the harshness of the weather he will face as a result of man's interference |

| Question | Expected Response | Max Mark | Additional Guidance |
|---|---|---|---|
| **35.** | Candidates should discuss the mood created in the last two verses. They should show understanding of the key ideas and analyse the use of poetic technique to create mood. One or more than one mood could be discussed.<br><br>For full marks there should be clear understanding of the key ideas and thoughtful analysis of how the mood is created.<br><br>Reference and a basic comment will be worth 1 mark. Reference and an insightful comment may be worth 2 marks. 0 marks for reference/quotation alone. | 4 | Possible answers include:<br>Mood(s):<br>• contemplative, wistful, melancholy, regretful, sympathetic, pessimistic, maudlin<br>References:<br>• "But Mousie" — the "but" suggests moving on from the bleak picture painted in preceding lines<br>• "thou art no thy lane" — offers some sympathy, fellow feeling that others suffer as well<br>• "the best-laid schemes" — no matter how well planned things are<br>• "o' mice an' men" — links man and beast, shows this happens to all<br>• "aft" — it is a frequent occurrence<br>• "grief an' pain" — very pessimistic picture of suffering<br>• "For promis'd joy!" — reminds us of the hopes, the expectations we once had<br>• "Still" — concedes that mouse has one advantage<br>• "thou art blest compar'd wi' me" — self-pity?<br>• "But och!" — tone of frustration perhaps<br>• "I guess an' fear!" finishes on an enigmatic note, but pessimism seems to dominate |
| **36.** | Candidates should discuss Burns' use of verse form in To a Mouse and at least one other poem and should refer to appropriate textual evidence to support their discussion.<br><br>0 marks for reference/quotation alone. | 10 | The generic marking guide, covering aspects of commonality, can be found on page 193.<br><br>In comments on other poems, possible references include:<br><br>• aspects of the Standard Habbie (*Holy Willie's Prayer*, *Address to the Deil*, *A Poet's Welcome* … )<br>• song and chorus in *A Man's A Man*<br>• rhyming couplet in *Tam o' Shanter*<br><br>Many other references are possible. |

## Text 2 — Poetry — *Mrs Midas* by Carol Ann Duffy

| Question | Expected Response | Max Mark | Additional Guidance |
|---|---|---|---|
| **37.** | Candidates should analyse the use of poetic techniques to create an ordinary, everyday atmosphere.<br><br>2 marks for an insightful comment and reference. 1 mark for a basic comment and reference. 0 marks for reference/quotation alone. | 4 | Possible answers include:<br><br>• the use of simple statement "It was late September", as if recounting a simple recollection<br>• the use of informal contraction "I'd just poured" suggests relaxed tone<br>• the absence of "and" between "wine and "begun" is informal, sounds comfortable<br>• everyday detail "a glass of wine" suggests relaxation, contentment<br>• word choice of "unwind" suggests calmness, composure<br>• imagery/personification "The kitchen/filled with the smell of itself" suggests warmth, pleasant smells, promise of good food<br>• "steamy breath/gently blanching the windows" — personification of kitchen as something alive, warm, tender<br>• conversational tone of "So I opened one" as if continuing a simple story |

| Question | Expected Response | Max Mark | Additional Guidance |
|---|---|---|---|
| 37. | *(continued)* | | • "wiped the other's glass like a brow" — affectionate, caring, unthreatening gesture<br>• simple description of what husband is doing "standing under a pear tree …"<br>• "snapping a twig" suggests a small, unthreatening action |
| 38. | Candidates should analyse the use of poetic techniques to convey the confusion beginning to arise in the speaker's mind.<br><br>2 marks for an insightful comment and reference. 1 mark for a basic comment and reference. 0 marks for reference/quotation alone. | 2 | Possible answers include:<br><br>• tone of "Now the garden was long and the visibility poor" — as if offering an excuse for possibly not seeing correctly<br>• the imagery of "the dark of the ground seems to drink the light of the sky" suggests something mysterious, dark, deprived of light, uncertain<br>• the delayed assertion "but that twig in his hand was gold" as if unwilling to state what she is seeing<br>• the parenthetical "- we grew Fondante d'Automne -" seems an unnecessary detail as if trying to hold onto reality by including it<br>• the minor sentence "On" conveys a sense of stupefaction, unable to say anything more than a single syllable<br>• question "Is he putting fairy lights in the tree?" suggests doubt, almost an attempt to rationalise |
| 39. | Candidates should explain how the poet conveys the strangeness of the husband's behaviour in these two stanzas.<br><br>2 marks for an insightful comment and reference. 1 mark for a basic comment and reference. 0 marks for reference/quotation alone. | 4 | Possible answers include:<br><br>• the juxtaposition of the ordinary ("He came into the house") with the extraordinary ("The doorknobs gleamed")<br>• the way his behaviour causes her mind to jump to a schoolroom memory<br>• the simile "like a king on a burnished throne" presents him as a regal figure amid great splendour<br>• "strange, wild, vain" — use of three monosyllables to convey a wide range of emotions<br>• "He started to laugh" suggests an almost irrational response to the situation<br>• "spitting out the teeth of the rich" — a grotesque image combining pain/discomfort with reference to wealth<br>• structure of "toyed with his spoon, then mine, then with the knives, the forks" suggests random actions, as if he is confused<br>• "glass, goblet, golden chalice" shows the progression from simple drinking vessel to exotic "chalice"; emphasised by the alliteration<br>• structure of "picked up the glass, goblet, golden chalice, drank" — suggests staccato movement, unusual behaviour |
| 40. | Candidates should discuss how Duffy creates and develops unusual or surprising ideas and/or situations and should refer to appropriate textual evidence to support their discussion.<br><br>0 marks for reference/quotation alone. | 10 | The generic marking guide, covering aspects of commonality, can be found on page 193.<br><br>In comments on other poems, possible references include:<br><br>• the rejection of the conventional in *Valentine*<br>• the prose/poetry types of love in *Anne Hathaway*<br>• the outspoken ideas/language of Miss Havisham<br><br>Many other references are possible. |

Text 3 — Poetry — *Last Supper* by Liz Lochhead

| Question | Expected Response | Max Mark | Additional Guidance |
|---|---|---|---|
| **41.** | Candidates should explain how the poet develops the metaphor of "this feast".<br><br>1 mark for each relevant reference and comment. 0 marks for reference/quotation alone. | 2 | Possible answers include:<br>• "leftover hash" — the idea of making something from the remaining scraps (of the relationship)<br>• "soup … render from the bones" — the idea of squeezing the last possible scrap of nutrition, also the idea of totally destroying the relationship, of grinding it to dust<br>• "something substantial … tasty" — idea of being able to provide an ample meal (i.e. worthwhile topic of conversation about the relationship) |
| **42.** | Candidates should analyse the use of sound to create a negative impression of "The Girls".<br><br>2 marks for an insightful comment and reference. 1 mark for a basic comment and reference. 0 marks for reference/quotation alone. | 4 | Possible answers include:<br>• alliteration in "cackling around the cauldron" suggests harsh, aggressive sound of their (witchlike) voices<br>• onomatopoeic effect from "spitting" — suggestion of contempt, disgust<br>• alliteration/series of plosive consonants in "spitting out the gristlier bits/of his giblets" suggests harshness, contempt, element of comedy also<br>• echoic nature of "bits of his giblets" — comic element, imitating their relish at the dismemberment<br>• alliteration in "gnawing on the knucklebone" — emphasised "n" almost imitates gnawing sound<br>• the rhythmical similarity of "intricate irony" echoes/mocks the faux-sophisticated conversation<br>• alliteration in "getting grave … -gout" suggests harsh, gritty nature of their voices |
| **43.** | Candidates should analyse the use of poetic techniques to describe the people at the Supper.<br><br>2 marks for an insightful comment and reference. 1 mark for a basic comment and reference. 0 marks for reference/quotation alone. | 4 | Possible answers include:<br>• irony/double meaning in "That's rich!" suggests self-consciously clever or unaware of what they're saying<br>• word choice of "splutter" suggests inelegant, lacking poise<br>• imagery of "munching the lies" suggests the enjoyment with which they accept/digest untruths about the man<br>• simile of "fat and sizzling as sausages" describes the "lies" as unhealthy but appealing<br>• word choice of "sink back" suggests a smug self-satisfaction<br>• metaphor "gorged on truth" suggests bloated, self-satisfied; also ironic since they've been consuming lies<br>• paradox in "savage integrity" suggests their hypocrisy<br>• word choice of "sleek" suggests glossy, superficial, slightly smug<br>• simile "preening/like corbies" suggests they are predatory |
| **44.** | Candidates should discuss, by referring to this poem and at least one other by Liz Lochhead, her ability to describe characters in a precise way and should refer to appropriate textual evidence to support their discussion.<br><br>0 marks for reference/quotation alone. | 10 | The generic marking guide, covering aspects of commonality, can be found on page 193.<br><br>In comments on other poems, possible references include:<br>• the mother in *View of Scotland/Love Poem*<br>• the grandmother (and other family members) in *For My Grandmother Knitting*<br>• the mother in *My Rival's House*<br><br>Many other references are possible. |

Text 4 — Poetry — *Assisi* by Norman MacCaig

| Question | Expected Response | Max Mark | Additional Guidance |
|---|---|---|---|
| 45. | Candidates should analyse how the use of sound enhances the description of the dwarf.<br><br>2 marks for an insightful comment and reference. 1 mark for a basic comment and reference. 0 marks for reference/quotation alone. | 2 | Possible answers include:<br><br>• sibilance in "sat, slumped" suggests lethargy, discomfort<br>• long vowel sounds in "sat, slumped" suggest heaviness, tiredness<br>• onomatopoeic effect in "slumped" to suggest heaviness, defeat, echoes of "lump", "dumped"<br>• alliteration in "tiny twisted" draws attention to the unpleasantness, ugliness<br>• line break between "which" and "sawdust" creates a small dramatic pause before the horrors of the description |
| 46. | Candidates should explain how the poet creates an ironic tone.<br><br>2 marks for an insightful comment and reference. 1 mark for a basic comment and reference. 0 marks for reference/quotation alone. | 2 | Possible answers include:<br><br>• juxtaposition of grand church ("three tiers") with St Francis' reputation ("brother/of the poor") and/or his simple lifestyle ("talker with birds")<br>• sardonic observation that dwarf has an "advantage" over St Francis, but only that he is "not dead yet" |
| 47. | Candidates should discuss what the speaker's statement suggests about his feelings at that moment.<br><br>2 marks for an insightful comment (reference is likely to be implicit). 1 mark for a basic comment. 0 marks for reference/quotation alone. | 2 | Possible answers include:<br><br>• presenting himself as the detached observer<br>• mock admiration for the "cleverness"<br>• hint of superiority (especially if read with emphasis on "I")<br>• a line of thought could be developed around the idea of a poet as user of words contemplating visual art communicating with the illiterate |
| 48. | Candidates should explain what the poet means by describing the dwarf as a "ruined temple".<br><br>For full marks, candidates should develop the implications of both words.<br><br>2 marks for an insightful comment and reference. 1 mark for a basic comment and reference. 0 marks for reference/quotation alone.<br><br>General statements comparing the dwarf to the church as described earlier in the poem will be worth 2 marks at most. | 4 | Possible answers include:<br><br>• "ruined" in the sense that he is physically deformed, a distortion of a "normal" human being:<br>  • "eyes wept pus" — not shedding tears in conventional way, but leaking infected fluid<br>  • ugly sound of word "pus"<br>  • heavy sound of three stressed syllables<br>  • "back ... higher/than his head" — distortion of the normal<br>• a "temple" in the sense of something with deep religious significance, often of immense beauty:<br>  • despite all the unpleasant surface appearances, the dwarf is polite "Grazie")<br>  • his voice is compared with that of a child (innocent) speaking to its mother (Madonna and child idea)<br>  • compared with a bird (nature, innocence) speaking to St Francis (icon of compassion, humility) |
| 49. | Candidates should discuss MacCaig's use of wry humour in *Assisi* and at least one other poem and should refer to appropriate textual evidence to support their discussion.<br><br>0 marks for reference/quotation alone. | 10 | The generic marking guide, covering aspects of commonality, can be found on page 193.<br><br>In comments on other poems, possible references include:<br><br>• the description of the drip in *Visiting Hour*<br>• the description of the shark in *Basking Shark*<br>• some of the imagery in *Aunt Julia*<br><br>Many other references are possible. |

**Text 5 — Poetry — *Hallaig* by Sorley MacLean**

| Question | | Expected Response | Max Mark | Additional Guidance |
|---|---|---|---|---|
| **50.** | (i) | Candidates should identify two central concerns of the poem. | 2 | Possible answers include: <br><br>• the influence of past <br>• landscape of Hallaig/Raasay <br>• poet's sense of connection to the history of the community <br>• celebration of tradition and heritage |
| | (ii) | Candidates should analyse how the poet's use of symbolism develops either or both of the concerns identified in 50(i). <br><br>2 marks for an insightful comment and reference. <br>1 mark for a basic comment and reference. <br>0 marks for reference/quotation alone. | 4 | Possible answers include: <br><br>• "their daughters and their sons are a wood" — connects generations to natural growth, organic development, continuity <br>• dislike/criticism of non-native species ("pine") seen as "proud", "crowing" <br>• "birch wood" as the natural, preferred species — poet is prepared to wait for it, sees it as something that will eventually provide comfort ("shade" for the whole area) |
| **51.** | | Candidates should explain how the poet creates a fusion of past and present. <br><br>2 marks for an insightful comment and reference. <br>1 mark for a basic comment and reference. <br>0 marks for reference/quotation alone. | 4 | Possible answers include: <br><br>• "Sabbath of the dead" — suggests an ongoing, present day celebration of the dead <br>• "people are frequenting" — suggests current presence, movement, community; use of present tense makes it appear to be happening now <br>• "every single generation gone" — emphasises extent of past destruction <br>• "They are still in Hallaig" — unambiguous assertion of presence <br>• "MacLeans and MacLeods" — use of local names in the plural suggests continuity, many generations <br>• "all who were there" — past tense draws attention to what is gone <br>• "the dead have been seen alive" — direct reference to the past in the present; clear contrast of "dead" and "alive" <br>• absence of verb in final stanza creates ambiguity <br>• "men lying" suggests death <br>• "girls a wood of birches" suggests no longer alive as people, but alive in nature <br>• "straight their backs" suggests alive, proud <br>• "bent their heads" suggests mourning |
| **52.** | | Candidates should discuss how MacLean explores ideas of tradition and heritage in *Hallaig* and at least one other poem and should refer to appropriate textual evidence to support their discussion. <br><br>0 marks for reference/quotation alone. | 10 | The generic marking guide, covering aspects of commonality, can be found on page 193. <br><br>In comments on other poems, possible references include: <br><br>• various descriptions in *Screapadal*, e.g. the effects of the Clearances, and of the warships <br>• the love of landscape in *Shores* <br>• the references to bygone heroes and warriors in *Heroes* <br><br>Many other references are possible. |

**Text 6 — Poetry — The Thread by Don Paterson**

| Question | Expected Response | Max Mark | Additional Guidance |
|---|---|---|---|
| 53. | Candidates should analyse the poet's use of imagery to describe his feelings about Jamie at the time of his birth.<br><br>2 marks for an insightful comment and reference.<br>1 mark for a basic comment and reference.<br>0 marks for reference/quotation alone. | 2 | Possible answers include:<br><br>• "made his landing" — compares baby with something arriving, descending from the sky, depicting his birth as something exciting, mystical<br>• "ploughed straight back into earth" — compares baby with something disastrous, hinting at death, burial<br>• "the thread of his one breath" compares his life to a single, fragile strand by which "they" held on to him and rescued him, expresses his wonder, his gratitude |
| 54. | Candidates should explain how the poet expresses his feelings now.<br><br>2 marks for an insightful comment and reference.<br>1 mark for a basic comment and reference.<br>0 marks for reference/quotation alone. | 4 | Possible answers include:<br><br>• "I thank what higher will/brought us" — gratitude to a higher power (expressed in a rather vague way: "what" seems to imply "whatever — I don't really know or care")<br>• "the great twin-engined swaying wingspan" — metaphor used to describe the appearance of him and his children's arms out and linked (him as fuselage, children as wings/engines), suggests a feeling of joy, power within the family unit<br>• "roaring down" — noisy, enjoying themselves thoroughly<br>• "out-revving/every engine in the universe" — exaggeration to convey his pride, relief, delight that the boy's lungs are healthy |
| 55. | Candidates should show understanding of the term "conclusion" and show how the content of the last sentence continues — or contrasts with — ideas and/or language from the rest of the poem.<br><br>4 marks can be awarded for four appropriate, basic comments. A detailed, insightful comment on one example may be awarded 2 marks.<br>0 marks for reference/quotation alone. | 4 | Possible answers include:<br><br>• continues image of the "thread" (from title and line 3) as what holds life together, but now applied to whole family not just Jamie<br>• "all of us" emphasises the unity within the family<br>• "tiny house" conveys the distance they are at the moment from home, but even so, the thread unifies them, holds them together<br>• very personal "us … our … son … your" continues personal nature of the whole poem<br>• image of the mother waving, despite her being only a "white dot", is welcoming, warm, a very optimistic, uplifting way to conclude the poem |
| 56. | Candidates should discuss Paterson's use of verse form to explore important themes in *The Thread* and at least one other poem and should refer to appropriate textual evidence to support their discussion.<br><br>0 marks for reference/quotation alone. | 10 | The generic marking guide, covering aspects of commonality, can be found on page 193.<br><br>In comments on other poems, possible references include:<br>• sonnet form in *Waking with Russell*<br>• rhyming couplets in *Two Trees*<br>• use of half rhyme/pararhyme in *11.00 Baldovan*<br><br>Many other references are possible. |

**[END OF MODEL MARKING INSTRUCTIONS]**

# HIGHER FOR CfE ENGLISH
# MODEL PAPER 2

## PAPER 1 — READING FOR UNDERSTANDING, ANALYSIS AND EVALUATION

**Marking Instructions for each question**

**Passage 1**

| Question | | Expected Response | Max Mark | Additional Guidance |
|---|---|---|---|---|
| 1. | (a) | Candidates should identify two ways the mall seems to encourage consumerism.<br><br>Candidates must use their own words. No marks are awarded for verbatim quotations from the passage.<br><br>*1 mark for each point from the "Additional Guidance" column.* | 2 | Possible answers include:<br><br>• retailers do not want consumers to sit down and take a break from shopping (explanation of "wooden bench purposely designed to be uncomfortable")<br>• deliberate/careful positioning of bench to maximise marketing opportunities (explanation of "placed alongside a digital screen")<br>• energetic use of technology to market products and tempt consumers (explanation of "screen pulsing ever-changing adverts")<br>• the mall offers diverse/seemingly endless methods for consumers to dispose of their income (explanation of "other outlets, other products, other ways")<br><br>or any other acceptable answer |
| | (b) | Candidates should analyse how the writer's use of language emphasises the intensity of consumerism in the mall.<br><br>Marks will depend on the quality of comment on appropriate language feature(s).<br><br>2 marks may be awarded for reference plus detailed/insightful comment; 1 mark for reference plus more basic comment; 0 marks for reference alone.<br><br>*Possible answers are shown in the "Additional Guidance" column.* | 2 | Possible answers include:<br><br>*Word choice*<br>• "purposely designed" suggests drive and focus on the part of retailers<br>• "pulsing" suggests screen is full of life, constantly moving; a heartbeat which empowers consumers<br>• "ever-changing" suggests incessant activity on screen, vast amount of items on offer<br>• "shoals" suggests the vast number of people who are in the mall/suggests that the consumers move in a darting, frantic manner similar to that of a shoal of fish<br>• "hurrying (in and out)" suggests pressurised, frenetic, single-minded activity<br>• "honouring" suggests that consumers view shopping as a duty to be carried out with devotion<br>• "creed" just as a creed is a set of religious beliefs or principles so the consumers in the mall place great faith in shopping<br>• "turbo-consumer" suggests the activity of the shoppers is super-charged<br>• "live to shop" suggests a fundamental importance, as if a motto of the "creed"; climactic, summative statement<br><br>*Sentence structure*<br>• list ("other … ways") emphasises the many options available to consumers<br>• repetition of "other" highlights the many ways in which consumers can spend /vast range of shopping choices<br>• repetition of "spend" mimics the furious exhortations of retailers/the fast pace of consumer transactions |

| Question | | Expected Response | Max Mark | Additional Guidance |
|---|---|---|---|---|
| | (b) | *(continued)* | | • juxtaposition of repeated options ("other... other...") and repetition of a single course of action ("spend") it could be argued that the juxtaposition of choice and single activity highlights the narrowing focus/determination of consumers as they shop in the mallcolon followed by "live to shop" creates a climactic, summative statement<br><br>or any other acceptable answer |
| 2. | (a) | Candidates should explain why, according to the writer, consumerism might be considered harmless but also unable to make us happy.<br><br>Candidates must use their own words. No marks are awarded for verbatim quotations from the passage.<br><br>*1 mark for each point from the "Additional Guidance" column. For full marks there must be at least one point from each list.* | 4 | Possible answers include:<br><br>*Harmless*<br>• it is not detrimental to one's health (explanation of "doesn't kill anyone")<br>• it contributes to the national wealth (explanation of "keeps the economy going")<br>• many people are employed in the retail industry (explanation of "it … provides one in six jobs")<br>• it creates contentment/pleasure (explanation of "it makes people happy")<br><br>*Unable to make us happy*<br>• there will always be new products which we crave (explanation of "Every time ... better than the one you have.")<br>• consumerism acts like an addictive drug (explanation of "the heroin of human happiness")<br>• consumerism can never fulfil our wishes (explanation of "our needs are never satisfied.")<br>• the happiness offered by consumerism is only temporary (explanation of "The brief high we feel ... just enough to keep us going")<br>• consumerism distracts us from what is really important (explanation of "... compensation for not having a richer, fuller life.")<br>• acceptable reference could be made to aspects of lines 6–10, e.g. the implications of "treadmill"<br><br>or any other acceptable answer |
| | (b) | Candidates should analyse how the writer's use of imagery emphasises her criticism of consumerism.<br><br>Marks will depend on the quality of comment on imagery. When dealing with imagery, answers must show recognition of the literal root of the image and then explore how the writer is extending it figuratively.<br><br>A detailed/insightful comment will be worth 2 marks; a more basic comment will be worth 1 mark. Mere identification of an image will be 0 marks.<br><br>*Possible answers are shown in the "Additional Guidance" column.* | 3 | Possible answers include:<br><br>• "Turbo-(consumerism)": just as a "turbo" is a supercharger which gives an engine or mechanical system much more power so the writer suggests that consumerism has become overpowering, having the potential to overwhelm other more meaningful aspects of life<br>• "voracious appetite": just as a voracious appetite describes an insatiable desire to consume food greedily/ravenously, so consumerism encourages an over-indulgent approach to shopping<br>• "seduced": to seduce is to tempt an individual, possibly into a sexual liaison or an unwise deed, so the writer suggests that the temptations of consumerism are hard to resist and may corrupt us<br>• "heroin": just as heroin is a highly addictive narcotic, so the writer suggests that we can become dependent on consumerism<br>• "(brief) high": just as a "high" is a temporary feeling of extreme happiness, so the writer suggests that consumerism offers only temporary happiness<br><br>or any other acceptable answer |

| Question | | Expected Response | Max Mark | Additional Guidance |
|---|---|---|---|---|
| **3.** | | Candidates should analyse how the writer's use of language conveys her disapproval of the large amount of space that is now devoted to shopping.<br><br>Marks will depend on the quality of comment on appropriate language feature(s).<br><br>2 marks may be awarded for reference plus detailed/insightful comment; 1 mark for reference plus more basic comment; 0 marks for reference alone.<br><br>*Possible answers are shown in the "Additional Guidance" column.* | 4 | Possible answers include:<br><br>*Word Choice*<br>• "giant" suggests that malls are an overwhelming or frightening presence<br>• "taking over" has connotations of conquest/invasion, suggests retail space is a hostile force winning a war<br>• "worldwide" suggests there is no escape from this takeover/global domination<br>• "mainstream" associates the vast amount of retail space with the humdrum/mediocre<br>• "footfall" suggests that so much retail space depersonalises us/shoppers become mere statistics<br>• "grazing time" suggests that exposure to more retail space has lessened our ability to think for ourselves: we become like animals, following the herd/latest trend<br>• "(retail) creep" to creep is to move forward stealthily, possibly with the intention of causing harm, suggesting that the growth of shopping space has been insidious and may be harmful to society<br>• "increasingly" suggests an on-going, almost unstoppable process<br>• "diminished" suggests reductive properties of increasing retail space<br><br>*Imagery*<br>• "monoculture": just as a monoculture is a crop of a single species, often grown in vast fields, so the enormous amount of shopping space lacks variety and restricts the growth of other activities which we could pursue<br>• "Kings as consumers, pawns as citizens": allows the writer to express the key idea that increased retail opportunities may lead us to believe we have power and control ("kings"), but the opposite is true: consumerism removes our ability to control our lives and, like "pawns" on a chessboard, we are manipulated by others and have very little power in the game as a whole/society<br><br>*Sentence structure*<br>• list of different types of retail space ("shops … malls") emphasises relentless expansion of shopping areas<br>• escalating nature of retail outlets within list ("shops, retail centres, giant malls") suggests an evolutionary process/growth which is difficult to stop or inevitable<br>• balanced structure/ contrast of "The more … the less …" allows the writer to highlight the spiralling negative consequences of increasing retail space<br>• "Kings as consumers, pawns as citizens" the very basic parallel structure of this final sentence emphasises the dismissive tone of "pawns as citizens", thereby allowing the writer to highlight her view that we are deluded into thinking we are important when in fact basic rights of citizenship are denied us |

| Question | | Expected Response | Max Mark | Additional Guidance |
|---|---|---|---|---|
| 3. | | (continued) | | *Tone* <br> • "... there's not much else to do but shop." creates a despairing/frustrated tone by using basic vocabulary in a matter-of-fact statement <br> • "citizens ... make decisions ... equally and collectively ... world ..." rather overblown language suggests that increased shopping space removes our higher values, leaving us intellectually poorer and deprived of our basic rights <br> • balanced structure of "It may be ... but we simply have ..." creates a dismissive/sceptical tone which allows the writer to highlight that more space devoted to shopping will ultimately deprive us of our liberty <br><br> or any other acceptable answer |
| 4. | | Candidates should discuss to what extent the writer's description of the shoppers suggests she is "over-catastrophising the consumer phenomenon". They may argue for either side or for both sides. <br><br> Marks will depend on the quality of evaluative comment. <br><br> 2 marks may be awarded for reference plus detailed/insightful comment; 1 mark for reference plus more basic comment; 0 marks for reference alone. <br><br> *Possible answers are shown in the "Additional Guidance" column.* | 3 | Possible answers include: <br><br> • "teeming with shoppers despite the credit crunch" suggests it's not a problem, because so many are still shopping and benefiting the economy (even in financially straitened times) <br> • "people don't look ... disempowered" suggests it's not a problem, because these shoppers still have the right to exercise control <br> • "people don't look ... depressed" suggests it's not a problem, because the shoppers do not appear to be unhappy <br> • "purposeful" suggests it's not a problem, because the shoppers are clear-sighted in their aims <br> • "teeming with shoppers despite the credit crunch" suggests it is a problem, because large numbers are shopping even though they can ill afford to <br> • use of qualifying adverb "particularly" before "disempowered or depressed" suggests that the writer cannot be whole-heartedly positive in her description of the shoppers <br> • "I suppose" suggests a reluctance on the writer's part to see consumers in a positive light <br> • "strangely distracted ... magnetic shop signs" suggests it is a problem, because the shoppers are not in control of their own actions, are in an almost hypnotic state <br><br> or any other acceptable answer |
| 5. | | Candidates should explain how "evolutionary psychology" can explain our need for material goods, but why "much of this is simply not true". <br><br> Candidates must use their own words. No marks are awarded for verbatim quotations from the passage. <br><br> *1 mark for each point from the "Additional Guidance" column, but at least one from each side.* | 4 | Possible answers include: <br><br> *"Can explain"* <br> • we think our outward appearance, as represented by a display of material goods (explanation of "self-marketing") ... <br> • ... has become the means by which we can indicate our suitability as a mate to the opposite sex (explanation of "practical tool for reproduction and survival") |

| Question | Expected Response | Max Mark | Additional Guidance |
|---|---|---|---|
| 5. | *(continued)* | | *"Not true"*<br>• most people are not aware of or concerned with what we wear (explanation of "the vast majority of people ... wearing" and/or "The fundamental consumerist delusion ...")<br>• it is people's ability to express themselves, to display lively intelligence and to express love which matters more than superficial adornments (explanation of "their conversation, their wit, or their affection")<br><br>or any other acceptable answer |
| 6. | Candidates should evaluate the final paragraph's effectiveness as a conclusion to the ideas of the passage as a whole.<br><br>Marks will depend on the quality of comment.  For full marks there must be appropriate attention to the idea of a conclusion.  A sophisticated intelligent answer may be awarded 3 marks; a sensible but not fully developed answer may be awarded 2 marks; a basic comment may be awarded 1 mark.<br><br>*Possible answers are shown in the "Additional Guidance" column.* | 3 | Possible answers include:<br><br>• the attitude and behaviour of the "two young shoppers" are the embodiment of "modern consumerism" as mentioned in the opening sentence; they follow the creed of "live to shop", illustrating the idea behind the title<br>• the "two young shoppers", as a device, allow the writer to return to the physical setting of the mall which is used at the beginning, in the middle and at the end, illustrating the scale of the shopping phenomenon<br>• the persistence of the "two young shoppers", as illustrated by the frivolous nature of their words, allows the writer to end the passage on a light-hearted note, perhaps suggesting she realises she is, to an extent, "over-catastrophising"<br><br>or any other acceptable answer |

## Passage 2

| Question | Expected Response | Max Mark | Additional Guidance |
|---|---|---|---|
| 7. | Candidates should identify key areas of disagreement in the two passages.<br><br>There may be some overlap among the areas of disagreement.  Markers will have to judge the extent to which a candidate has covered two points or one.<br><br>Candidates can use bullet points in this final question, or write a number of linked statements.<br><br>Evidence from the passage may include quotations, but these should be supported by explanations.<br><br>*Approach to marking is shown in the "Additional Guidance" column.*<br><br>*Key areas of disagreement are shown in the grid below.  Other answers are possible.* | 5 | The mark for this question should reflect the quality of response in two areas:<br><br>• identification of the key areas of disagreement in attitude/ideas<br>• level of detail given in support<br><br>The following guidelines should be used:<br><br>**Five marks** — comprehensive identification of three or more key areas of disagreement with full use of supporting evidence<br>**Four marks** — clear identification of three or more key areas of disagreement with relevant use of supporting evidence<br>**Three marks** — identification of three or more key areas of disagreement with supporting evidence<br>**Two marks** — identification of two key areas of disagreement with supporting evidence<br>**One mark** — identification of one key area of disagreement with supporting evidence<br>**Zero marks** — failure to identify any key area of disagreement and/or total misunderstanding of task |

| | Area of Disagreement | Carol Midgley | Will Hutton |
|---|---|---|---|
| 1. | general | damages individuals and society — an addiction | actually benefits individuals and society (a problem only in the minds of the minority) |
| 2. | happiness | gives short-term pleasure but longer-term unhappiness as consumers can never be satisfied | is fun and gives continuous pleasure through seeing and/or acquiring new "things" |
| 3. | architecture | makes town and city centres look the same | can (at its best) create attractive buildings |
| 4. | public space | restricts public space where people can meet to participate in the democratic process | creates public space where people do something imaginatively and economically important |
| 5. | motivation | is motivated by people's need to attract a mate (but is not effective in that respect) | is motivated by people's need to express themselves through what they buy/own |
| 6. | values | makes people superficial, obsessed with appearance rather than things that really matter | provides people with the opportunity to do something important for themselves as individuals and for society as a whole |
| 7. | manipulation | the market is all-powerful, manipulative, degrading to shoppers | consumer as individual has free will, retains autonomy |

**[END OF MODEL MARKING INSTRUCTIONS]**

# HIGHER FOR CfE ENGLISH
# MODEL PAPER 2

**PAPER 2 — CRITICAL READING**

**SECTION 1 — Scottish Text**

**SCOTTISH TEXT (DRAMA)**

Text 1 — Drama — *The Slab Boys* by John Byrne

| Question | Expected Response | Max Mark | Additional Guidance |
|---|---|---|---|
| 1. | Candidates should explain how the audience is made to feel sorry for Hector. <br><br> 2 marks for an insightful comment and appropriate reference(s). 1 mark for a basic comment and reference(s). 0 marks for reference/quotation alone. | 4 | Possible answers include: <br><br> • the general idea that Hector is facing humiliation in his new clothing <br> • the fact that the attempt by Alan to warn him is thwarted by Phil's threat with the pen … <br> • … such that (even) Alan is obliged to lie to him <br> • Hector's pathetic enthusiasm: "Will I go now and ask her? Will I?" <br> • Phil's and Spanky's apparent determination that he face humiliation at the hands not just of Lucille, but Willie Curry also <br> • Hector's enthusiasm for "swanking" and his belief that his clothes are "up to date" <br> • the way he is forced into putting on the coat and the balaclava, showing him as at the mercy of others <br> • Phil's justification for the balaclava ("it's draughty in Willie's room") verges on the insulting <br> • the stage direction *"Slightly bamboozled"* paints him as a sad, put-upon figure <br> • the glibness of Phil's invented story for him shows how much contempt he has for Hector, how much he enjoys manipulating him <br> • the " Triple pneumonia … Double rupture … " knockabout might amuse Phil and Spanky, but it is further evidence of their having fun at someone else's expense <br> • Hector's "I'll away along then" is pathetic in its simplicity and naivety <br> • the insincerity of Phil and Spanky's good wishes <br> • their bursting into uncontrollable laughter the moment he leaves |
| 2. | Candidates should explain how the language of lines 30—32 allows Phil and Spanky to make fun of Alan. <br><br> 2 marks for an insightful comment and appropriate reference(s). 1 mark for a basic comment and reference(s). 0 marks for reference/quotation alone. | 2 | Possible answers include: <br><br> • they take the rather "public school" turn of phrase "a lousy trick" … <br> • … and echo it sneeringly in similar terms: "by jove" and "you cad" <br> • they mock Alan's (to them) posh way of speaking by pretending to speak in the same way |

| Question | Expected Response | Max Mark | Additional Guidance |
|---|---|---|---|
| **3.** | Candidates should explain how the playwright emphasises the animosity between Alan and Phil.<br><br>2 marks for an insightful comment and appropriate reference(s). 1 mark for a basic comment and reference(s). 0 marks for reference/quotation alone. | 4 | Possible answers include:<br><br>• Alan's quite aggressive, forceful "Hey, watch it! Chuckit!"<br>• knows he's "speaking out of turn", but is prepared this time to stand up to Phil<br>• (for Alan) the use of "poor little bastard" shows how angry he is, trying to make Phil see how awful things are going to be for Hector<br>• he reels off what is going to happen to Hector ("thinking … he really does cut a dash … he'll probably stop off … doff the coat and hat") to paint a full scenario of Hector's humiliation as a result of Phil behaviour<br>• the rather extreme "she'll wet herself" shows just how amoral he think's Phil's behaviour is<br>• contempt in "you and your crummy friend"<br>• Phil's response is couched in mock public school language, implying that the ethics of the public school don't operate here<br>• refers to Alan as Steerforth Minor, reducing to a public school stereotype (with the added barb of "Minor")<br>• throws Alan's words "poor little bastard" back at him, as if to say "don't you dare call him that"<br>• claims he and Spanky have some sort of right to humiliate Hector<br>• as if there are situations Alan could never understand<br>• Alan has the staying power to come back with "More than a bit" showing he doesn't accept Phil's argument. |
| **4.** | Candidates should discuss the importance of the conflict between Phil and Alan in exploring at least one theme in the play, and should refer to appropriate textual evidence to support their discussion.<br><br>0 marks for reference/quotation alone. | 10 | The generic marking guide, covering aspects of commonality, can be found on page 193.<br><br>In comments on the rest of the play, possible references include:<br><br>• Alan is the butt of many of Phil's jokes and sarcasm<br>• Alan represents the successful, privileged middle class whom Phil despises<br>• Alan is the antithesis of Phil in terms of work ethic, conventional manners, respect for "superiors"<br><br>Many other references are possible. |

**Text 2 – Drama – *The Cheviot, the Stag and the Black, Black Oil* by John McGrath**

| Question | Expected Response | Max Mark | Additional Guidance |
|---|---|---|---|
| 5. | Candidates should explain how the playwright creates a relaxed mood.<br><br>1 mark for each acceptable explanation. 0 marks for simply identifying an aspect of the plan. | 4 | Possible answers include:<br><br>• the "quiet" song will be peaceful, calm<br>• "It begins, I suppose" sounds like a natural speaking voice, not assertive, almost diffident<br>• "and all that" is very colloquial<br>• "in a bit of a mess" is very understated, not being dramatic<br>• light humour in the response of the singer to information about Gaelic and the plaid<br>• "So …" is very conversational<br>• the visually amusing appearance of the cottage<br>• two girls singing in Gaelic – unthreatening, pleasing<br>• "making it all seem fine" suggests there was no panic, no unrest<br>• "invented … introduced" underplaying the severe impact of the Cheviot<br>• "not too pleased about it" is something of an understatement in the light of what actually happened |
| 6. | Candidates should explain how the playwright conveys the difference in outlook between the Young Highlander and the Two Women.<br><br>2 marks for an insightful comment and reference. 1 mark for a basic comment and reference. 0 marks for reference/quotation alone. | 4 | Possible answers include:<br><br>the Women are unconcerned, don't complain, shown by:<br>• the dismissive "blethers" which suggests idle talk, not to be taken seriously<br>• defence of the Countess as having been "kind" to them<br>• sees no problem with the Countess living the high life ("Why wouldn't she be?")<br>• invalidates the Y.H.'s criticism of misuse of rent by claiming he never pays any<br>• not interested in Y.H.'s news about 150 soldiers; ignore its and tell him (or the other woman?) to get on with the work<br><br>the Young Highlander criticises the Duchess, is full of complaints, is agitated about idea of soldiers, shown by:<br>• sneering remark about the Countess an absentee ("away in England")<br>• obvious antipathy at "fancy palaces and feasts for Kings and fine French wines" – sees her as living in luxury (while they have to scrape a living)<br>• accuses her of doing so at their expense ("it's our rent she's spending")<br>• sense of accumulating grievance in structure of ("If it's not bad weather … it's mildew … and last year it was both together … And now they're talking about …") |
| 7. | Candidates should explain how the extract ends on a humorous note.<br><br>2 marks for a clear explanation. 1 mark for a basic explanation. 0 marks for reference/quotation alone. | 2 | Possible answers include:<br><br>• the apparently innocuous "You might find a good use for this" when he hands her the bucket, is actually inviting her to throw the urine at Sellar and Loch, the approaching representative of authority<br>• the tongue-in-cheek use (and repetition) of "gentlemen" to describe two notoriously cruel and heartless characters |

| Question | Expected Response | Max Mark | Additional Guidance |
|---|---|---|---|
| 8. | Candidates should discuss how effective they find the unconventional staging of the play in exploring at least one key idea in the play and should refer to appropriate textual evidence to support their discussion.<br><br>0 marks for reference/quotation alone. | 10 | The generic marking guide, covering aspects of commonality, can be found on page 193.<br><br>In comments on the rest of the play, possible references include:<br>• audience participation (e.g. in the "Walla Walla Wooskie" section)<br>• reciting/quoting detailed statistics (e.g. about population decline)<br>• musical extravaganzas such as Texas Jim's square dance<br>Many other references are possible. |

## Text 3 — Drama — *Men Should Weep* by Ena Lamont Stewart

| Question | | Expected Response | Max Mark | Additional Guidance |
|---|---|---|---|---|
| 9. | (i) | Candidates should explain what important aspects of Maggie's character are revealed in these lines.<br><br>2 marks for an insightful comment and reference. 1 mark for a basic comment and reference. 0 marks for reference/quotation alone. | 4 | Possible answers include:<br>• defensive of her role: "Ye canna help …", "I dae the best I can"<br>• defensive of her family: "You leave John alane", "He does his best for us"<br>• sentimental: "I still love John. And whit's more, he loves me"<br>• self-deluding: "Aye! I'm happy!", "I'm sorry for you, Lily" |
| | (ii) | Candidates should explain one important aspect of Lily's character which is revealed in these lines.<br><br>2 marks for an insightful comment and reference. 1 mark for a basic comment and reference. 0 marks for reference/quotation alone. | 2 | Possible answers include:<br>• she speaks her mind, not afraid to be negative: "midden", "No much o a best", "nae" repeated<br>• quick to placate, conciliate: "OK. OK. …"<br>• sense of humour: "photies to the Sunday papers … Is this a record?" |
| 10. | | Candidates should analyse how lines 16–28 are structured in such a way as to provide a lively dramatic exchange between Maggie and Lily.<br><br>2 marks for an insightful comment and reference. 1 mark for a basic comment and reference. 0 marks for reference/quotation alone. | 4 | Possible answers include:<br>• the key ideas are (i) the back and forth, "tennis match", balanced nature of the exchanges, and (ii) the way each pair of lines is linked to the next by a word or an idea:<br>  • balance: "Servin …" — "Livin …"; "in a Coocaddens pub" — "in a slum"; "brutes o men" — "a useless man"<br>  • link: "weans"<br>  • balance: "his greetin weans" — "They're *my* weans!"<br>  • link: "workin … work"<br>  • balance: "*paid* for my work" — "paid wi love"<br>  • link: "airms roon ye/me"<br>  • balance "a man's …" — "*Men*!"<br>  • link: "They're a dirty beasts" — "a lumped thegither"<br>  • balance: "Ye're daft!" — "You're *saft*! |
| 11. | | Candidates should discuss to what extent men in the play are presented as weak and should refer to appropriate textual evidence to support their discussion.<br><br>0 marks for reference/quotation alone. | 10 | The generic marking guide, covering aspects of commonality, can be found on page 193.<br><br>In comments on the rest of the play, possible references include:<br>• John's less than convincing efforts to support his family<br>• John's inability to cope with Jenny<br>• Alec's submissiveness to Isa<br>Many other references are possible. |

ANSWERS TO HIGHER FOR CfE ENGLISH

**Text 1 — Prose — *The Painter* by Iain Crichton Smith**

| Question | Expected Response | Max Mark | Additional Guidance |
|---|---|---|---|
| 12. | Candidates should explain how the narrator's account creates an ambiguous impression of how serious the fight is. <br><br> For full marks there must be acknowledgement of both sides. 2 marks for an insightful comment and reference. 1 mark for a basic comment and reference. 0 marks for reference/quotation alone. | 4 | Possible answers include: <br><br> • suggestions that it is serious: <br>   • the ferocity suggested by word choice of "kill … enraged … frustrated … tortured" <br>   • metaphor in "gradually grew more demoniac" suggests father-in-law as almost possessed <br>   • detail of actual injury in "cutting his son-in-law's left leg so that he fell to the ground" <br><br> • suggestions that it may not be serious: <br>   • inclusion of "perhaps", "to a certain extent" suggest narrator's uncertainty <br>   • "however" (used twice) shows a willingness to contradict himself, lessen the seriousness of what has just been said <br>   • "ponderously" suggests rather lethargic movement <br>   • "looked as if …" suggests speculation, lack of certainty <br>   • "odd … as if each was trying to cut corn" — they're merely "odd", not frightening, and appear as if engaged on everyday activity <br>   • description of wife is essentially comic |
| 13. | Candidates should analyse how the writer makes clear the contrast between William and the two fighters. <br><br> For full marks there must be reference to both William and the fighters. 2 marks for an insightful comment and reference. 1 mark for a basic comment and reference. 0 marks for reference/ quotation alone. | 4 | Possible answers include: <br><br> *William* <br> • "sitting comfortably" suggests he is relaxed, at ease <br> • "no expression on his face at all" suggests he is emotionless <br> • "a cold clear intensity" suggests a deep, almost disturbing concentration <br> • "as if he were asleep" suggests he is detached <br> • "he sat there" suggests he is passive <br> • "nor … did he make any attempt to pull his chair back" suggests he is unaware of (or not bothered by) any danger <br><br> *the fighters* <br> • "the scythes swung to and fro" suggests repeated intense and dangerous activity <br> • "faces … contorted" suggests the effort is twisting the shape of their faces <br> • "in the fury of battle" suggests a sense of ferocious engagement <br> • "suffused with blood and rage" suggests a sense of all-consuming anger <br> • "teeth were drawn back in a snarl" suggests an animal-like savagery |
| 14. | Candidates should describe in their own words why the narrator is so incensed at William. <br><br> 1 mark for each acceptable point. 0 marks for quotation alone. | 2 | Possible answers include: <br><br> • revulsion at his coldness, callousness <br> • thinks he is as unfeeling as a natural predator <br> • compares his response with a rat, i.e. aggressive when challenged <br> • resents his apparent assumption that events had been organised for his benefit <br> • his attitude reduces human participants to inanimate objects ("house … wall") <br> • [possibly] recognises in William the urge to capture the moment, which he, as a writer, shares |

| Question | Expected Response | Max Mark | Additional Guidance |
|---|---|---|---|
| 15. | Candidates should discuss the impressions Crichton Smith creates of life in a small community in *The Painter* and at least one other story and should refer to appropriate textual evidence to support their discussion.<br><br>0 marks for reference/quotation alone. | 10 | The generic marking guide, covering aspects of commonality, can be found on page 193.<br><br>In comments on other stories, possible references include:<br><br>• the tensions between the two women in *The Telegram*<br>• the son's sense of isolation in *Mother and Son*<br>• the pressure to conform in *The Red Door*<br><br>Many other references are possible. |

### Text 2 — Prose — *The Eye of the Hurricane* by George Mackay Brown

| Question | Expected Response | Max Mark | Additional Guidance |
|---|---|---|---|
| 16. | Candidates should explain the various methods the Captain uses to convince the narrator to buy him alcohol.<br><br>2 marks for an insightful comment and reference. 1 mark for a basic comment and reference. 0 marks for reference/quotation alone. | 4 | Possible answers include:<br><br>• very matter of fact opening ("Now, Barclay, about this cold of mine.") as if the whole conversation will be business-like, not admitting of any disagreement.<br>• disparages Miriam early on, an attempt to neutralise her influence on the narrator, to get him "on-side"<br>• tells narrator that his drinking is not something he can control, claims it's a natural phenomenon which has to be faced up to<br>• addresses him like teacher/pupil: "Do you understand that, Barclay?"<br>• flatters the narrator with a reference to his writing<br>• ingratiates himself to the narrator ("I like you. I'm very glad you're living in this house.")<br>• uses an elaborate sea-going metaphor to justify asking narrator to help<br>• asserts his dominant role as "skipper"<br>• tries to make it simple: "And the first thing I want you to do ..."<br>• completely ignores the narrator's repeated refusals<br>• resorts to open threat of raising rent, evicting him |
| 17. | Candidates should analyse how the narrator uses imagery to explain his views on charity.<br><br>2 marks for an insightful comment and reference. 1 mark for a basic comment and reference. 0 marks for reference/quotation alone. | 4 | Possible answers include:<br><br>• "Charity is no hard-minted currency ... a shilling here and a sovereign there": it is not a simple matter of tangible coinage, cash to be handed out as and when you wish<br>• "it is the oil and wine that drop uncertainly through the fingers": it is like liquid, not easily defined, not easily controlled<br>• "the wounds of the world": the idea that suffering can happen at any time in any place<br>• "wherever the roads of pity and suffering cross": compares pain and the compassion to alleviate it to roads which, when they intersect, allow "charity" to be delivered |
| 18. | Candidates should explain what the last three lines suggest about the narrator's feelings for the Captain.<br><br>2 marks for an insightful comment and reference. 1 mark for a basic comment and reference. 0 marks for reference/quotation alone. | 2 | Possible answers include:<br><br>• pity — sees him as a lonely, lost figure, caught up in his own fantasies<br>• concern — the constant pacing must be indicative of mental struggle |

| Question | Expected Response | Max Mark | Additional Guidance |
|---|---|---|---|
| 19. | Candidates should discuss how George Mackay Brown creates confrontations between characters in *The Eye of the Hurricane* and at least one other story and should refer to appropriate textual evidence to support their discussion.<br><br>0 marks for reference/quotation alone. | 10 | The generic marking guide, covering aspects of commonality, can be found on page 193.<br><br>In comments on other stories, possible references include:<br>• Bill and Sinclair in *A Time to Keep*<br>• Flaws and the minister in *The Whaler's Return*<br>• the Vikings and the villagers in *Tartan*<br>Many other references are possible. |

### Text 3 — Prose — *The Trick is to Keep Breathing* by Janice Galloway

| Question | Expected Response | Max Mark | Additional Guidance |
|---|---|---|---|
| 20. | Candidates should explain how the writer establishes an unwelcoming atmosphere at the start of the extract.<br><br>2 marks for an insightful comment and reference.<br>1 mark for a basic comment and reference.<br>0 marks for reference/quotation alone. | 3 | Possible answers include:<br>• the doctor's lateness suggests a lack of care<br>• "sea-coloured corridor" — the sea has unpleasant associations for Joy<br>• "no pictures and all the curtains closed" suggests cold, dark, claustrophobic, inhospitable<br>• "smells like dog in the rain" suggests pungent, non-human, sickening<br>• the absence of any preliminary chat suggests a very functional, bureaucratic approach<br>• "Well?" suggests a very abrupt, uncaring tone<br>• "horrible jacket" suggests even his clothing is off-putting<br>• "gloom" reinforces the darkness in the room<br>• "his eyes are all iris" suggests something unnatural, creepy, threatening |
| 21. | Candidates should analyse how the exchange between the Patient and Dr Three highlights the lack of communication between them.<br><br>2 marks for an insightful comment and reference.<br>1 mark for a basic comment and reference.  0 marks for reference/quotation alone. | 4 | Possible answers include:<br><br>reference to general points such as:<br>• the profusion of short questions<br>• the "stage directions" about Patient being "Mesmerised", "Confused", not able to speak, tears welling<br><br>reference to specific points in the dialogue such as:<br>• "Well what" — her response to Dr's opening shows she doesn't understand<br>• "I thought you would start" — shows she doesn't know what's going on<br>• "Start what?" — Dr is (deliberately?) showing he doesn't want to engage<br>• "Yes.  So what …" — a very perfunctory response to Patient's statement<br>• "I want to know …" — "I don't know …" — total breakdown of communication<br>• "So." — as if it's all been explained, nothing further to say<br>• "Any other questions?" — with a hint that they will be dismissed as quickly as the first<br>• "How long have you been here did you say?" — she's already told him |

| Question | Expected Response | Max Mark | Additional Guidance |
|---|---|---|---|
| 22. | Candidates should explain how the Doctor's uncaring approach is made clear.<br><br>2 marks for an insightful comment and reference.<br>1 mark for a basic comment and reference.<br>0 marks for reference/quotation alone. | 3 | Possible answers include:<br>• "Sighing" suggests impatience, as if dealing with a stupid child<br>• "I suppose" as if he's having to do the thinking for her<br>• "To go home for the weekend?" questioning intonation as if explaining something very simple to someone not very bright<br>• "...all right?" — patronising tone<br>• "I don't know what that's supposed to mean" — unhelpful reply to someone obviously distressed<br>• "Take your time. [Silence] Right then" — invites her to take her time and then doesn't give her any<br>• "... taps the bundle of papers ... folds his arms" — making his impatience obvious<br>• "The interview is over." — very abrupt |
| 23. | Candidates should discuss how *The Trick Is To Keep Breathing* explores the way the individual is treated within the Mental Health system and should refer to appropriate textual evidence to support their discussion.<br><br>0 marks for reference/quotation alone. | 10 | The generic marking guide, covering aspects of commonality, can be found on page 193.<br><br>In comments on the rest of the novel, possible references include:<br><br>• the Health Visitor<br>• Joy's experiences in the hospital<br>• Doctor Two and the *Courage and Bereavement* pamphlet<br><br>Many other references are possible. |

Text 4 — Prose — *Sunset Song* by Lewis Grassic Gibbon

| Question | Expected Response | Max Mark | Additional Guidance |
|---|---|---|---|
| 24. | Candidates should analyse how the writer's use of language emphasises the offensiveness of Ewan's behaviour.<br><br>2 marks for an insightful comment and reference.<br>1 mark for a basic comment and reference.  0 marks for reference/quotation alone. | 4 | Possible answers include:<br>• "sneered" suggests contempt in his voice<br>• *"Hell, Chris, what a bloody place!"* the coarse language suggests a lack of respect<br>• "flung his pack one way and his hat the other" suggests a lack of care, self-respect<br>• "as though she were a tink" compares Chris to someone to be looked down on, of no value<br>• "hot and questing and wise" suggests he is being sexually aggressive, selfish, that he is more experienced now than he was and isn't afraid to make Chris aware of it<br>• "the hot smoulder fire in his eyes" suggests he is almost demonic, malevolent<br>• "red with other things" suggests he is sexually aroused in a frightening way<br>• *"Well, we'll hope so, eh Chris?"* crude, sexual innuendo<br>• *"unless you're too bloody stand-offish"* open insult to his wife coarsened by use of offensive language<br>• "picked the thing up and flung it ..." — such lack of respect for his own child's picture book (emphasised by "thing" and "flung") is an especially upsetting detail<br>• the commanding tone of *"Here, give us some tea."* as if Chris were a servant to be bossed about |

| Question | Expected Response | Max Mark | Additional Guidance |
|---|---|---|---|
| **25.** | Candidates should analyse how the writer makes the reader aware of Chris's perception of Ewan.<br><br>2 marks for an insightful comment and reference. 1 mark for a basic comment and reference.  0 marks for reference/quotation alone | 4 | Possible answers include:<br><br>• "like a beast at a trough" suggests she sees him as non-human, merely satisfying basic needs, no self-respect; the harsh, plosive consonants at "beast" and "trough" add a hint of disgust<br>• "coarse hair that sprang like short bristles" suggests she sees him a rough, unrefined, compares him with an inanimate object<br>• "red and angry circle about the collar" shows that she can sense his aggressiveness in the chafing left by his uniform<br>• "a great half-healed scar ... glinted putrescent blue" — a revolting description of something deeply unhealthy, unnatural, almost alive |
| **26.** | Candidates should identify the change in young Ewan's reaction to his father.<br><br>1 mark for identifying/explaining each reaction. 0 marks for reference/quotation alone. | 2 | Possible answers include:<br><br>• at first, he is cautious, but acknowledges Ewan as his father<br>• at the end he is scared/seeks Chris's protection, calling him "that soldier", i.e. denying any relationship |
| **27.** | Candidates should discuss the development of the relationship between Chris and Ewan and should refer to appropriate textual evidence to support their discussion.<br><br>0 marks for reference/quotation alone. | 10 | The generic marking guide, covering aspects of commonality, can be found on page 193.<br>In comments on the rest of the novel, possible references include:<br><br>• the nervousness of the initial wooing<br>• early passion, happy domestic life with young Ewan<br>• the disparity in intellect, e.g. attitude to history at Dunnottar Castle<br><br>Many other references are possible. |

**Text 5 — Prose — *The Cone-Gatherers* by Robin Jenkins**

| Question | Expected Response | Max Mark | Additional Guidance |
|---|---|---|---|
| **28.** | Candidates should analyse how the sentence structure helps to convey how Calum is feeling.<br><br>2 marks for an insightful comment and reference. 1 mark for a basic comment and reference.  0 marks for reference/quotation alone. | 2 | Possible answers include:<br><br>• the balancing around the semicolon helps to convey the idea that Calum has changed from being a beater to thinking of himself as a deer<br>• the sentence beginning "He could not, however ..." serves to introduce the contrast between the deer's agility and Calum's clumsiness<br>• the structure of the sentence beginning "He fell and rose again ..." imitates the frantic, headlong action it describes with a list of movements ("fell ... rose avoided ... collide"); it also lists all the things Calum feels are ignoring him and the deer, so many that he feels completely cut off from help or sympathy |

| Question | Expected Response | Max Mark | Additional Guidance |
|---|---|---|---|
| 29. | Candidates should analyse how the writer's use of language creates a sense of "commotion".<br><br>2 marks for an insightful comment and reference. 1 mark for a basic comment and reference. 0 marks for reference/quotation alone. | 4 | Possible answers include:<br><br>• some of the many references to sound (e.g. "barked …roared … shouts … bellowed … bawled" etc.) could be dealt with collectively with a comment suggesting the way they create a sense of confusion of cacophonous sound<br>• "barked fiercely" suggests harsh, loud, aggressive noise<br>• "rush into the danger" suggests a reckless dash<br>• "roared to him" suggests an impassioned, panicked cry<br>• "resounded with their exultant shouts" suggests an echoing effect, all the calls mixing together<br>• "bellowed" suggests loud, deep, fanatical<br>• "bawled" suggests frantic, hysterical<br>• list of adjectives "silent, desperate, and heroic" suggests the extent of their plight<br>• "guns banged" suggests loud, aggressive noise, associated with death/violence<br>• "wails of lament" suggests high-pitched exclamations of mourning<br>• "dashed on at a demented speed" suggests reckless speed, desperate, almost out of control<br>• "shot out" suggests a sudden, dramatic appearance<br>• "a deer screaming" suggests high-pitched, suffering, in pain<br>• "scrabbling about" suggests agitated, distressed movement<br>• "feverishly reloading" suggests excited, tense movement<br>• the rather paradoxical "Screaming in sympathy" suggests the confusion at the scene<br>• list of actions "flung … clasped … tried to comfort" suggests a rush of actions"<br>• "flung" suggests acting with passion, no thought of consequences<br>• "dragged him about with it in its mortal agony" suggests frantic movement back and forth at the moment of death |

| Question | Expected Response | Max Mark | Additional Guidance |
|---|---|---|---|
| 30. | Candidates should explain how the reader is made aware of Duror's state of mind at this point.<br><br>2 marks for an insightful comment and reference. 1 mark for a basic comment and reference. 0 marks for reference/quotation alone. | 4 | Possible answers include:<br><br>• the contrast between the immobility of Forgan, Roderick and Lady Runcie-Campbell, and Duror "leaping out of the wood" like something possessed emphasises Duror's disturbed state of mind<br>• the paradoxical "berserk joy" depicts him as out of control, unaware of what his real emotions are<br>• the blunt abruptness of the simple sentence "There was a knife in his hand" focuses attention on it and foreshadows the violence he is about to carry out<br>• "he never heard her" suggests he is "switched off", so caught up in his emotions that he cannot process the sound of her words<br>• "Rushing … he threw … with furious force, … seizing … cut its throat savagely" combine to depict someone in a uncontrolled, violent bloodlust, acting with tremendous strength and energy<br>• the ambiguity of his pose after the kill, not proud, but apparently grieving suggests a confusion in his own mind<br>• clinging onto the knife suggests he is in shock, doesn't know what to do |
| 31. | Candidates should discuss how the writer explores the theme of death and should refer to appropriate textual evidence to support their discussion.<br><br>0 marks for reference/quotation alone. | 10 | The generic marking guide, covering aspects of commonality, can be found on page 193.<br><br>In comments on the rest of the novel, possible references include:<br><br>• the War — the death and suffering it is causing<br>• the contrast between Duror's and Calum's attitude to the death of animals<br>• the deaths of Duror and Calum at the end of the story<br><br>Many other references are possible. |

### Text 1 — Poetry — *Tam o' Shanter* by Robert Burns

| Question | Expected Response | Max Mark | Additional Guidance |
|---|---|---|---|
| 32. | Candidates should analyse how the extended simile creates a vivid picture of what is happening.<br><br>For full marks there must be reference to all three of the comparisons. 1 mark for a comment and reference. 0 marks for reference/quotation alone. | 3 | Possible answers include:<br><br>• "As bees … " suggests a sense of outrage, a need to escape assault; idea of the small and vulnerable ("bees") being threatened by something larger ("herds")<br>• "As open pussie's … " suggests a sudden ("pop") attack close at hand ("before their nose") which causes extreme alarm<br>• "As eager … " suggests a concerted response to a rallying cry, one being chased by many |
| 33. | Candidates should explain how Burns makes this part of the poem dramatic.<br><br>2 marks for an insightful comment and reference. 1 mark for a basic comment and reference. 0 marks for reference/quotation alone. | 4 | Possible answers include:<br><br>• the pause to lecture Tam creates tension by delaying the continuation of the story<br>• direct address to Meg ("do thy speedy utmost") reminds reader of the urgency involved<br>• setting a sort of target for Meg/Tam ("There at them …") sets up the dramatic chase, creating uncertainty about their fate |

| Question | Expected Response | Max Mark | Additional Guidance |
|---|---|---|---|
| 33. | *(continued)* | | • idea of Nannie being way out in front of the other witches creates fear that she will catch Tam<br>• referring to Maggie as "noble" increases the sense of good versus evil in the chase<br>• the frantic efforts by Nannie ("flew at Tam wi' furious ettle") increase the tension<br>• "But little wist she … " — a last minute turn of fortune, the hero has a trick up his sleeve<br>• "Ae spring" — a single leap, one last final effort<br>• "But left behind …" the sacrifice involved in saving her master |
| 34. | Candidates should discuss to what extent they think lines 27–32 are meant as a serious warning to the reader.<br><br>Marks will depend on the thoughtfulness of the discussion and the appropriateness of reference. 2 marks for an insightful comment 1 mark for a basic comment. 0 marks for reference/quotation alone. | 3 | Possible answers include:<br><br>• Not serious: it's just a conventional conclusion, with the expected element of moralising and instruction ("take heed … Think … Remember"); it can't really be a "tale o' truth" so any reluctant moral isn't convincing; it's just a bit of fun, developing the idea of men as in need of guidance, playing on superstitions of witchcraft<br><br>• Serious: it warns reasonably enough about over-indulgence (in drink or lascivious thoughts), of paying a high price for unwise behaviour; it is addressed only to men, the weaker sex as far as irresponsible behaviour is concerned |
| 35. | Candidates should discuss the extent to which Burns passes judgements in *Tam o' Shanter* and at least one other of his poems, and should refer to appropriate textual evidence to support their discussion.<br><br>0 marks for reference/quotation alone. | 10 | The generic marking guide, covering aspects of commonality, can be found on page 193.<br><br>In comments on other poems, possible references include:<br><br>• judgement on Hamilton and on Holy Willie himself in *Holy Willie's Prayer*<br>• on the upper classes and the pompous in *A Man's a Man for a' That*<br>• on his detractors (and on himself) in *A Poet's Welcome to his Love-Begotten Daughter*<br><br>Many other references are possible. |

**Text 2 — Poetry — *Anne Hathaway* by Carol Ann Duffy**

| Question | Expected Response | Max Mark | Additional Guidance |
|---|---|---|---|
| 36. | Candidates should analyse how the first sentence establishes the speaker's passion.<br><br>There must be reference to two techniques. 1 mark for an acceptable comment and reference. 0 marks for reference/quotation alone. | 2 | Possible answers include:<br><br>• metaphor/imagery comparing the bed to:<br>　• "a spinning world …" suggests lively, exhilarating, breathless<br>　• "forests, castles, torchlight, clifftops" (collectively or singly) suggests romantic, exotic, thrilling, dangerous<br>　• "seas/where he would dive for pearls" suggests both depth and thrilling activities with potential for wealth<br>• list structure:<br>　• "forests, castles, torchlight, clifftops, seas" suggests a vast range of different things, as if she is reeling them off with pleasure |

| Question | Expected Response | Max Mark | Additional Guidance |
|---|---|---|---|
| 37. | Candidates should explain how the poet uses references to writing to convey the speaker's feelings.<br><br>2 marks for an insightful comment and reference. 1 mark for a basic comment and reference. 0 marks for reference/quotation alone. | 4 | Possible answers include:<br><br>• the general idea is about the blurring of the distinction between life and art, that Anne sees their love as being as vital, exciting, as fulfilling as her husband's work; this idea should be developed by specific references such as:<br>• "words/were shooting stars" could possibly refer to written words, hence suggesting she sees them as exciting, romantic<br>• "my body now a softer rhyme" creates a sense of their being joined together, of belonging together (Duffy is also touching on the idea of masculine and feminine rhyme)<br>• "now echo, assonance" continues the idea of things being joined together in a pleasing way (imitated by the string of words linked by assonance: "on", "body", "softer", "to", "echo", "assonance", "touch" and "noun")<br>• "a verb dancing in the centre of a noun" suggests joyous action, sexually suggestive; hints at Shakespeare's fondness for creating verbs from nouns and therefore suggests energy, freshness in their lovemaking<br>• "I dreamed he'd written me" suggests how her love has sparked her imagination, she loves him so much that she dreams of being one of his creations<br>• "the bed/a page" continues the conflation of his creativity and their lovemaking; almost punning on idea of sheets of paper/sheets on a bed; his creativity on paper is matched by his creativity in bed<br>• "Romance/and drama played" elevates their love to a full theatrical production; as if they are acting out a dramatic (and poetic) script |
| 38 | Candidates should evaluate the effectiveness of lines 11—14 as a conclusion to the poem.<br><br>Candidates should show understanding of the term "conclusion" and show how the content of the last four lines continues — or contrasts with — ideas and/or language in lines 1—10.<br><br>4 marks can be awarded for four appropriate, basic comments. An insightful comment on one example may be awarded 2 marks. 0 marks for reference/quotation alone. | 4 | Possible answers include:<br><br>• the contrast between the exuberant love of Anne and her lover and the dullness of the guests, seen in "dozed" which suggests they are inactive and in "dribbling their prose" a disdainful reference to the difference between the everyday nature of "prose" and the excitement, energy of poetry<br>• the vitality suggested in "living, laughing love" — emphasised by the alliteration, the smooth, liquid sound of the repeated "l" (which contrasts with the harsher sounds of "dozed", "dribbling" and "prose")<br>• the dash leads into the conclusion, a dramatic separation of the descriptions of her husband alive and the acknowledgement that he lives on in her imagination<br>• the consonance in "hold" and "held" recalls that the lovers rhymed with each other<br>• the imagery of "casket" suggests that like a strongbox for valuables her memories are precious<br>• the final rhyming couplet (in imitation of the Shakespearean sonnet) brings the poem to an aural conclusion |

| Question | Expected Response | Max Mark | Additional Guidance |
|---|---|---|---|
| 39. | Candidates should discuss how Duffy explores the theme of love in *Anne Hathaway* and at least one other poem, and should refer to appropriate textual evidence to support their discussion.<br><br>0 marks for reference/quotation alone. | 10 | The generic marking guide, covering aspects of commonality, can be found on page 193.<br><br>In comments on other poems, possible references include:<br>• the destructive power of love in *Havisham*<br>• the unusual take on love in *Valentine*<br>• the relationship between husband and wife in *Mrs Midas*<br><br>Many other references are possible. |

**Text 3 — Poetry — Some Old Photographs by Liz Lochhead**

| Question | Expected Response | Max Mark | Additional Guidance |
|---|---|---|---|
| 40. | Candidates should explain how the poet creates a dream-like atmosphere.<br><br>For full marks there should be reference to more than one technique. 2 marks for an insightful comment and reference. 1 mark for a basic comment and reference. 0 marks for reference/quotation alone. | 4 | Possible answers include:<br>• the lack of punctuation/the ungrammatical nature of each line creates a muddled, dreamlike impression; it's like one enormous list of impressions<br>• the uneven, irregular lines give it a distorted, random feel<br>• the synaesthesia in "weather evocative as scent" suggests a confusion, in which something inanimate can be described as strong, lingering<br>• paradox in "romance of dark stormclouds" describes what is usually seen as threatening ("stormclouds") in terms of pleasure, passion<br>• stress pattern in "low wide river", three consecutive long vowel sounds creates a heavy, slowed down effect<br>• word play in "long … and longer" suggests confusion, uncertainty (+ hint of "long" = yearning)<br>• the enjambment in "of light/of smoke" draws out the sound as if one image is piling up on another<br>• "fabulous film-noir stills" conjures up images of stylish Hollywood movies; also suggests a hint of menace, anything can happen<br>• slightly incongruous comparison of Central Station with Hollywood chic<br>• the repeated "f" sound in "fabulous film … freezing fog" creates an echo effect<br>• assonance and rhyme in "silvering the chilled, stilled" continues the echo effect<br>• "the glamorous past" suggests a world/time where everything was stylish, no flaws or problems<br>• metaphor in "drops on a rainmate are sequins" turn something prosaic ("rainmate") into something dazzling, sophisticated |

| Question | Expected Response | Max Mark | Additional Guidance |
|---|---|---|---|
| 41. | Candidates should explain how the poet reminds the reader that these photographs are old. <br><br> 1 mark for an acceptable comment and reference. 0 marks for reference/quotation alone. | 2 | Possible answers include: <br><br> • "still-lovely mother" indicates the photograph shows the mother before she aged/lost her youthful beauty <br> • "before you were born" as if the poet is talking to herself about a very distant time <br> • reference to "all" dads being "in hats" must be a time (50s at the latest) when all adult males wore hats <br> • "Central at five past five" suggests a bygone time when all offices and businesses closed at five o'clock <br> • "belted dark overcoats" suggest, again, the 50s or earlier |
| 42. | Candidates should explain what impression the poet creates of George Square. <br><br> 2 marks for an insightful comment and reference. 1 mark for a basic comment and reference. 0 marks for reference/quotation alone. | 2 | Possible answers include: <br><br> • a sense of movement/bustle in "starlings swarming" <br> • a sense of urban grit in "noise and stink and smoky breath" <br> • a sense of relentless activity in the list "all the passing now/and noise and stink and smoky breath" <br> • a slightly surreal impression from "above what was/never really this photograph" — as if the photograph has vanished and she is/thinks she is actually in the Square |
| 43. | Candidates should explain how the poet creates a sense of excitement in the last three lines of the poem. | 2 | Possible answers include: <br><br> • the apparently random list "wee boays, a duchess, bunting" as if there's something out of the ordinary about to happen <br> • using local speech in "wee boays" creates a lively, realistic picture of the scene <br> • "a/big launch" — idea of something starting off fresh, new <br> • "that boat is yet to sail" — slightly enigmatic, but hints at the future, good things to come |
| 44. | Candidates should discuss whether criticism of Liz Lochhead for being overly nostalgic is fair, by referring to *Some Old Photographs* and at least one other poem, and should refer to appropriate textual evidence to support their discussion. <br><br> 0 marks for reference/quotation alone. | 10 | The generic marking guide, covering aspects of commonality, can be found on page 193. <br><br> In comments on other poems, possible references include: <br><br> • the depiction of a past way of life in *For My Grandmother Knitting* <br> • the description of the mother's preparations in *View of Scotland/Love Poem* <br> • the recollections of Hogmanay traditions in *View of Scotland/Love Poem* <br><br> Many other references are possible. |

Text 4 — Poetry — *Memorial* by Norman MacCaig

| Question | Expected Response | Max Mark | Additional Guidance |
|---|---|---|---|
| 45. | Candidates should analyse how one of the images conveys how the speaker has been affected by the death.<br><br>2 marks for an insightful comment. 1 mark for a basic comment. 0 marks for reference/quotation alone. | 3 | Possible answers include:<br>• "The silence of her dying sounds through/the carousel of language"<br>  • compares silence with something that can make a sounds, suggesting confusion or heightened awareness of her absence; compares language to a carousel — something associated with joyful sound and happy experiences, suggesting she is felt/sensed at all times, albeit in an incongruous way [this image is not easy to pick apart — there is no "correct answer"; candidates should be rewarded for all plausible comment]<br>• "It's a web/on which laughter stitches itself"<br>  • compares the silence with an intricate pattern, and imagines laughter as capable of attaching itself to the web, suggesting her presence/absence is capable of causing happiness ("laughter"), an apparently contradictory emotion [this image is not easy to pick apart — there is no "correct answer"; candidates should be rewarded for all plausible comment] |
| 46. | Candidates should explain how the poet uses contrast to reveal the persona's feelings.<br><br>2 marks for an insightful comment and reference. 1 mark for a basic comment and reference. 0 marks for reference/quotation alone. | 4 | Possible answers include:<br>• various contrasts of living/dying suggest confusion, unwillingness to accept the death<br>• contrast of the vivid and natural ("bird … sun … fish … crocus") with sense of death, emptiness ("black words … the sound/ of soundlessness … nowhere")<br>• contrast between what "she tells … " and what "I hear … " suggests he is living with both happiness and sadness<br>• contrast between beauty of "No crocus is carved more gently" and the bleakness of "the nowhere/she is continuously going into" shows the persona feels the death in a contradictory way<br>• contrast/contradiction in "sound/of soundlessness" suggests confusion, or a heightened awareness of the absence |
| 47. | Candidates should explain how the persona makes clear the impact the death has had on him.<br><br>2 marks for an insightful comment and reference. 1 mark for a basic comment and reference. 0 marks for reference/quotation alone. | 3 | Possible answers include:<br>• he says she "can't stop dying" — in his mind he relives her death all the time<br>• she has the power to make him "her elegy" — he personifies everything he would want to say about her death<br>• the extended "artistic" metaphor ("elegy … masterpiece … fiction … music") creates an elaborate sense of how her death/memory permeates every aspect of his life and his creativity<br>• the apparently contradictory nature of "walking masterpiece" and "true fiction" suggests bewilderment, disorientation<br>• the enigmatic last line suggests they have almost merged in personality |

| Question | Expected Response | Max Mark | Additional Guidance |
|---|---|---|---|
| 48. | Candidates should discuss Norman MacCaig's exploration of deeply emotional situations in *Memorial* and at least one other poem, and should refer to appropriate textual evidence to support their discussion.<br><br>0 marks for reference/quotation alone. | 10 | The generic marking guide, covering aspects of commonality, can be found on page 193.<br><br>In comments on other poems, possible references include:<br><br>• the feelings experienced by the persona in *Visiting Hour*<br>• the sense of loss in *Sounds of the Day*<br>• the relationship between persona and the aunt in *Aunt Julia*<br><br>Many other references are possible. |

**Text 5 — Poetry — *Shores* by Sorley MacLean**

| Question | Expected Response | Max Mark | Additional Guidance |
|---|---|---|---|
| 49. | Candidates should analyse how the poet conveys the power of natural features.<br><br>2 marks for an insightful comment and reference. 1 mark for a basic comment and reference. 0 marks for reference/quotation alone. | 3 | Possible answers include:<br><br>• imagery: "great white mouth … two hard jaws" personifies the bay as capable of devouring; the promontories as the powerful "jaws" ready to snap shut<br>• "beside the sea/renewing love" suggests healing power of the sea, able to renew something as powerful as love<br>• "the ocean was filling/Talisker bay forever" suggests eternal power of the ocean<br>• "Prishal bowed his stallion head" compares landscape feature to a powerful, graceful animal |
| 50. | Candidates should explain how the poet conveys his commitment to the person he is addressing.<br><br>2 marks for an insightful comment and reference. 1 mark for a basic comment and reference. 0 marks for reference/quotation alone. | 3 | Possible answers include:<br><br>• "I would stay there till doom" — i.e. until the end of time, a strong, if conventional, promise of fidelity<br>• "measuring sand, grain by grain" — an exaggerated notion of counting out an almost infinite number<br>• "the sea draining drop by drop" — another infinite task |
| 51. | Candidates should evaluate the last verse as a conclusion to the poem as a whole by referring to structural similarities and differences.<br><br>Up to 2 marks for identification of similarities/differences. 2 marks for an insightful comment on the last verse as a conclusion. 1 mark for a basic point. 0 marks for reference/quotation alone. | 4 | Possible answers include:<br><br>• Structural similarities:<br>　• "And if I were … I would … I would";<br>　• use of "shore" in first line of each verse<br>• Structural differences:<br>　• "And if we" (vv 1 and 2) but "And if I" (v 3)<br>　• "And if …" appears once in vv 1 and 2 but twice in v 3<br>　• vv 1 and 2 are single sentences but v 3 is two sentences<br>　• "I would …" in vv 1 and 2 is followed by stasis ("stand … stay … wait") but by action in v 3 ("put up … build"<br>• Comments:<br>　• brings together "I" and "we" — sense of resolution<br>　• continues idea of power of nature, but combines elements from previous verses ("ocean and the sand, drop and grain"<br>　• continues idea of commitment ("synthesis of love for you")<br>　• introduces a desire to protect ("I would build the rampart wall")<br>　• conclusion could be argued as pessimistic contrary to previous sense of hope, commitment |

| Question | Expected Response | Max Mark | Additional Guidance |
|---|---|---|---|
| 52. | Candidates should discuss the importance of landscape in MacLean's poetry and should refer to appropriate textual evidence to support their discussion.<br><br>0 marks for reference/quotation alone. | 10 | The generic marking guide, covering aspects of commonality, can be found on page 193.<br><br>In comments on other poems, possible references include:<br>• Cnoc an Ra and Beinn na Lice in *Hallaig*<br>• Carn Mor and Creag Mheircil in *Screapadal*<br>• the effects of the Clearances in both *Hallaig* and *Screapdal*<br><br>Many other references are possible. |

**Text 6 — Poetry — *Two Trees* by Don Paterson**

| Question | Expected Response | Max Mark | Additional Guidance |
|---|---|---|---|
| 53. | Candidates should explain how the poet makes the first verse sound like the start of a simple folk tale or parable.<br><br>2 marks for an insightful comment and reference. 1 mark for a basic comment and reference. 0 marks for reference/quotation alone. | 4 | Possible answers include:<br>• typical story opening "One morning … "<br>• simplicity of  "… got out of bed"<br>• focuses on his "one idea" and states it simply "to graft … "<br>• the hint that there is something potentially symbolic in what he is doing, i.e. attempting to bring together two different entities<br>• keeps it focuses on one person and his activities: "work … lay open … lash"<br>• "twelve months" pass — the story moves on quickly<br>• "nothing" for a while, "but one day … ", i.e. the next stage in the story has arrived<br>• "Over the years …" — another long passage of time leading to …<br>• … the wondrous outcome: "each bough looked like it gave a double crop"<br>• Miguel becomes a figure famous for his "magic tree" i.e. he has (or appears to have) supernatural attributes |
| 54. | Candidates should explain how lines 13—16 act as a link or turning point in the poem as a whole.<br><br>1 mark for establishing link with what goes before; 1 mark for establishing link with what follows. | 2 | Possible answers include:<br>• the new purchaser's lack of a "dream" links back to Don Miguel's "one idea" and forward to the potentially destructive nature of his action<br>• his splitting of the tree links back to Don Miguel's successful grafting and forward to the effect of the separation<br>• the "fused seam" links back to Don Miguel's "lash[ing]" them together and forward to the "split[ting]"<br>• "two holes" links forward to the separation of the two trees and recalls Don Miguel's enthusiasm to turn two into one |

| Question | Expected Response | Max Mark | Additional Guidance |
|---|---|---|---|
| 55. | Candidates should explain how the poet subverts the idea that the poem is a parable or a tale with a message.<br><br>2 marks for an insightful comment and reference. 1 mark for a basic comment and reference. 0 marks for reference/quotation alone. | 4 | Possible answers include:<br><br>• "And no … " sounds almost as if addressed directly to readers who might be jumping ahead, warning them not to engage in fanciful interpretations<br>• "they did not … nor did … nor did" provides a list of the kind of interpretations readers might be expecting, a is forcefully negative about each one<br>• the possible interpretations are all a little romanticised, whimsical (all involve anthropomorphism of a sort) almost in mockery of what readers might be expecting<br>• concludes with two one-line sentences (the only ones in the poem) as if making a very simple, direct point<br>• repetition of "trees" emphasises that they are (he claims) the only topic of the poem<br>• denies bluntly the possibility of tress having human qualities ("don't weep or ache or shout")<br>• the assertiveness of the last two lines is emphasised by the straightforward, conclusive rhyme |
| 56. | Candidates should discuss Paterson's use of symbolism to explore important themes and should refer to appropriate textual evidence to support their discussion.<br><br>0 marks for reference/quotation alone. | 10 | The generic marking guide, covering aspects of commonality, can be found on page 193.<br><br>In comments on other poems, possible references include:<br><br>• the stone in *Nil Nil*<br>• the pool table or the ferry in *The Ferryman's Arms*<br>• the bus journey in *Baldovan 11.00*<br><br>Many other references are possible. |

**[END OF MODEL MARKING INSTRUCTIONS]**

# HIGHER FOR CfE ENGLISH
# MODEL PAPER 3

## PAPER 1 – READING FOR UNDERSTANDING, ANALYSIS AND EVALUATION

Marking Instructions for each question

Passage 1

| Question | | Expected Response | Max Mark | Additional Guidance |
|---|---|---|---|---|
| 1. | (a) | Candidates should analyse how the writer's word choice emphasises the "conventional wisdom" that reading books is better than playing video games.<br><br>Marks will depend on the quality of comment on appropriate language feature(s).<br><br>2 marks may be awarded for reference plus detailed/insightful comment; 1 mark for reference plus more basic comment; 0 marks for reference alone.<br><br>*Possible answers are shown in the "Additional Guidance" column.* | 2 | Possible answers include:<br><br>• "enriches" suggests that reading adds to one's knowledge, awareness; is rewarding, beneficial; improves one<br>• "the mind" suggests reading is influencing something greater than just the brain; it influences our consciousness: thought, perception, emotions and imagination<br>• "deadens" suggests video games make kids less aware, less sensitive, less vigorous; they make kids think less; lifeless<br>• "zoning out" suggests video games make kids detached from people and things around them, unresponsive, unstimulated<br><br>or any other acceptable answer |
| | (b) | Candidates should explain "the question" the writer asks about "other forms of culture".<br><br>Candidates must use their own words. No marks are awarded for verbatim quotations from the passage.<br><br>*Depending on clarity of explanation, 1 mark or 2 marks for the suggested answer "Additional Guidance" column.* | 2 | Possible answers include:<br><br>• the writer is asking if these other forms of culture involve discrete thinking skills / have qualities which benefit, stimulate, challenge, stretch our minds in ways which are different from – but just as important as – reading<br><br>or any other acceptable answer |
| | (c) | Candidates should analyse how the writer uses at least two language features to emphasise the contrast between his positive view of "other forms of culture" and the negative view held by "most critics".<br><br>Marks will depend on the quality of comment on appropriate language feature(s).<br><br>2 marks may be awarded for reference plus detailed/insightful comment; 1 mark for reference plus more basic comment; 0 marks for reference alone.<br><br>*Possible answers are shown in the "Additional Guidance" column.* | 4 | Possible answers include:<br><br>*Imagery*<br>• "(progressive) story": just as a "story" is a developing, organised narrative, so the writer sees the positive influence of popular culture as gradual, logical, coherent, interesting…<br>• "our brains sharper": just as sharpening involves giving cutting tools a better edge, this suggests making our brains keener, more accurate…<br>• "we soak in": soaking in is a process of absorption, of taking in as much liquid as possible; this suggests we become immersed in popular culture, that its influence is natural, irresistible, all-consuming, profound, deep…<br>• "(lowbrow) fluff": fluff is light, downy material (for example, small pieces of wool); its use suggests critics believe popular culture is light, trivial, worthless, superficial, irrelevant, trifling…<br>• "honing": just as honing is a (refined) process of giving cutting tools a perfect edge, this suggests gradually making our brains as sharp as possible, more and more precise, accurate, productive…<br><br>*Word choice*<br>• "allege" suggest doubt, calls the critics' views into question<br>• "dumbing down" suggests popular culture offers people a reduced intellectual challenge **or** is responsible for making people less educated, less intelligent, more lowbrow |

| Question | | Expected Response | Max Mark | Additional Guidance |
|---|---|---|---|---|
| | (c) | *(continued)* | | • "progressive" suggests developing, advancing, moving forward steadily, leading to improvement<br>• "steadily" suggests reliable, consistent progress<br>• "imperceptibly" suggests change is gradual, subtle<br>• "sharper" suggests keener, more precise, more accurate<br>• "soak in" suggests it's not a superficial process; influence is deep; we are fully engaged, absorbed<br>• "dismissed" suggests brushed aside, considered beneath contempt, irrelevant, unimportant, trivial<br>• "lowbrow" suggests vulgar, anti-intellectual, uncultured, plebeian<br>• "fluff" suggests worthless, trivial, inconsequential, superficial<br>• "honing" suggests sharpening, perfecting, refining<br><br>*Sentence structure*<br>• balanced structure/contrast of "Where … story" allows the writer to trump the critics' argument; this is heightened by the greater certainty of his "see" set against the dubious nature of what they "allege"<br>• use of colon to introduce a full development of his "progressive story" argument<br>• use of parenthesis "but … imperceptibly" to explain that this positive development is so gradual that it's easy for the less astute (like the critics) to miss it<br>• positioning of "I hope to persuade you" at the start of the final sentence alerts the reader to the fact that the writer is about to make what he believes is his most important point<br>• positioning of "increasingly" just before his key statement stresses that the point he is about to make is more and more relevant, true<br>• balanced nature of final statement, hinging on the "just as important as" comparison stresses skills developed by popular culture are of a comparable standard to the skills developed by reading<br><br>or any other acceptable answer |
| 2. | | Candidates should analyse how the writer conveys the difficulty of playing video games by his use of sentence structure and imagery.<br><br>Marks will depend on the quality of comment on appropriate language feature(s).<br><br>For full marks there must be reference to both features. 2 marks may be awarded for reference plus detailed/insightful comment; 1 mark for reference plus more basic comment; 0 marks for mere identification of a feature of sentence structure.<br><br>*Possible answers are shown in the "Additional Guidance" column.* | 4 | Possible answers include:<br><br>*Sentence structure*<br>• the positioning of **and/or** rhythmic/repetitive nature of "And the first and last thing" conveys the definitive 'Alpha and omega' nature of this phrase, especially when placed at the start of the sentence, suggests the difficulty of video games is a fundamental point to the writer<br>• use of parenthesis "the thing … hear" adds to the mystery, adds to the dramatic build-up to the final announcement of video games' difficulty<br>• additional phrase "sometimes maddeningly" has two functions: again adds to the build-up **and/or** ramps up the notion of extreme difficulty that "fiendishly" has introduced |

| Question | Expected Response | Max Mark | Additional Guidance |
|---|---|---|---|
| 2. | *(continued)* | | • use of climax in the sentence "The dirty ... fun." — the somewhat awkward/unusual construction of this sentence is designed to stress the "not having fun" element of its conclusion<br>• repetition of the "you may be" structure stresses — and this is heightened by the use of the inclusive direct address — the variety of problems playing video games may cause<br>• repetition of adjectives ("frustrated", "confused", "disorientated", "stuck") — rat-a-tat run of adjectives suggests 'the sea of troubles' playing video games may involve<br>• anticlimax of "you may be stuck" in its definitive downbeat simplicity, it is a stark summation of the seemingly insoluble challenge these games present<br>• use of the continuous tense in final sentence — an argument might be made that this reflects the ongoing, nagging nature of the problems involved<br><br>*Imagery*<br>• "wrestling": just as wrestling involves close, physical combat with a single opponent, so it suggests a demanding, exhausting battle with an unforgiving enemy<br>• "worrying a loose tooth": just as this involves the constant working away at a persistent physical annoyance, so it suggests that the difficulties presented by video games are nagging frustrations that constantly prey on one's mind<br>• "stuck": just as to be stuck is to be fixed immovably, so it suggests being trapped in a situation which offers no escape<br>• "dirty little secret": usually used in the realms of ethics or morality, a deliberate attempt to hide the truth, a cover-up of some sort, a hidden scandal; used in relation to the difficulty of video games, it heightens the potentially damaging nature of this feature, suggests it is a very negative feature that is deliberately glossed over<br><br>or any other acceptable answer |
| 3. | Candidates should identify three reasons why "reward" is so important to the learning process involved in playing video games.<br><br>Candidates must use their own words.  No marks are awarded for verbatim quotations from the passage.<br><br>*1 mark for each point from the "Additional Guidance" column.* | 3 | Possible answers include:<br><br>• people are hard-wired to respond strongly to rewards<br>• people find rewards a great stimulus to action, learning etc.<br>• video games are designed to be full of rewards<br>• rewards in video games are precise, with clear outcomes (explanation of "clearly defined")<br>• the rewards are attractive<br>• the rewards are presented in a variety of forms<br>• players are constantly reminded about the rewards<br>• the rewards are vitally important to achieving success in the games<br>• the rewards are more intense, striking, colourful than in real life<br>• players aren't always aware that they are learning (explanation of "without realising ...")<br><br>or any other acceptable answer |

| Question | | Expected Response | Max Mark | Additional Guidance |
|---|---|---|---|---|
| 4. | | Candidates should identify two criticisms and two defences the writer makes of video games. | 4 | Possible answers include: |
| | | Candidates must use their own words.  No marks are awarded for verbatim quotations from the passage. | | *Criticisms* |
| | | | | • the games may seem attractive but the attractions flatter to deceive, are rather superficial, blind one to the truth (explanation of "dazzled") |
| | | *1 mark for each point from the "Additional Guidance" column; maximum of 2 marks for criticism and 2 marks for defence.* | | • the games are addictive (explanation of "hooked") |
| | | | | • the subject matter is infantile, petty, puerile, trivial... (explanation of "actual content ... childish") |
| | | | | • unnecessarily threatening, unjustifiably scary (explanation of "gratuitously menacing" — but explanation of "menacing" alone: 0) |
| | | | | • the subject matter is very limited **and/or** moves between the two extremes of violence and childish fantasy (explanation of "alternates ... princess-rescuing") |
| | | | | • the games are violent (explanation of "drive-by shooting") |
| | | | | • the games are pure fantasy (explanation of "princess-rescuing") |
| | | | | *Defences* |
| | | | | • the activities involved are beneficial for mental training/development ("good for the brain") |
| | | | | • the skills developed will be of use in other spheres ("come in handy elsewhere") |
| | | | | • it resembles learning algebra, which might seem pointless and abstract but exercises the brain |
| | | | | • like chess, games might seem very basic (and aggressive in concept), but they are every bit as cerebral and mind-developing as chess; they develop strategic, tactical thinking |
| | | | | or any other acceptable answer |
| 5. | (a) | Candidates should explain in their own words the key distinction the writer makes between reading a novel and playing a video game. | 2 | Possible answers include: |
| | | | | *reading a novel* |
| | | Candidates must use their own words.  No marks are awarded for verbatim quotations from the passage. | | • can get us thinking in a creative way, transport us to in different situation (explanation of "activate our imagination") |
| | | | | • can affect our feelings, arouse passions (explanation of "conjure up powerful emotions") |
| | | *1 mark for each point from the "Additional Guidance" column.* | | *playing a game* |
| | | | | • makes you explore, study carefully (explanation of "analyse") |
| | | | | • makes you weigh up options (explanation of "choose") |
| | | | | • makes you evaluate options (explanation of "priotitise") |
| | | | | • makes you reach a conclusion (explanation of "decide") |
| | | | | or any other acceptable answer |

| Question | Expected Response | Max Mark | Additional Guidance |
|---|---|---|---|
| (b) | Candidates should analyse how the writer's use of language conveys the contrast between what a gamer looks like from "the outside" and what is happening "inside the gamer's mind". <br><br> For full marks there must be reference to both "outside" and "inside"; 2 marks may be awarded for reference plus detailed/insightful comment; 1 mark for reference plus more basic comment; 0 marks for reference alone. <br><br> *Possible answers are shown in the "Additional Guidance" column.* | 4 | Possible answers include: <br><br> *the gamer from "the outside"* <br> • "looks like" suggests this may be an unreliable perspective, a superficial, unquestioning way to approach an analysis of gamers <br> • "fury" suggests the gamer is behaving in an impulsive, uncontrolled way; everything is being done at top speed, in a blur of unthinking activity <br> • "clicking" suggests mindless, repetitive activity <br> • "shooting" suggests destructive, homicidal activity <br> • "clicking and shooting" automatic, unthinking, mechanical, robotic, repetitive... <br> • the general simplicity of the penultimate sentence (especially when compared to the much more complex final sentence) heightens the impression that this is a naïve, simplistic way to view gamers <br><br> *the gamer on the inside* <br> • "peer" suggests an active approach involving close examination <br> • "turns out" suggests a sense of some kind of revelation, surprise, discovery <br> • "another creature" suggests something mysterious, surprising, unexpected, interesting but hard to define, a new form of life we didn't know existed <br> • use of colon introduces a detailed description of the full range of intellectual activities involved in gaming <br> • balance/repetition of "some of them" stresses range of activities involved <br> • contrast in "snap judgements ... long-term strategies" shows range of important decision-making skills involved from quick, smart thinking to overall planning <br> • "judgements" suggests wise, fair thinking <br> • "strategies" suggests considered, creative thinking <br><br> or any other acceptable answer |

Passage 2

| Question | | Expected Response | Max Mark | Additional Guidance |
|---|---|---|---|---|
| **6.** | | Candidates should identify key areas of disagreement in the two passages.<br><br>There may be some overlap among the areas of disagreement.  Markers will have to judge the extent to which a candidate has covered two points or one.<br><br>Candidates can use bullet points in this final question, or write a number of linked statements.<br><br>Evidence from the passage may include quotations, but these should be supported by explanations.<br><br>Approach to marking is shown in the "Additional Guidance column.<br><br>Key areas of disagreement are shown in the grid below.  Other answers are possible. | 5 | The mark for this question should reflect the quality of response in two areas:<br><br>• identification of the key areas of disagreement in attitude/ideas<br>• level of detail given in support<br><br>The following guidelines should be used:<br><br>**Five marks** — comprehensive identification of three or more key areas of disagreement with full use of supporting evidence<br>**Four marks** — clear identification of three or more key areas of disagreement with relevant use of supporting evidence<br>**Three marks** — identification of three or more key areas of disagreement with supporting evidence<br>**Two marks** — identification of two key areas of disagreement with supporting evidence<br>**One mark** — identification of one key area of disagreement with supporting evidence<br>**Zero marks** — failure to identify any key area of disagreement and/or total misunderstanding of task |

| | Area of Disagreement | Steven Johnson | Boris Johnson |
|---|---|---|---|
| 1 | general status | they are viewed as pointless, but they are not | they are harmful, narcotically addictive |
| 2 | intellectual benefits | they develop the brain in a number of ways | they require no thought or effort |
| 3 | educational benefits | high level thinking skills are developed | they may pretend to be educational but are totally lacking in educational value; a threat to literacy |
| 4 | the challenge involved | they can appear simple but are often very complex<br>the process is more important than the (often simplistic) content | they encourage slovenly behaviour and thinking |
| 5 | the reward(s) involved | they are at times extremely hard unlike other entertainment, pleasure is not immediate | they offer immediate and simple pleasures |

**[END OF MODEL MARKING INSTRUCTIONS]**

# Acknowledgements

Permission has been sought from all relevant copyright holders and Hodder Gibson is grateful for the use of the following:

The article 'Cutting down a tree is worse than fox hunting' by Janice Turner © The Times/News Syndication, 12 January 2013 (SQP Reading for Understanding, Analysis and Evaluation pages 2 & 3);
Article is adapted from 'Trees, me, and all of us' by Colin Tudge. Reproduced by kind permission of Colin Tudge (SQP Reading for Understanding, Analysis and Evaluation page 5);
Extract is taken from 'The Slab Boys Trilogy' © John Byrne 2003, published by Faber & Faber Ltd. All right whatsoever in this play are strictly reserved and application for performance etc. should be made to the Author's agent: Casarotto Ramsay & Associates Limited, Waverley House, 7–12 Noel Street, London W1F 8G (rights@casarotto.co.uk). No performance may be given unless a licence has been obtained. (SQP Critical Reading pages 2 to 4);
An extract from 'The Cheviot, the Stag, and the Black, Black Oil,' by John McGrath. Published by Methuen Drama, an imprint of Bloomsbury Publishing Ltd. © John McGrath (SQP Critical Reading pages 5 & 6);
An extract from 'Men Should Weep' by Ena Lamont Stewart. Reproduced with permission of Alan Brodie Representation Ltd (SQP Critical Reading pages 7 & 8);
An extract from 'In Church' by Iain Crichton Smith, taken from 'The Red Door: The Complete English Stories 1949-76', published by Birlinn. Reproduced by permission of Birlinn Ltd. www.birlinn.co.uk (SQP Critical Reading pages 10 & 11);
An extract from 'A Time to Keep' by George Mackay Brown, published by Polygon. Reproduced by permission of Birlinn Ltd. www.birlinn.co.uk (SQP Critical Reading page 12);
An extract from 'The Trick is to Keep Breathing' by Janice Galloway, published by Vintage, reprinted by permission of The Random House Group Limited (SQP Critical Reading pages 14 & 15);
An extract from 'Sunset Song' by Lewis Grassic Gibbon, published by Jarrold Publishing, 1932. Public Domain. (SQP Critical Reading page 16);
An extract from 'The Cone Gatherers' by Robin Jenkins published by Canongate Books Ltd. (SQP Critical Reading pages 18 & 19);
An extract from 'Holy Willie's Prayer' by Robert Burns. Public Domain. (SQP Critical Reading pages 20 & 21);
The poem 'Originally' by Carol Ann Duffy from 'The Other Country' (Anvil, 1990). Reproduced by permission of the author c/o Rogers, Coleridge & White Ltd., 20 Powis Mews, London W11 1JN (SQP Critical Reading page 22);
An extract from the poem 'For My Grandmother Knitting' by Liz Lochhead from 'A Choosing: Selected Poems' published by Polygon. Reproduced by permission of Birlinn Ltd. www.birlinn.co.uk (SQP Critical Reading pages 24 & 25);
The poem 'Sounds of the Day' by Norman MacCaig from 'The Poems of Norman MacCaig' published by Polygon. Reproduced by permission of Birlinn Ltd. www.birlinn.co.uk (SQP Critical Reading page 26);
The poem, 'Heroes' by Sorley Maclean taken from 'Sorley Maclean Selected Poems' (edited by Whyte and Dymock), published by Polygon. Reproduced by permission of Birlinn. (SQP Critical Reading pages 28 & 29);
An extract from 'The Ferryman's Arms' by Don Paterson taken from 'Nil Nil' (Faber & Faber 1993) Reproduced by permission of the author c/o Rogers, Coleridge & White Ltd., 20 Powis Mews, London W11 1JN (SQP Critical Reading page 30);
An extract from 'The Last Veteran' by Peter Parker, published by Fourth Estate, reprinted by permission of HarperCollins Publishers Ltd. © Peter Parker 2009 (Model Paper 1 Reading for Understanding, Analysis and Evaluation pages 2 & 3);
A passage adapted from 'Why World War I Resonates' by William Boyd from The New York Times, 21 January 2012 © The New York Times. All rights reserved. Used by permission and protected by the Copyright Laws of the United States. The printing, copying, redistribution, or retransmission of this Content without express written permission is prohibited (Model Paper 1 Reading for Understanding, Analysis and Evaluation pages 5 & 6);
An extract from 'The Slab Boys Trilogy' © John Byrne 2003, published by Faber & Faber Ltd. All right whatsoever in this play are strictly reserved and application for performance etc. should be made to the Author's agent: Casarotto Ramsay & Associates Limited, Waverley House, 7–12 Noel Street, London W1F 8G (rights@casarotto.co.uk). No performance may be given unless a licence has been obtained. (Model Paper 1 Critical Reading pages 2 & 3);
An extract from 'The Cheviot, the Stag, and the Black, Black Oil,' by John McGrath. Published by Methuen Drama, an imprint of Bloomsbury Publishing Ltd. © John McGrath (Model Paper 1 Critical Reading pages 4 & 5);
An extract from 'Men Should Weep' by Ena Lamont Stewart. Reproduced with permission of Alan Brodie Representation Ltd (Model Paper 1 Critical Reading page 6);
An extract from 'The Crater' by Iain Crichton Smith, taken from 'The Red Door: The Complete English Stories 1949-76', published by Birlinn. Reproduced by permission of Birlinn Ltd. www.birlinn.co.uk (Model Paper 1 Critical Reading page 8);
An extract from 'The Bright Spade' by George Mackay Brown taken from 'A Time To Keep' published by The Hogarth Press Ltd, 1969. Reproduced by permission of The Estate of George Mackay Brown/Jenny Brown Associates (Model Paper 1 Critical Reading page 10);
An extract from 'The Trick is to Keep Breathing' by Janice Galloway, published by Vintage, reprinted by permission of The Random House Group Limited (Model Paper 1 Critical Reading page 12);
An extract from 'Sunset Song' by Lewis Grassic Gibbon, published by Jarrold Publishing, 1932. Public Domain. (Model Paper 1 Critical Reading page 14);
An extract from 'The Cone Gatherers' by Robin Jenkins published by Canongate Books Ltd. (Model Paper 1 Critical Reading page 16);
The poem 'To a Mouse' by Robert Burns. Public Domain. (Model Paper 1 Critical Reading page 18);
The poem 'Mrs Midas' by Carol Ann Duffy, taken from 'The World's Wife', published by Picador 1999. Reproduced by permission of Pan Macmillan © Carol Ann Duffy 1999 (Model Paper 1 Critical Reading page 20);
An extract from the poem 'Last Supper' by Liz Lochhead from 'A Choosing: Selected Poems', published by

Polygon. Reproduced by permission of Birlinn Ltd. www.birlinn.co.uk (Model Paper 1 Critical Reading page 22);
The poem 'Assisi' by Norman MacCaig from 'The Many Days: Selected Poems of Norman MacCaig' published by Polygon. Reproduced by permission of Birlinn Ltd. www.birlinn.co.uk (Model Paper 1 Critical Reading page 24);
An extract from 'Hallaig' by Sorley MacLean, taken from'Caoir Gheal Leumraich/White Leaping Flame: collected poems in Gaelic with English translations', edited by Christopher Whyte and Emma Dymock 2011. Reproduced by permission of Carcanet Press Ltd (Model Paper 1 Critical Reading page 26);
The poem 'The Thread' by Don Paterson from 'Landing Light' (Faber & Faber 2003). Reproduced by permission of the author c/o Rogers, Coleridge & White Ltd., 20 Powis Mews, London W11 1JN (Model Paper 1 Critical Reading page 28);
The article 'Buying Stuff is the Heroin of Human Happiness' by Carol Midgley, taken from The Times © The Times/News Syndication, 22 July 2009 (Model Paper 2 Reading for Understanding, Analysis and Evaluation pages 2 & 3);
The article 'Shopping and Tut-tutting' by Will Hutton, taken from The Observer 4 September 2005. Copyright Guardian News & Media Ltd 2005. (Model Paper 2 Reading for Understanding, Analysis and Evaluation pages 5 & 6);
Extract is taken from 'The Slab Boys Trilogy' © John Byrne 2003, published by Faber & Faber Ltd. All right whatsoever in this play are strictly reserved and application for performance etc. should be made to the Author's agent: Casarotto Ramsay & Associates Limited, Waverley House, 7-12 Noel Street, London W1F 8G (rights@casarotto.co.uk). No performance may be given unless a licence has been obtained. (Model Paper 2 Critical Reading pages 2 & 3);
An extract from 'The Cheviot, the Stag, and the Black, Black Oil,' by John McGrath. Published by Methuen Drama, an imprint of Bloomsbury Publishing Ltd. © John McGrath (Model Paper 2 Critical Reading pages 4 & 5);
An extract from 'Men Should Weep' by Ena Lamont Stewart. Reproduced with permission of Alan Brodie Representation Ltd (Model Paper 2 Critical Reading page 6);
An extract from 'The Painter' by Iain Crichton Smith, taken from 'The Red Door: The Complete English Stories 1949-76', published by Birlinn. Reproduced by permission of Birlinn Ltd. www.birlinn.co.uk (Model Paper 2 Critical Reading pages 8 & 9);
An extract from 'The Eye of the Hurricane' by George Mackay Brown, taken from 'A Calendar of Love' published by Polygon. Reproduced by permission of Birlinn Ltd. www.birlinn.co.uk (Model Paper 2 Critical Reading page 10);
An extract from 'The Trick is to Keep Breathing' by Janice Galloway, published by Vintage, reprinted by permission of The Random House Group Limited (Model Paper 2 Critical Reading page 12);
An extract from 'Sunset Song' by Lewis Grassic Gibbon, published by Jarrold Publishing, 1932. Public Domain. (Model Paper 2 Critical Reading page 14);
An extract from 'The Cone Gatherers' by Robin Jenkins published by Canongate Books Ltd. (Model Paper 2 Critical Reading page 16);
The poem 'Tam o' Shanter' by Robert Burns. Public Domain. (Model Paper 2 Critical Reading page 18);
The poem 'Anne Hathaway' by Carol Anne Duthy, taken from 'The World's Wife', published by Picador 1999. Reproduced by permission of Pan Macmillan © Carol Ann Duffy 1999 (Model Paper 2 Critical Reading page 20);
An extract from the poem 'Some Old Photographs' by Liz Lochhead from 'A Choosing: Selected Poems' published by Polygon. Reproduced by permission of Birlinn Ltd. www.birlinn.co.uk (Model Paper 2 Critical Reading page 22);
The poem 'Memorial' by Norman MacCaig from 'The Many Days: Selected Poems of Norman MacCaig' published by Polygon. Reproduced by permission of Birlinn Ltd. www.birlinn.co.uk (Model Paper 2 Critical Reading page 24);
An extract from 'Shores' by Sorley MacLean, taken from'Caoir Gheal Leumraich/White Leaping Flame: collected poems in Gaelic with English translations', edited by Christopher Whyte and Emma Dymock 2011. Reproduced by permission of Carcanet Press Ltd (Model Paper 2 Critical Reading page 26);
The poem 'Two Trees' by Don Paterson taken from 'Rain' (Faber & Faber 2010) Reproduced by permission of the author c/o Rogers, Coleridge & White Ltd., 20 Powis Mews, London W11 1JN (Model Paper 2 Critical Reading page 28);
An extract from the article 'Want to exercise your mind? Try playstation' by Steven Johnson © The Times/News Syndication, 13 May 2005 (Model Paper 3 Reading for Understanding, Analysis and Evaluation pages 2 & 3);
The article 'The Writing Is On The Wall' by Boris Johnson, taken from The Daily Telegraph © Telegraph Media Group Limited (28 December 2006) (Model Paper 3 Reading for Understanding, Analysis and Evaluation page 5).

Hodder Gibson would like to thank SQA for use of any past exam questions that may have been used in model papers, whether amended or in original form.